DUDE ! WHERE'S MY CURE?

FOOD AS MEDICINE
USING AYURVEDIC BODY TYPING

VOLUME TWO

MIND/SPIRIT CONSCIOUSNESS
&
ADVANCED SUBJECTS

✳

LIFE IS LIKE A TAXI RIDE

Spirit
hails a taxi and jumps into the back seat
of whatever body comes along.

Spirit gives the mind a destination,
and leans back to watch through the window
as life passes by.

The mind
navigates life's highways, alleys, and potholes,
and dodges crazy drivers,
but only sometimes
goes where Spirit asks.

The body
is maintained by the mind
for better or for worse
'til illness and death bring it
to its earthen recycling center.

There, the Spirit-passenger
gives the mind-driver a tip, exits the body-vehicle,
and waits patiently by the cosmic roadside
reflecting on what's been seen
and learned.

After a while,
Spirit raises a tentative hand
and hails another ride
through yet another life adventure!

Dude! Where's My Cure?

Food as Medicine
Using Ayurvedic Body Typing

Volume Two

Mind/Spirit Consciousness
&
Advanced Subjects

by Paul. L Hoffman. M.D.

✳

Editors: Jaisri M. Lambert, Jerri-Jo Idarius, Della L. Tracy Davis
                 Ray N. Hoffman,

Cover LayoutAssistance: Danielle Knight

Illustrations: Referenced authors

Photography: Paul L. Hoffman

Design and Page Layout: Jerri-Jo Idarius

Legal: Timothy Walton, Mark Hazelbaker, Lee F. Hoffman

ATTRIBUTIONS: All images not created by the author are public domain material or used with permission or licence and are denoted by a numerical superscript or subscript referencing the bibliography.

DISCLAIMER: This book is a reference and not intended to treat, diagnose or prescribe. The information contained herein is in no way to be considered a substitute for consultation with a duly licensed health-care provider. All hail, lawyers.

First Edition: 2013   Printed in the United States of America

Library of Congress Cataloging-in-Publication-Data 2013903573

Dude, Where's My Cure?

Includes bibliographical references
Includes Index

ISBN   Paperback 978-0-9890211-0-4
        Electronic 978-0-9890211-2-8
        ePDF   978-0-9890211-4-2

Published by Impressive Press & Alternative Health Services
  235 Dorrance Road, Boulder Creek, CA 95006

TABLE OF CONTENTS

※

VOLUMES ONE AND TWO

Contents - Volume One
The Body

CONTENTS - VOLUME ONE

Contents - Volume Two

Mind/Spirit Consciousness & Advanced Subjects

Volume Two

Mind/Spirit Consciousness
&
Advanced Subjects

✷

PART THREE:
THE MIND
DRIVER

CHAPTER 17:
CAB DRIVER
BETWEEN
YOUR EARS

The Mind

MIND GAMES

Hey, there! It's me, Margo. Hopefully, you've already read about me, Reggie, and ayurveda in Volume One of "Dude, Where's My Cure?" We run a taxi company here in Santa Cruz serving the sick, and a few members of the general public. Reggie's the oldest driver in the company and I'm the dispatcher, office manager, and general Earth-mother.

If you *do* know about us, you already understand the basic principles of AIR, FIRE, and EARTH body-typing that form the basis of the ayurvedic viewpoint of the world. If you haven't, I've outlined them for you in Table 15-3 on page 514.

Just remember this: We all have different qualities, and we can understand most of what's going on in our lives by understanding whether things around or within us have qualities that are like AIR, FIRE, or EARTH. Read Volume One, dude!

Anyway, Reggie's bad habits have finally caught up with him. He's been making himself pretty sick, so he finally had some testing done down at Dominical Hospital. He's got some serious behavioral issues too! Believe me. He's on the phone right now… Let's see how he's doing now that he's had the lab tests done…

"So, Regg. What happened?"

"Oh, they think I've got a damn stomach ulcer."

"Uh huh… Does that surprise you?"

"Not really. I guess it makes sense. They've booked me for some procedure thing where they drug you up and stick a scope-thing down your throat and look around."

"Oh, yeah. I had one of those up my butt. It was kinda gross, because they…"

"Yo! Spare me the details, girl!"

"Sorry."

"It's OK."

"So, how long are you gonna be in the hospital?"

"Just the morning."

"That's all? Damn cheap-ass-HMO-bastard-SOB's. You'd think they'd give you some support. Ulcers are some serious shit, Regg! Dude, you need some major beach time! You gotta get some serious counseling and unwind!"

"Don't we all?!"

"Amen to that. It took me so damn long to learn not to let my mind screw up my health."

"So, how'd you do it, Margo?"

"Long story, my man, very long story. The mind is totally tricky and powerful! Learning the ways to get it working for you, instead of the other way around… that's a tough one."

"Mind games, huh?"

"Exactly. Learning how to play. That's the game."

"I wish I could learn about all that shit without having to deal with the shrinks. Those guys really rankle my ass with their $250 an hour parrot act… 'Well, what do YOU think about that?' (Ka-ching!)."

"Oh, lighten up, Regg. Shrinks can be a big help."

"If you can find a sane one!"

True, but it's worth the effort, dude! Getting your mind to shut up and take a break is a big part of what its all about."

TABLE 15-1 (Review):
PRINCIPLES OF AYURVEDIC
PHYSICAL BODY TREATMENT

1. Everyone is different. Everyone has different qualities.

2. The three basic qualitiy groups are AIR, FIRE, and EARTH.

3. Identifying a person's 'Body Quality-Type' is important.

4. Health is a largely a state of balanced qualities.

5. When a person's qualities are balanced, health is more likely. Imbalanced qualities cause illness.

6. Balancing qualities is achieved by adding the opposite quality, and avoiding an excess of the same quality.

7. Ayurveda provides the knowledge of a substance's specific qualities, and the use of that knowledge to achieve balance.

8. Excess qualities, toxins, or energy imbalances can affect the tissues, wastes, and systems and cause illness.

9. Qualities of substances can be made acceptable to an individual by cooking, drying, hydrating, combining, etc. with other qualities.

10. Most illness is caused by wrong digestion: physical, mental or both.

11. Wrong digestion produces toxic Incorrect Products of Digestion (IPODs).

12. Toxic IPODs can cause illness.

13. Proper digestion requires proper 'Digestive Transformational Energy' (DTE).

14. Everyone's illness is unique to the individual.

15. Removing toxins and excess qualities can help restore health.

16. Chronic illness often requires chronic therapy.

17. Serious illness requires stronger medicine.

18. The physical body is a condensation of spiritual & mental energy.

19. Body, mind, and spirit are closely interconnected.

20. Cause brings effect. Effect reveals cause.

CAB DRIVER BETWEEN YOUR EARS
MIND

Taxis don't drive themselves. They need drivers to turn the steering wheel, watch the road, avoid the obstacles, and push all the buttons and pedals. Someone has to take care of the cab. Someone has to know how it handles, what it can and can't do, what kind of gas to use, and when to take it in for tune-ups and repairs.

Drivers need to be able to identify which cab in the parking lot is theirs and protect it. They need to get along with the other drivers, and still be able to provide competitive service to the airport. A good driver does all these things and many more. A driver with problems will have difficulty caring for the vehicle, and difficulty delivering his passenger where he or she wants to go.

The *mind is the driver of the human vehicle*. Like a cab driver, it maintains and guides its body-vehicle through all situations.

The mind cannot do all these chores for everyone. It must give priority to its own vehicle. This separation from other vehicles and drivers results in a sense of individual "self" or "ego." THIS is MY cab. THAT is NOT my cab. The awareness of what is "self" and what is "other" is a large part of what the mind is all about.

This separation often takes on a defensive or competitive nature, and is the basis of the insecurity and fear which make up a large part of the mind's activities. This dysfunctional separation is what leads to many diseases and conflicts.

The mind needs direction and guidelines in much the same way that a cab driver needs to be told where (and sometimes how) to drive. These directions can come from many different sources including the environment in which the mind is trained. Minds trained to drive aggressively in Manhattan will be different from those trained to haul freight from Seattle to Los Angeles.

But a good cab driver also follows the directions of his passenger and goes where the *passenger* requests, not where the mind wants to go. If the passenger dozes off and gives no instructions, the driver will take the vehicle to places he prefers while waiting for the passenger to regain consciousness.

The passenger in the back seat determining the destination is the spirit, consciousness, soul, or conscience. Yoga, ayurveda and many other philosophies and systems acknowledge the existence of such a directing force. The "Spirit-Passenger" is discussed at length in Part Four.

The question of whether the mind or the spirit is in control is a central issue that governs not only an individual's philosophy, but also the manner in which his or her body-vehicle is cared for and driven.

If left on its own, the mind will always be attracted to sensual things. For the young child, these are typically short-term pleasures. Eating, drinking, sleeping and being held and loved are among the basic pleasures the young mind seeks. Many minds grow no further.

The mind's primary job is survival, and its circuitry is hard-wired to obtain and hold survival essentials. A person who is raised in poverty may have a difficult time outgrowing the need for necessities. Someone who is raised on Park Avenue may have a difficult time outgrowing the need for lavish but "essential" toys. A mind raised in a generous religious community may be more accustomed to sharing.

As time goes on, the mind develops an internal sense of security that allows it to pursue non-survival ends. At that point, non-essential pleasures and social power become more important. With greater security, the mind can advance to *giving*, as well as gathering, hoarding, and protecting. It can even move on to advanced communication and harmony with other minds.

The development of the *"Higher Self,"* a governing spirit, conscience, or consciousness is evidence of an even more secure existence. The nature of this Higher Self is different from the nature of the mind. The mind must deal with the hard, everyday, practical issues. The spirit deals with long-term abstracts and concepts. The mind is active and assertive. The spirit is subtle, observing, and guiding.

The active and assertive nature of the mind often allows it to dominate the spirit. After all, which is more important, food or brotherhood? The hungry body helps the insecure mind shout down any argument from the spirit that "Man does not live by bread alone." On the other hand, the *satisfied* body and *secure* mind may allow a deeper consideration of the cosmic questions that the spirit seeks to reconcile.

TABLE 17-1:
ESSENTIAL MIND ASPECTS

Survival	Immediate Gratification
Security	Activity
Fear	Identification
Pain (avoiding)	Separation
Pleasure (seeking)	Judgment
Sensory Stimulation	Control

HEALTHY DRIVER, HEALTHY CAR
MIND/HEALTH RELATIONSHIP

Regrettably, most minds stay trapped in the pursuit of basic necessities, and remain in the pleasure/pain circus.

Exactly where the mind-driver goes, and what kind of care it takes of the body depends on the physical and mental messages it receives, and how it processes them. An understanding of the way the mind receives and digests input is crucial for those who wish to regain control of the mind and the body it manages.

According to ayurvedic principles, ***most illness is caused by wrong digestion; physical digestion, mental digestion or both.*** The treatment of illness with "mind-body medicine" is now an accepted principle in most health sciences.

When the mind incorrectly processes the input it receives, the toxic results are detrimental to both the mental and physical systems. Mental confusion and disorder are often the result.

The mind prefers *any* predictable order to disorder, so when it is confused, the mind frequently creates a *different* or unusual *order* out of what it perceives to be chaos and loss of control. That unusual mental re-ordering may be dys-functional in the practical world (a *dys*-order), but it is still a form of order.

These mental "dys-orders" can take many forms. They can be short-term responses to difficult life situations, such as the loss of a loved person or object, or they can become extended, and turn into long-term patterns of behavior. The mind's new mental approach may be helpful or dysfunctional, and the mind may jump from one thought system to another.

Just as there are different types of physical body-vehicles with different qualities and characteristics, there are also different types of mind-drivers with identifiable qualities. In the School of Life, learning to appreciate and deal with the plethora of different mind-drivers is a major part of the curriculum. Ayurvedic psychology can help.

PINOCCHIO
IRRESPONSIBLE MIND

The process of maintaining and directing the body-vehicle on a moment-to-moment basis can be so overwhelming that the mind can lose track of the passenger's spiritual destination in the maze of details and desires.

After hours of difficult and confused mind travel, the spiritual passenger may give up on its lofty goals, and fall asleep in the back of the cab. The mind is then free to take the body and spirit to any carnival its senses, whims, and emotions may choose.

The mind then creates its own agenda that is usually related to practical and sensory issues. Does the cab need gas? Did I get the registration renewed? Is the traffic bad up ahead? Shall I smoke a cigarette?

Long-term, religious and philosophical questions are not primary mind concerns because spiritual answers and achievements often seem out of reach in the real world:

> "I can't be a great stock car driver because I don't have the money, the guts, or the time. I have too many responsibilities, yada, yada …"

So the mind gives up on the spirit's destination and becomes overwhelmed by day-to-day issues. It gives up trying to get somewhere significant, and repeatedly stops at the ESPN Zone. It's easy. It's simple. The mind distracts itself from the fact that it doesn't have the fortitude to make it to the mountain top. So it settles for Mickey D's, the tube, and a Bud.

After a long struggle, the spirit-passenger my also give up and let the mind take over. Where the spirit is taken is often the result of the type of mind that has been left in charge.

In Ayurvedic thinking, the different quality-types of mind are AIR, FIRE, or EARTH.

SPIRITUAL BEINGS & SPACE CADETS
AIR-TYPE MIND

AIR-type mind-drivers are like Sally in Chapter 2. Their minds have light, mobile, unpredictable AIR-like qualities (see Table 17-2).

Their thinking is agile and fast. Their interests change frequently and quickly. They can be talkative and unfocused, and their minds can easily wander out of control. Because they have quick minds, they are often very creative and informed, and can understand many different points of view. But because their minds change direction quickly, they can lack depth in their understanding. They can also be fairly superficial in their interests, and their opinions often waver.

When balanced, AIR-type minds tend to be good at communication, thinking, writing and creating. They tend to be artistic and to live in imaginative, changeable worlds. They are often sociable, but they can also become loners if overwhelmed. They are sensitive and often rebellious. They are the most flexible and adaptable of the mind types.

AIR minds are frequently indecisive and unsteady. Their focus and determination are irregular, and they are often inconsistent. Self-confidence is frequently a struggle, and they develop images of themselves that can quickly change from positive to negative.

Fear can be a dominant emotion for imbalanced AIR-types. It is often their first reaction to new and different situations. Worry, anxiety and instability are often hallmarks of their emotional states.

AIR-type memory is often erratic and is most effective in the short-term. People with AIR minds are often described as "spacey" and "absent-minded." Their mental endurance is more limited than other mind-types, and they tend to over-extend themselves even though they get exhausted from extra mental work.

Britney Spears, Lindsay Lohan and Paris Hilton may be good examples of light-weight AIR-type minds.

Robin Williams, Andy Worhol and Chris Rock may represent positive creative AIR type Minds.

TABLE 17-2:
MIND QUALITIES

AIR-Mind	FIRE-Mind	EARTH-Mind
Light	Sharp	Satisfied
Mobile	Penetrating	Passive
Unpredictable	Creative	Stable
Fast	Driven	Slow
Agile	Winning	Long Memory Good
Creative	Intellectual	Accepting
Informed	Perceptive	Persistent
Verbal	Organized	Building
Unfocused	Systematic	Romantic
Superficial	Discriminating	Sentimental
Memory Erratic	Judgmental	Loving
Memory Short-term	Opinionated	Emotional
Worry	Self-righteous	Devoted
Anxiety	Angry	Attached
Instability	Aggressive	Hoarding
Spacey	Domineering	Greedy
Absent-minded	Goal-Oriented	Procrastinating
Mental fatigue	Obsessed / Rigid	Consistent
Flexible	Intelligent	Reliable

MY-WAY-OR-THE-HIGHWAY GENIUS
FIRE-TYPE MIND

FIRE-type minds have the same qualities as FIRE-type bodies. Like Bertold from Chapter 2, these minds are sharp, penetrating, creative and driven (see Table 17-2).

They are competitive. They are winners - or else! They are often highly intelligent, perceptive, organized, systematic, discriminating and judgmental. They can be very opinionated and self-righteous. They are often prone to heated discussions and to anger if their point of view is not accepted. They can be aggressive, domineering and fanatic. They make effective leaders. They are strong-willed, sometimes to the point of obsession.

521

FIRE-type minds are often rigorous, probing, and scientific. They tend to be good at organizational, mechanical and mathematical endeavors. They are innovative and creative. They like order, rules, laws and discipline. They are highly intelligent and quick-witted.

Because of their drive and strength, FIRE-type minds may become rigid and exclusive. They gravitate toward systems of hierarchy and authority. They are hard driving and goal oriented.

Hilary Clinton, Donald Trump, and George Will might be examples of FIRE-type minds.

LOVERS & COUCH POTATOES
EARTH-Type MIND

Big-bellied, truck driving EARTH-type minds tend to be more satisfied and passive. Like the physical EARTH qualities, these minds may be a bit slower, but they are stable and retain much of what comes their way (see Table 17-1).

EARTH minds tend to be accepting and non-rebellious rather than creative or inventive, although once things get started, the EARTH mind is often good at building and finishing projects. They like familiarity and predictability. They tend to be loving, romantic, sentimental and emotional. They are often loyal and devoted.

Because they like stability and are less fond of change, EARTH-type minds tend to become attached, possessive, and even greedy. They like wealth and will use power to control the road.

EARTH minds can also stagnate, and they often have problems with motivation and procrastination. They are consistent.

Loving, EARTH-like minds may be exemplified by Mother Theresa and Oprah.

FREEWAY PERSONALITIES
MENTAL/SPIRITUAL CHARACTER

When quality descriptions are applied to the mind or spirit, the implications and terminology change. Not only can the mind have AIR, FIRE, or EARTH-like *qualities*, it can also be described as having developed a *personality or character* that is dominated either by PURITY, ACTIVITY, or NEGATIVITY. These character traits are described in greater detail in Chapter 24.

NEGATIVE minds have personalities that are often described as dark, threatening, or evil. Most neighborhood gang members don't don't go around helping people feel safe and secure. These personalities are often dominated by NEGATIVITY ("Tamas"). They often have minds that are dominated by the EARTH or FIRE tendencies.

In contrast, church school bus drivers tend toward a character or personality that is dominated by charity, sharing, and spiritual concerns. These traits of PURITY ("Satva") are often associated with a mind that has balanced AIR qualities.

Highway engineers, on the other hand, tend to be super practical, very active, and good at creating, directing, and achieving. Their personalities are aptly described as being dominated by ACTIVITY ("Rajas"), and their minds often have traits associated with the FIRE quality.

523

DUDE, WHAT'S YOUR SIGN?
MENTAL STEREOTYPING

Some of this mental quality grouping sounds like a horoscope from the back of a tabloid newspaper. These Ayurvedic descriptions of mind qualities are *observations* of mental trait groupings that have been noted repeatedly over the centuries.

Observe the people you know. They are all interesting mixtures of mind qualities, to be sure. But some are definitely parked on the couch, while others are straining at the starting line, and still others are off in the clouds.

Of course, as situations and moods change, our mental qualities change with them. Although we do move from one mental quality or personality to another, the majority of the time there is a tendency to be one of the specific mind types.

It is easier to get a handle on the many individual qualities of mind if those qualities can be organized into some recognizable recurring pattern. Ayurveda says that certain qualities tend to occur together as described above. Any individual mind can have any of the above-mentioned qualities.

DALE ERNHARDT ON A MOTOR SCOOTER
BODY-MIND MATCHING

Each type of motor vehicle is designed to be driven in a certain way by a driver with a certain mental personality.

Race cars are usually driven by people with excellent attention, focusing ability, eye-hand coordination, and quick responses. Truck drivers, on the other hand, are often those who are patient, can tolerate boredom, and have the ability to stay awake. Scooters and motorcycles are often driven by those who are good at quickly changing directions and starting and stopping.

In the same way, each physical body-type is designed to be managed by a mind with certain characteristics. Fortunately, human vehicles are usually matched at birth with minds that correspond to their physical characteristics. As a result, they run more efficiently and effectively. At birth, each person has a natural, genetic mind quality ("Manas Prakruti").

People with AIR-like bodies usually have mobile and changeable AIR-like minds. Motocross racers have quick responses. FIRE-type bodies usually have minds that are sharp, accurate and goal-oriented. Sports car drivers are precise and determined. EARTH-type bodies are matched with minds that are steady, patient and persistent, and good for the long haul.

Although it is less common, people of one body-frame type can have minds that are of a different type. This is often the result of powerful circumstances of their environments that are of a quality different from their body type.

Big, heavy, EARTH-type people can have AIR-like minds that move quickly and unpredictably. Truck drivers may take too much stimulating medication and become mentally AIR-like. They talk a mile a minute, don't remember things well, and become spacey in their expressions and decisions.

Hot, medium-build FIRE-type bodies are sometimes run by minds that are AIR-like and unpredictable as a result of excessive, over-extended efforts at achievement. An executive can take on too much responsibility and become scattered. The same FIRE-like executive can become mentally EARTH-like; heavy and slow as a result of taking sedative medication to balance the stress of his or her achievement efforts. AIR or EARTH-types can develop razor-sharp tongues, critical manners and unstoppable career drives that are typical of FIRE-type minds.

When this type of mismatch occurs, problems often develop. If a race car driver like Dale Ernhardt or Jeff Gordon were forced to drive a motor scooter or a truck all the time, they might push the vehicle beyond its natural abilities. In a similar way, minds that do not match their bodies may cause mismatched behavior that may not be healthy over time.

The identification of a person's mind type by the characteristics of his body can be deceiving. In the same way, trying to determine a person's body type by his or her mind characteristics can be misleading as well. It is important to separate the two. Excess mind qualities can be problematic. They can be balanced by increasing their opposite mental or physical qualities. A frenetic AIR mind can be calmed by heavy EARTH-quality foods, medicines, and activities. Aggressive FIRE minds can be cooled by AIR or EARTH interventions, and a sluggish EARTH mind in be stimulated by adding AIR or FIRE.

Conversely, correcting a physical quality excess with a different and counter-balancing mind-quality may be beneficial. Physical heaviness may be aided by an AIR-like mind that demands movement, an over-heated body may be cooled by a quiet EARTH-type mind, and a fragile AIR body may be strengthened by the habits of an EARTH or FIRE-type mind.

ROAD WEARY
LIFE EFFECT ON MIND

More often, however, it is the experience of driving life's highways that changes the qualities of our mind-driver. One might start out as an alert and attentive driver but, over time, one may lose one's edge. At that stage, a mind-driver becomes heavy and EARTH-like, and lacks the ability to run a speed vehicle.

We may also put unhealthy mental fuel into our own mind-engines and cause them to become unbalanced. If we feed ourselves violence, sex, power, and greed every day, we will become over-heated FIRE-brand minds. If we smoke, drink alcohol, and do speed all the time, we'll wind up driving our Mack trucks down the interstate at a hundred miles an hour! If we watch soap operas and food commercials on TV all day long, our mental engines can become selfish, greedy and clogged. If we wind up working the same boring, mentally stagnating job day after day, our mind engines can get sluggish and may not manage our bodies well.

Since the mind-driver governs the body-vehicle, *what we feed the mind is absolutely crucial.* There is little else in the mechanics of our journey through life that is more important.

We may believe that we can tolerate a mental junk food diet, but, like the physical body:

The mental body is what it eats and digests.

Maternal deprivation syndrome, in which a child does not grow physically for lack of a caretaker's attention, is an example of the mind's need for nourishment. Brain washing is another example of force feeding the wrong things to a needy mind and coming out with a bizarre result.

In ayurveda, the out-of-balance mind condition is simply known as the *mental imbalance state* ("Manas Vikrukti"). Either TOXINS or one of the three qualities (AIR, FIRE, or EARTH) build up in our mental engine until it runs too fast, too hot, too slow, or too sticky.

On the other hand, if our minds are exposed to healthy mental fuels for our specific needs, rebalancing happens, and a healthy mind can guide us to greater achievements.

DRIVER PERFORMANCE EVALUATIONS
MIND EVALUATION CHECKLISTS

As with the body, the mind can be evaluated to determine whether its qualities are like AIR, FIRE, or EARTH. Circle the qualities in the columns in Tables 17-3 and 17-4 below. Then, add up the number of circles in each column to see which mind-type is dominant, secondary, and tertiary for your **Genetic** Mind-type, and your **Current** Mind-state.

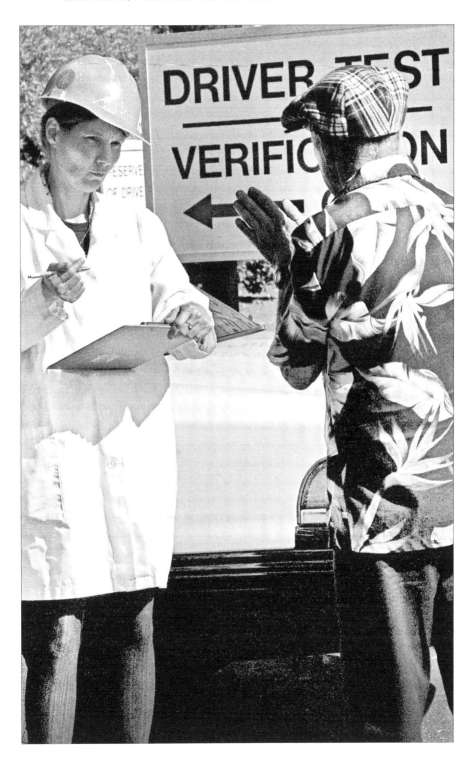

TABLE 17-3:
MIND-TYPE EVALUATION CHECKLIST

GENETIC STATE - THE MIND DURING THE MID 20s

Circle the description in one of the three categories that most closely applies.

Mind Quality / Characteristic	AIR	FIRE	EARTH
Speed	Fast	Quick	Slow
Precision	Random	Accurate	Certain
Compulsion	Common	Common	Rare
Memory, Short-Term	Changeable	Excellent	Fair
Memory, Long-Term	Poor	Precise if useful	Excellent
Sleep Quantity	Less	Moderate	More
Sleep Quality	Active	Good	Heavy
Temper	Unpredictable	Fiery, reactive	Cool
Spirituality	Changeable	Goal-oriented	Deep
Attachment	Little	Moderate	High
Ego	Fickle	High	Low
Competitiveness	Moderate	High	Low
Status Concern	Low	High	Moderate
Clothing	Creative	Neat	Relaxed
Generosity	High	Purposeful	Low
TOTAL	_____	_____	_____

TABLE 17-4:
MIND-TYPE EVALUATION CHECKLIST

YOUR CURRENT MIND CONDITION

Circle the description in one of the three categories that most closely applies.

Mind Quality / Characteristic	AIR	FIRE	EARTH
Speed	Fast	Quick	Slow
Precision	Random	Accurate	Certain
Compulsion	Common	Common	Rare
Memory, Short-Term	Changeable	Excellent	Fair
Memory, Long-Term	Poor	Precise if useful	Excellent
Sleep Quantity	Less	Moderate	More
Sleep Quality	Active	Good	Heavy
Temper	Unpredictable	Fiery, reactive	Cool
Spirituality	Changeable	Goal-oriented	Deep
Attachment	Little	Moderate	High
Ego	Fickle	High	Low
Competitiveness	Moderate	High	Low
Status Concern	Low	High	Moderate
Clothing	Creative	Neat	Relaxed
Generosity	High	Purposeful	Low
T O T A L	_____	_____	_____

MENTAL QUALITIES

Fill in the totals for AIR, FIRE, and EARTH from Tables 17-3 and 17-4

(17-3) Mid-20s or GENETIC - MENTAL QUALITIES

	AIR	FIRE	EARTH
TOTAL	_____	_____	_____

Circle your **dominant quality** (highest number above): AIR FIRE EARTH
Circle your **secondary quality** (next highest number): AIR FIRE EARTH
Circle your **tertiary quality** (lowest number): AIR FIRE EARTH

(17-4)   Current or IMBALANCE STATE - MENTAL QUALITIES

	AIR	FIRE	EARTH
TOTAL	_____	_____	_____

Circle your **dominant imbalance quality** (highest): AIR FIRE EARTH
Circle your **secondary quality** (next highest number): AIR FIRE EARTH
Circle your **tertiary quality** (lowest number): AIR FIRE EARTH

Summarize yourself by circling one quality on each line below:

Your **dominant MENTAL GENETIC quality**: AIR FIRE EARTH

Your **dominant CURRENT
        MENTAL IMBALANCE quality**: AIR FIRE EARTH

With this knowledge of your mental qualities, you can begin to choose methods to bring yourself back into balance with your desired mental state. Meditation is an excellent tool for developing an awareness of one's mental state.

MENTAL IPODS
MENTAL POLLUTION

If we eat bad food, we can expect to get sick. If we take in negative mental messages that are filled with pain, fear, violence, anger, hate, greed, etc., it should be no surprise that we would feel mentally uncomfortable.

Negative mental images may not immediately affect us overtly, but over time, they can build up and create an agitated, painful, or depressed state. Once this mental junk is ingested, it must be digested. If it isn't, it festers in the subconscious in much the same way that undigested food ferments in the digestive tract and causes problems.

Mental digestion involves a transformation of experience into awareness and wisdom. If we have an intellect that is strong, and the strength to look directly at our mental issues, then our mental trash can be disposed of more easily. The process consists of techniques such as controlled breathing, focused attention, awareness, meditation (see Chapter 8) and other practices (see Part Five).

Why do we eat mental junk food? Usually, for the same reasons we take bad physical food; it's available, plentiful, easy, stimulating, and current. Saying "no" to negative and violent movies, TV and ideas means missing out on what's popular. Being left out of cesspool swimming parties may not feel good initially, but in the long run, a healthier life will result.

SNAIL MAIL
INERTIA

If we drive in the mud all the time, we're going to get stuck. According to ayurveda, much of our inability to get going on activities or projects is the result of mental mud. Avoiding mental pollution and participating in uplifting activities is an important way to keep moving.

Of course, one needs a *reason* to get out of the mud. If there's nowhere to go, then there's no need to push the car out of the rut. Goals, hope, and direction are needed for there to be any chance of mental progress. They are derived from planning and spiritual development (see Part Four on Spirituality).

Because the mind and body are interrelated, physical heaviness can also be a source of mental inertia. Just as an overloaded vehicle is harder to drive, many EARTH quality imbalances can result in mental immobility.

An excess of the mental AIR quality is like a vehicle that is spinning its wheels in dry sand. This type of immobility requires increased mental grounding for there to be any traction and progress.

If too much FIRE quality has caused a vehicle to overheat or burn out, then no movement is likely. Treatment of this type of breakdown often requires a cooling down period consisting of mental rest and rebuilding.

In all of these cases, some type of cleanup is indicated. The *Five Cleansings* technique (see Chapter 15, Volume One) can be very useful in removing the mud, heat, or sand in which we get stuck. It can calm, clear and re-set the mind. Breathing techniques can help put the wind back in our sails, and meditation can help us get grounded and rested.

SENDING THE DRIVER TO REHAB
MENTAL COUNTERBALANCING

In the same way that we correct physical imbalances by decreasing the qualities that are present in excess and adding the opposite qualities, we can correct our mental problems with similar re-balancing techniques.

High doses of active FIRE-like mind qualities may be very helpful to move a depressed and passive EARTH-quality mind. In contrast, the calming EARTH-type quality of natural beauty and meditation may be needed to ground a spacey AIR-type mind. In a similar way, cooling ocean images and meditations may be needed to cool and soften an aggressive FIRE-type mind.

Because the mind and breath are closely connected, breathing practices can be especially helpful in controlling and improving the mind. Slow breathing and meditation techniques can help quiet the mind. Rapid breathing can help awaken the mind, and yoga postures can help move both blood and subtle energy to the brain.

Many of the other ayurvedic treatment techniques such as yoga postures, polarity, acupressure, yogic locks, sound, color, foods, herbs, disciplines, austerities, and the Five Cleansings process, can be helpful. (See Chapter 23)

CHAPTER 18:

WORKING FOR
THE POSTAL SERVICE

Mind as Organizer

PREDICT-ABILITY

Things are so disorganized these days...

...and things get done so differently around here every damn time!

...and you never f-ing know how fast to drive some of these sick people...

...whether to talk or shut up...

...what kind of disease they're carrying...

...always moaning away about their problems!...

...

You can't even figure out who to risk picking up off the street...late at night ... !

... no cops around...

It used to be a lot easier. Back when I was driving for the Post Office up in Boulder Creek, everything was defined and predictable. You knew who your supervisor was, and what you werere supposed to be doing...

If you had trouble with the truck, you left it for Chuck. If you had problems with the sort, you gave 'em to Mort. If the mail got mangled, then Millie would untangle it...

There's something about a well-established business that does things the same way every damn time! You know what to expect. It's organized. It's automatic. One bin for the incoming mail, one bin for the outgoing bundles...

In an organized business, if things get hectic, there are established ways to deal with it, both approved and unapproved. It reminds me of the time Arlen, me, and Jesus got stoned after lunch one day, and came back all messed up! So we walk back into the sorting room, and there, right in frikin' front of us, is the District Postal Inspector with a plastic bag of urine collection cups! Well, ...

"Reggie? ... Hey, Reggie!"

... See... Nothing predictable...

... Except being interrupted...

FIGURE 18-1: **GETTING TO THE POST OFFICE**

WORKING FOR THE POSTAL SERVICE
MIND AS ORGANIZER

The mind is like a post office. It handles many different types of sensory and thought input in much the same way that a post office handles many different types of mail. Just as a post office has specific ways of collecting, categorizing, and sorting many different types of mail, the mind has its own complex ways of collecting and sorting sensory and thought input.

Definite routines are developed in both the post office and the mind that aid in the efficiency of this sorting process. When problems arise, adjustments are made. These adjustments can help solve, cover up, continue, or worsen the problems.

This postal organization is housed in a physical building, and that organization is responsible for the building's maintenance, in much the same way that the mind is responsible for the physical body. Understanding the mind's organization is essential for maintaining the health of the mental and physical bodies. There are many theories of mind organization. Not surprisingly, ayurveda and yoga have their own viewpoints.

The mind is closely associated with the nervous system, so an understanding of nervous system function is also important for understanding the mind.

LETTERS, MAILBOXES, & HIGHWAYS
SENSORY STIMULI, RECEPTORS, & IMPULSES

The body interacts with the sensory world by receiving the physical stimuli of light, sound, touch, taste and smell. It receives these stimuli through sensory receptors in much the same way that a mailbox receives letters.

There are many different types of stimuli-letters and many types of sensory-receptor-mailboxes. If the mailbox-receptors are defective, then the sensations are not received and nothing is noticed. Some metabolic and neurological conditions can cause a loss of sensation at this level.

The stimuli that are successfully received are transported to the central nervous system in much the same way that postal vans transport letters to the central postal station for sorting. These impulses travel over smaller nerves to larger and larger ones just as postal collection vans travel from small roads to larger highways on the way to the mind/brain post office. If the nerve-highways are damaged by illness or disease, then the impulses will have difficulty reaching the post office. Poor nutrition, disease, and under-use of the sensese can cause troubles all along the nerve route to the post office.

In Ayurvedic thinking, the road to the sensation sorting center can be dried or cracked by excessive AIR quality, burned by extra FIRE quality, or clogged by mudslide-like EARTH quality. Multiple sclerosis is an example of AIR-drying and/or FIRE-burning of the nerve pathways. Diabetic neuropathy is another example of a burned nerve route. Some genetic diseases such as glycogenoses can cause an EARTH-like clogging of the nerve pathways.

MAIL COLLECTION VANS
ELECTRICAL IMPULSE TRANSMISSION

Much of what the mind is about is the movement and organization of electricity. The post-office-mind loves activity and stimulation! The more delivery vans that come through the post office gates the happier (to a point) the activity-hungry mind becomes. If no mail is delivered, the mind becomes agitated and makes activity of its own.

Often, it doesn't even matter whether the electrical impulses the mind receives result in pain or pleasure. As long as there are impulses, the mind can do busy-ness. The mind can create plenty of problems for itself and the physical body in the process of avoiding the dreaded boredom (peace) that comes from lack of stimuli.

In ayurvedic thinking, the electricity in the nervous system
with the AIR quality. If there is excess AIR quality in the h.
symptoms of extra nervous activity are often seen including t
nervousness, anxiety, neuroses, and even convulsions.

If excess FIRE activity is present, then the nerves may become infla.   .ng
in burning pain (neuritis), or numbness and tingling. Excess EAR. . quality
in the nerves may result in a loss of sensitivity or a sluggishness of impulse
transmission.

ROUTINE MAIL
AUTONOMIC NERVOUS SYSTEM

The handling of the electrical messages in the nervous system is largely automatic. Just as a race car driver must focus on the track and the other cars and not
on the mechanics of the car, many everyday body functions that do not require
the attention of the mind are continuously controlled subconsciously. Breathing, heart rate, blood vessel tone, secretions, sphincters, temperature, and many
other activities are all removed from routine consciousness so that the mind's
attention can be given to other activities.

These automatic functions are governed by the *autonomic* nervous system. Within
that system, two separate subsystems, the *sympathetic* and *parasympathetic*
systems, work together to balance the nervous activity in the body so that it runs
smoothly.

A knowledge of the ways that these systems work is helpful in understanding the
workings of the mind.

STIMULATING MAIL
SYMPATHETIC NERVOUS SYSTEM

When letters marked "URGENT!" or "OPEN IMMEDIATELY" are received,
they elicit an immediate response. In the mind and body, dangerous or threatening
messages stimulate a "fight or flight" response from the body's sympathetic
nervous system.

In much the same way that a burglar alarm sounds warnings to the residents, the
neighbors, and the police, the body's sympathetic nervous system automatically
sounds alarms in many parts of the body.

When the sympathetic system is stimulated, the adrenal glands secrete epinephrine
(a.k.a. adrenalin) that speeds up the heart and dilates the pupils in the eyes.
Blood vessels are opened to supply more blood to vital organs such as the heart
and brain, while other blood vessels are narrowed to take blood away from less

response organs such as the skin and the gastrointestinal tract. Sugar is released from the liver into the blood stream to power the emergency response. Blood clotting ability is increased in case injury occurs, muscle strength and sweating are increased.

When the sympathetic nervous system is stimulated, the mind becomes more alert. This state of alertness is energizing and invigorating. For that reason, stimulating the sympathetic nervous system becomes pleasurable and desirable. Many dangerous behaviors can be explained as an attempt to get this "adrenalin rush."

In Ayurvedic thinking, the sympathetic nervous system also has many characteristics of the AIR quality, so activities and substances that stimulate the AIR quality are likely to stimulate the sympathetic nervous system. Conversely, things that calm the AIR quality tend to calm the sympathetic nervous system. Using the techniques for calming the AIR quality, or increasing the EARTH quality (see Chapter 15) will often help in dealing with a flood of stimulating mail, or the desire for stimulation.

CALMING MAIL
PARASYMPATHETIC NERVOUS SYSTEM

In contrast to the stimulating messages that start activity in the sympathetic nervous system, messages that are calming trigger the "slow down" *parasympathetic* nervous system.

The heart rate is slowed, the pupils are constricted, and the sphincters are relaxed. The intestines go back to work absorbing food, and routine glandular secretions are discharged. Nor-epinephrine (a.k.a. noradrenalin) is released, and the blood supply is returned to non-emergency areas in the body such as the gastrointestinal tract and the kidneys.

According to ayurvedic theory, EARTH quality is responsible for the activity of the parasympathetic nervous system. Substances and activities that affect the EARTH quality can alter the activity and effects of the sympathetic nervous system.

BATTERIES
CHEMICAL NEUROTRANSMITTERS

Another primary means of mind stimulation or sedation involves adjusting the levels of the various chemical neurotransmitters (NTs) circulating in the body. These chemicals act primarily on the nervous system, and, therefore, on the mind. They are like tiny batteries that have been charged with chemical energy by the body's electrical and/or metabolic resources.

In the nervous system, there is a gap between individual nerve cells. Because it is difficult for regular electrical impulses to bridge this "synaptic gap," neuro-

transmitter batteries are used to transport electrical/chemical energy across it. Like ferries crossing a river of intracellular fluid, bundles of neurotransmitter batteries are transported across the nerve gap where they release their energy messages to the nerve cells.

These NT chemicals do not need to remain in the nervous system. Once released they can also travel in the body-fluid-streams to many different parts of the body and brain. When they arrive, the different types of chemical batteries have many different effects on the nerves, the brain, and the mind. Many of these batteries fit into specific receptor sockets in the brain, and light up activities that eventually result in either PAIN or PLEASURE!

The post office mind is therefore very concerned about the supply of these neurotransmitter batteries, and their distribution to different parts of the body. If the number of PAIN-producing batteries exceeds the number of PLEASURE-producing ones, then states of discomfort or depression occur. Messages are then sent directing that more of the pleasing, energizer-bunny-type batteries be produced or obtained from outside the body.

This effort to obtain higher net levels of PLEASURE-producing neurotransmitters is the basis of pleasure-seeking, addiction, and many other behaviors.

It is therefore important to understand what gets the different neurotransmitter batteries charged up and what drains them. One answer is the mind itself! If our attitudes and circumstances are positive, then more pleasurable NTs are created, and we feel even better. If attitudes and conditions are difficult and negative, then our happy battery levels are more rapidly drained.

Another factor that affects the way that NT batteries are created and charged is the type of chemicals that are available to make neurotransmitters. The body's NT chemistry is heavily influenced by the type of food that is taken. Chemicals and drugs that affect NTs are the basis of the pharmacological treatment of depression and anxiety.

There are dozens different neurotransmitter batteries that serve different functions in the nervous system. Some are stimulating, some stabilizing, and some depressive.

In ayurvedic thinking, most neurotransmitters are of the FIRE type, so if we want to FIRE ourselves up, then taking FIERY foods can often be helpful. If stimulating NT's are desired, then AIR foods often work as well. To calm things down, heavy EARTH foods are needed.

Once again, it's all about balancing qualities.

In any event, because we are primarily concerned with pain and pleasure impulses, we must be primarily concerned with whatever tweaks our NTs.

MANAGING THE MAIL
ORGANIZING STIMULI

One function of the mind is to sort and organize all the chemical and electrical communications that come through the brain's intake portals.

There are many theories that attempt to explain the workings of the mind and its responses to everyday and unusual events. In yoga and ayurveda, various aspects of mind organization are identified, and explanations of how the mind works are given.

The following represents the author's interpretation of the aspects of the mind according to yoga philosophy. The interested reader is referred to the Yoga Sutras of Patanjali and other materials in the bibliography for the basis of this description and for other interpretations.

TABLE 18-1: **THE FOUR MINDS**

MIND	MAIL ANALOGY
SENSORY	POST OFFICE INTAKE
EGO	POSTMARK
DISCRIMINATORY	SORTING
AWARENESS	QUARTERLY REPORT

SORTING THE MAIL
INPUT ORGANIZATION

Once the sensory impulses and thoughts are dumped on the post office sorting room table, the organizational process begins. This sensory input mind is known as "Manas" in yoga philosophy. It receives and prepares the sensations for the other sorting tasks of the mind that follow.

Sensations, impressions, thoughts, and beliefs are circulated throughout the mind-post office until they find their locations in one or more of the many specialty mail rooms. In each individual mail room, the mail is placed into a series of filing cubicles. It is eventually filed either as "pain," "pleasure," or "neutral." From there, mail is sent out of the post office in the form of "responses."

A disorder of any of the qualities of AIR, FIRE, or EARTH, can result in sensory intake errors. AIR disorders often result in oversensitivity, FIRE excess yields hyperintensity, and EARTH excess brings blurring and a lack of sensitivity.

HAZARDOUS MAIL
URGENT/DANGEROUS STIMULI

If a piece of mail is received that registers "DANGER!" then that stimulus is sent directly to the mental security department. From there, alarms can be sounded that can result in a "fight or flight" response to danger. The anxiety/security status of the mind can be raised or lowered from yellow to orange to red, and various sphincters can then be tightened or loosened in response.

Artificially triggering the danger alarm is one way the mind can get some stimulation and excitement. Such false alarms also result in the mental post office being temporarily cleared of bothersome psychological problems. Of course, many times, creating a dangerous crisis just adds to the list of problems, but facing any current problems is conveniently postponed due to the immediate crisis.

The AIR quality is usually associated with urgent situations, so excesses of AIR qualities in a person's life can result in more frequent pushing of the panic button. FIRE excess can also cause inappropriate demands for action.

POSTMARKING DEPARTMENT
PERSONAL IDENTIFICATION

Once the stimulus-mail has successfully passed through the dangerous materials detector, it is sent to the postmarking department and stamped with a mark that identifies it as having been handled by that particular individual's mind.

This identification with the stimuli, thoughts, or beliefs is the first part of the mind's ego process. "These are *MY* thoughts" or "This is what *I* feel." The FIRE quality is usually involved in most ego issues.

UNION SHOP
EGO

The ego mind (known in yoga philosophy as "Ahamkar") identifies the sensory mail as "MY" smell, taste, touch, sound, or vision. Thoughts and beliefs are stamped with the "I think" and "I believe" postmark. They are separated from the sensations and thoughts experienced by others.

Because the workers in a particular post office are there all the time, they quickly identify the place as "MY post office!" Then, they unionize! The ego-mind is a lot like a worker's union, in which self-interest is often the primary concern. In order to protect itself, complex procedures and priorities are created, rules are established, and the politics of individuality begins.

The goal of the postal ego-union is to get the most for itself. Since the mind loves and needs stimulation, the ego-union works to make sure that there's plenty of sensory and thought mail for it to handle. If the sensory mail stops flowing, then mind-workers could be laid off. This fear of mind inactivity ("boredom") can cause mental panic, and creation of needless and counter-productive mental and physical "make work" activity.

The volume of mental and sensory mail can become excessive, and serious strain on the mental sorting machinery may occur. For this reason, the ego-union uses many different tactics, and plays many games in an effort to deal with difficult sensory and thought realities.

There are positive and negative ways for the mind to deal with stresses and anxieties. The ego-union can negotiate in a straight forward and constructive way, or it can play dangerous anesthetic and diversionary games that create internal confusion, maladaptive behavior, and poor physical health.

The defenses that the ego puts up to protect itself create the conflicts that are the subjects of classical psychology (see Chapters 20-22).

The main areas of ego-mind concern are:

1. Pleasure & Pain	(Physical & Mental)
2. Safety/Fear/Anxieties	(Real & Imagined)
3. Emotions & Feelings	(Helpful & Difficult)
4. Reality & Fantasy	(External & Internal)
5. Needs & Desires	(Imagined & Actual)
6. Impulses & Restraints	(Primary & Created)
7. Conflict & Compromise	(External & Internal)
8. Relationships	(Self & Non-Self)

These subjects constitute the core studies of life's educational curriculum. They are the reason we are on this planet. If constructive and logical approaches to these issues are used, then ego-mind acceptance responses are increased. If individual power is denied in thes union will rebel, and conflicts will be created in the environmen mind itself.

These areas of ego-mind games have been discussed extensively by many experts over the years, and many different points of view have been expressed. But the primary and overriding mental principle is that:

The ego-mind will do just about anything to avoid or modify pain or a threat to its own existence.

The effort to defend the ego-mind can easily eclipse the spirit-fulfilling purposes for which the mind was created in the first place. Mind games frequently become more important than achieving life goals. The ever present struggle between union and management, between individuality and community, is one of the fundamental health-depleting conflicts of life.

SAFETY & HAZARDS IN THE POST OFFICE
PLEASURE & PAIN

One of the mind's major preoccupations is safety and security. The mind system is specifically designed to promote survival. Any sensation or thought that brings a sense of safety to the mind satisfies this instinctual need, and is identified as "good" or "pleasurable."

In contrast, anything that threatens safety and security causes fear. Fear is the basis of mental "pain." In order to satisfy its primary job of securing safety, the mind will do almost anything to *insure that feelings of safety and security dominate its activity.*

Safety = Pleasure
Fear = Pain

The search for safety/pleasure sensations, and the avoidance of fear/pain impressions is the dominant goal of all postal mind workers.

*Life is About
How We Respond to Pleasure and Pain*

TYPES OF PAIN MAIL
PAIN QUALITY TYPING

It is important to study the nature of the pain as it arrives. By understanding its purpose, and becoming more comfortable with it, we reduce it.

Some pain is AIR-like. It is sudden and rough, and it hits quickly. It comes from out of the blue, is on and off, and is worsened by cold and dry emotional conditions. Other pains are more burning, angry, penetrating and FIRE-like in nature. Still others are heavy, dull and depressing EARTH-type pains.

We can then become aware of how much of each type of pain we receive, create, find comforting, abhor and so forth. This identification helps us feel that the pain is more familiar and that we have some control over it. *Labeling* our pain can become a complication if that process results in pigeonholing the pain and not facing it.

At the identification mind level, we can ask whether the pain we are feeling is something that we *are*, something we *own*, something to which we were simply *exposed*, or something that we "*deserve*."

At the awareness mind level, we can look at the spectrum of our mind behaviors and the pain that those behaviors bring. We can draw further conclusions or illusions about the meaning or the causes of the pain.

AIR MAIL
AIR-TYPE MENTAL PAIN

Mental pain that is based primarily on fear is identified in ayurveda as AIR-type mental pain. The subtypes of fear that include anxiety and worry are also AIR-like in nature. If the mental pain is irregular, unpredictable, and occurs in several areas of concern, then it is more likely to be of the AIR type.

Mental pain that is bitter in nature and exhausting in its effect is also typical of AIR-type mental pain.

If we can identify our mental pain as AIR-like, then we can approach it with therapies that are specific for that type of pain. We can also use the approaches to physical AIR problems to help with mental AIR difficulties because of the connections between the mind and body.

EXPRESS MAIL
FIRE-TYPE PAIN

Mental pain that is dominated by anger and/or hatred is more typical of FIRE-type pain.

Painful emotions that are sharp, penetrating, burning and intense have a significant element of the FIRE quality in them. When painful mental processes develop a spreading quality that carries the anger over into other areas, then this can also be a FIRE-type of mental pain.

As with other types of pain, FIRE pain can be identified and approached from the physical perspective with cooling therapies, as well as with mental treatments that are cooling.

GROUND MAIL
EARTH-TYPE PAIN

If the mental pain has heavy, attached, depressive qualities, then it is viewed as EARTH-type pain, and approached with treatments that are specific for EARTH excess.

Mental difficulties that are numbing, immobilizing, and constant are typical of this kind of pain. Thoughts and emotions that are melancholic, overwhelming, prolonged, and dominated by sadness and melancholy are EARTH-like in nature. They respond to physical management that encourages the introduction of lightness, movement, and energy into physical and mental environments.

MAIL SUBJECTS
THOUGHTS

Some philosophers hold that the essence of a person is in what they do. Others believe that a person's essential nature can be found by examining their thoughts.

What are thoughts? Roughly speaking, *thoughts are the mind's attempt to organize the input it receives*. Those organizational attempts may be further labeled "ideas," "concepts," "expectations," "emotions," "considerations," "beliefs," or "opinions."

The mind is largely a *collection* of thoughts that shape our internal and external worlds. Thoughts also create relationships and attachments. An understanding of common thought patterns can, therefore, be helpful in understanding the mind. This is a crucial step in the process of making positive mental and physical health changes.

What do we think about?

At an early age, we think only of survival basics such as food and protection. We progress in our thought patterns depending on our parenting, cultural, and personal circumstances. Table 18-1 gives a basic listing of some of the more common thought subjects by age.

As life moves on, the subjects of our thoughts and concerns progress in a common pattern as estimated in Table 18-1. While it is certain that there are many variations in this progression, it is interesting to note that several areas consistently take up much of our thought time. Social and family concerns consistently rank high throughout life. Entertainment (diversion) is also consistently important.

Health is not often an issue until later in life when it becomes a nearly all-consuming problem. Paying greater attention to health in the earlier years when we often feel invulnerable is an sign of uncommon wisdom and maturity.

Many people do not follow this age progression of thought activity. They remain stuck in areas that are more typical of younger, less mature people. Possessions and sensory gratifications are examples of thought-activities that are usually of less importance with advancing age when legacy and spiritual/after-life considerations often become more pressing.

TABLE 18-2: COMMON THOUGHT SUBJECTS BY AGE

IN APPROXIMATE ORDER OF IMPORTANCE

YOU ARE WHAT YOU THINK ABOUT

Infant (0 – 2 yrs.)	Toddler (2 – 5 yrs.)	Child (5 – 12 yrs.)	Adolescent (12 – 18 yrs.)	Young Adult (18 – 35 yrs.)	Working adult (35 – 62 yrs.)	Older Adult (62 – 80 yrs.)	Old Adult (over 80)
Sensory	Family	Family	Social	Education	Work	Family	**Health**
Food	Sensory	Social	Sensory	Work	Family	**Health**	Family
Sleep	Food	Entertainment	Entertainment	Social	Money	Social	Social
Family	Learning	Creativity	Food	Sensory	Entertainment	Money	Food
	Social	Food	Sleep	Sex	Social	Chores	Money
	Sleep	Sleep	Money	Money	Creativity	Entertainment	Spirituality
		Chores	Sex	Adventure	Chores	Spirituality	Legacy
			Family	Politics	Food	Politics	Sex
			Creativity	Family	Sex	Creativity	
			Education	**Health**	**Health**	Legacy	
			Chores	Spirituality	Education	Sex	
			Health	Chores	Sensory		
					Spirituality		

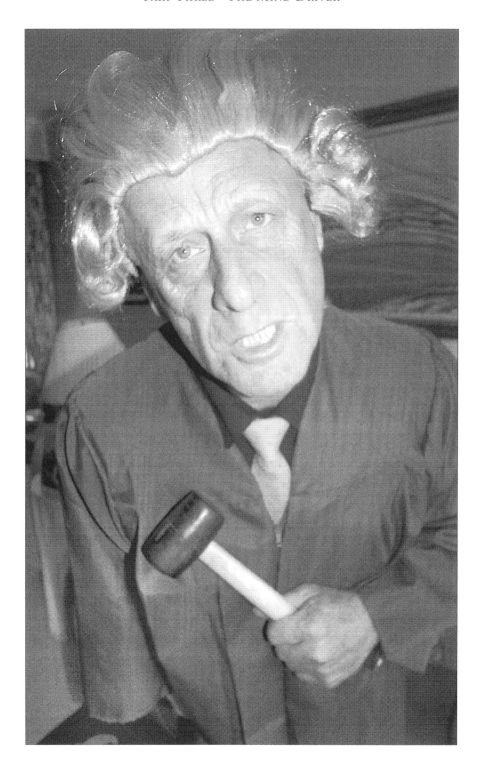

Activity is a favorite food of the mind, so we tend to think about things that are active that stimulate us. Subjects such as education and spirituality that are quiet and relatively inactive are labeled as "boring." Yoga and ayurveda both hold that fewer and quieter thoughts bring a quieter mind, which brings a healthier body, mind, and spirit. "Boredom" can be very healthy!

JUDGING THE MAIL
BELIEFS

After sorting numerous letters, post cards and junk mail, the mind starts to form "opinions" about the information that passes through the mental post office. Eventually, generalizations are created about the value of most thoughts. These patterns of thought are known as "judgments," "conclusions," or "beliefs."

Once these beliefs have been created, similar thoughts are no longer given the same objective consideration. They are filed (judged) on the basis of previously created categories. When this happens, no new views of a subject are created, and old patterns are reinforced. To avoid this type of mental stagnation, yoga philosophy suggests that situations should simply be *observed* and *accepted* for what they are, and not labelled and pigeonholed.

Despite this admonition, much of our living is based on conclusions and beliefs. It is hard not to draw conclusions. Reconsidering every thought every time it occurred would leave no time. The challenge is to pause every now and then, and look at routine things in a new light.

We must also be careful that we do not identify our true selves with our belief patterns. On one level, we may actually be what we believe, but on another:

We are also something more enduring than a collection of mental conclusions.

THE MOST COMMON PAIN-LETTERS
THREE NEGATIVE MESSAGES

While there are many negative messages that the mind receives or creates, there are three common ones that are consistently difficult to manage.

From an early age, we are often told that what we do is "*not good enough,*" or that we "*didn't do it right.*" We get these messages from our teachers, sports coaches, friends, the media, or our parents. If we hear those negative messages often enough, we begin to believe them. We begin to look at everything we do as incorrect or not good enough for *ourselves*! We send ourselves internal memos that are supercritical of our own behavior.

Another common negative message is "*There isn't enough.*" The idea that there are not enough resources in our lives for everyone to share results in the need to hoard and create defenses.

The contrary philosophy is that there is always *infinite abundance*.

If we keep receiving those "didn't do it right" or "not good enough" or "there isn't enough" messages, we are forced to do something with them so that our mental supervisor (conscience, superego) doesn't lose it. Often, we find unhealthy ways to hide from those messages, or to kill the pain of receiving them. (See Chapters 20, 21.)

RUSH HOUR
MODERN LIFE

Modern life comes with plenty of pain (and pleasure as well). Our efforts toward survival in a painful modern world result in many challenging issues and behavioral responses.

The ability to support oneself and one's family often depends on enduring something painful. Every day we are reminded about the need to achieve and acquire. Getting up day after day and going to a difficult workplace that may be competitive and filled with ego dramas can be terribly stressful. Yet we need to create financial equity and security, so we endure the pain. In the process, we become emotionally involved and deeply attached to our creations and efforts.

The pace of modern life is becoming faster and faster. It is *activity-centered*, and quiet behavior is rarely encouraged. This pace often induces many AIR-quality disorders. The media is always bombarding us with worrisome news, reports of violence, and suggestions of personal inadequacy. As a result, maintaining good interpersonal interactions and relationships can become a major challenge.

The toll these and other stresses take on the physical body cannot be underestimated. It is like the daily wear and tear of driving down a road that can be filled with potholes. The mental friction of life's highway is one reason the life experience is often called "the grind!"

WORK IS HARD
LIFE HAS PAIN

When dealing with pain, one of the first steps, from an Eastern philosophical point of view, is to *acknowledge* and *accept* that much of life is indeed painful. Wherever there is pleasure, there is also pain - the two go together and cannot be separated. They are described as the two sides of the same coin.

It is the way that we *respond* to pain and pleasure that is key in yoga/ayurvedic philosophy. The Buddhist orientation is especially directed toward dealing with pain.

An understanding of what pain actually is (Table 18-3) can be helpful in finding ways to deal with it.

TABLE 18-3:

ABOUT PAIN

1. LIFE ALWAYS COMES WITH SOME PAIN.

2. PAIN IS UNIVERSAL.

3. OTHERS OFTEN HAVE GREATER PAIN.

4. PAIN IS TRANSIENT.

5. PAIN IS OFTEN SITUATIONAL.

6. PAIN AND PLEASURE ARE CONNECTED.

7. PAIN AND PLEASURE OFTEN ALTERNATE.

8. PAIN IS A MIND CONCLUSION.

9. PAIN IS NON-ACCEPTANCE BY THE MIND.

10. PAIN IS A OFTEN A REFLECTION OF SELF-INTEREST.

11. ATTACHMENT BRINGS PAIN.

12. PAIN IS A LIFE-LESSON.

13. PAIN IS OFTEN A CALL FOR SELF-CONTROL.

PAPER CUTS
PHYSICAL PAIN

Anything that generates an impulse from a pain receptor through its impulse tracts results in a painful message being filed in the brain.

If the nerve highway to the brain is blocked, or is in a poor state of repair, then fewer pain (or pleasure) impulses get through to the processing post office of the mind. Severe physical pain can be controlled by simply cutting the nerve that runs from the pain source to the brain. This is the basis of some extreme forms of pain surgery. Of course, good messages are also carried by the nerves, so therapeutic cutting of the nerve to avoid the pain messages brings problems of its own.

If the nerve itself is damaged, then a steady stream of emergency repair vehicles carrying pain messages may begin to flow from the damaged area to the postal pain reception center. When certain mail bins receive too much pain mail, they become enlarged. If they can't handle the pain load, then additional *internal* pain messages are added to the list of problems.

Actions need to be taken to deal with this pain increase, and creative patterns of managing the excess pain are rapidly developed. Creating these Defense Mechanism patterns is one of the mind's primary functions.

These response patterns to pain messages are often the result of long-standing habits. These habits can also be patterns of behavior that were present when the new post office mind first opened at birth, according to yoga philosophy.

In Ayurvedic thinking, the AIR quality is involved in registering pain sensations, so taking steps to reduce the AIR quality can result in less pain. Inflammation from FIRE excess can also cause pain.

LET THE GAMES BEGIN!
DEFENSE MECHANISMS

The body and mind respond to pain in many different ways. The actual sensory reception can be modified at the environmental or brain level to reduce or eliminate pain messages coming in (sensory withdrawal).

At the mind level, an erroneous conclusion can be reached that the pain problem simply does not exist (denial) in spite of evidence to the contrary. Another way to deal with pain is to numb it away. Anesthetic defenses constitute this approach. (See Chapter 20.)

Thought patterns can be created that change the nature of the pain to make it less difficult. Thoughts, beliefs and stories can explain away the painful prob-

ₒh diversionary defenses. (See Chapter 21.) Constructive, long-term de-
...se mechanisms can also be created to deal more effectively with pain.

REMOVING THE MAIL BOXES
SENSORY WITHDRAWAL

Because sensory receptors are like mailboxes, they are the starting point for
receipt of nerve activity. If one eliminates the sensory mailboxes, or changes
them so that they cannot receive stimuli, then pain messages do not even get
into the nerve tract highways and no pain occurs.

Desensitizing these nervous receptors is one way to cope with too much pain.
Removing oneself from problematic physical situations and from sensations
that trigger pain responses is an important method to control pain problems.
However, after a while, this type of purposeful isolation can result in a decreased ability to function in the real, sensory world.

LOCKING THE POST OFFICE FRONT DOOR
DENIAL

The mind can ignore painful messages altogether when they arrive, even though
they may be piling up outside the post office entrance. Internal thought and
belief memos then dominate the mind's activity, and keep the mind busy ignor-
ing what's going on outside. Sooner or later, this denial defense results in more
external pain mail being sent by dissatisfied customers on the outside.

Once the pain-mail has forced its way in through the post office front door, the
mind employees must deal with it. Many times, denial responses are transformed into intense emotions.

SHUTTING DOWN FOR THE NIGHT
SLEEP

Another way to avoid dealing with painful life-messages is to sleep through them.
Sleep is necessary to give the mind a rest, as well as to give the physical body time
to recuperate. But mental activity doesn't stop with sleep, and dreams can be far
from restful if the mind remains filled with painful issues in need of resolution.

Dreams can be seen as an attempt to process or digest those mental and emotional
concerns. As with physical food, mental meals must be properly digested. If
there is inadequate mental digestion, then mental TOXINS can build up and
disrupt the mental and physical systems.

Dreams are usually less effective at processing mental issues than are conscious,
waking efforts. If we have unresolved mental issues, we will continue to work

556

on them like a postal employee staying at work after closing. If there is a ton of mental mail to process, more mind energy will be required to work into the night, and sleep may be even less restful.

There are several levels of sleep that are notable. The most restful is the stage of quiet, dreamless sleep, so ayurveda suggests getting adequate amounts of this sleep stage. Avoiding excessive stimulating mental activity and food before sleep is recommended to avoid extra night-time mental activity.

The qualities we bring to our sleep from daytime activity will influence the quality of the sleep itself. If we bring extra EARTH qualities, then our sleep will be heavy, long, dull, and quiet. Water is a common EARTH theme in dreams. AIR sleep is light, short, interrupted, active, and filled with movement. This manifests with dream themes such as flying, running, fear, and inspiration. FIRE qualities in our lives may well result in restless, violent, colorful, creative, and achievement themes.

As a person ages, the amount of sleep normally decreases. Babies (high EARTH quality) normally sleep quite a bit. Older people (high AIR quality) often sleep much less.

Sleep normally accounts for a full third of our lives. If an average person lives for about 66 years, 22 years will have been spent asleep. How we spend those twenty-two years is huge! If we have done adequate mental digestion by facing life's pain, we will usually sleep more restfully.

Quieting the mind with meditation before sleep is a good way to lower the mental activity level and produce sound sleep. Balanced neurotransmitter levels may be necessary to correct sleep problems.

CHAPTER 19:
POSTAL DRIVER'S PASSION

Emotions

GOING POSTAL

I just can't stand it anymore!

I'm tired of it.

Sick and tired.

Sick.

I bust my hump driving these flakes wherever they want to go twelve hours a day, and for what? So that at the end of the month, I get to watch every god-damn cent I earn go to some deadbeat who doesn't deserve it!

The frikin' banks, and their frikin' credit cards. They've got me hooked, now. Every month. Twelve, eighteen, twenty-two, and now thirty percent interest on credit cards! And then, I get to give all my morning shifts to the bastards in the government who let the banks get away with that crap! Republican'ts, Demagogues, third-party freaks – what's the difference?! They're on the take, in control, and they're robbing me frikin' blind every month!

Just look at this weak-ass paycheck! You'd think I barely showed up instead of worked a seventy-hour week. Federal, State, City, SSI, and for what? So they and the frikin' corporate pigs the politicos work for can retire to Palm Springs and play golf every day. The government freaks could give a crap about all the hard working people they sucker into voting for the flags and the crosses they wave in the air every time an election rolls around!

A man can work his whole life and end up with nothing because women control the planet! P.C. or not, it's true! Every damn month. My ex gets hers up front, off the top of my paycheck! And for what? She's already milked me dry! It's been eight frikin' years now that she's been sticking it to me, even after the kids have grown and gone. Just what did she do to deserve a free ride beside sit on her fat ass, watch Oprah, do crossword puzzles, and plan how to use the Great State of California's justice-free legal system to do some good old-fashioned gold digging?

Every time those ego-tripping bastards puts on their judge's robes and look in the mirror, they should apologize to the world for the self-serving legal system they're too goddamn lazy to change.

What a frikin' joke. Presidents can commit perjury, wiretap without warrants, get drunk and shoot someone in the face and get away with it! But let me just try and support myself, and the system is right there to screw me over for the benefit of some blood-sucking crybaby!

,udge now! "Reggie! You did such a great job driving all those
. all week long! You showed up on time, you smiled, you helped
.e, and you drove safely all week long. Now… give all your cash to
ctle bitch over here. And don't forget to SMILE!"

My ᴄ ᴊe was simple enough. I was stupid enough to get married and keep working. If only I could have gotten myself pregnant, and just stayed home with the kids and made sure that Jerry Springer and Judge Judy behaved. If only I'd pretended to care just long enough to find some ugly-ass lawyer to get rid of all my responsibilities, and get me my very own personal income slave!

And do you know what the frikin' Inferior Court of the State of Calinsanity did then? They gave that bitch the house, the furniture, the car, the kids, and left me with the obligation to work myself into an early …

"Hey, Reggie. You got a phone call."

(Piss!)… "Who was it, Margo?!"

"It was June, dude. She said to tell you if you don't get her the alimony check that …"

"Goddamit, Margo! That's none of your damn business! Don't be calling me with that crap!"

"Well, excuse the hell out of me, asshole! See if I take any more messages for you! Don't you think it's about time that you …"

"Quit lecturing me, goddamit! I get enough of that from June?"

"Have a nice day (jerk)."

[click]

MOODY PROBLEM DRIVERS
EFFECT OF EMOTIONS ON HEALTH

Mind activity has a direct effect on health from the physical behavior it elicits, and from its energetic effect on the tissues themselves. *Emotional* mind activity has even more profound physical effects. The intensity of many emotions affect tissues on a deeper physical level than many other mind activities. Specifically, emotions lodge in the connective tissues of the body according to ayurveda.

It is difficult for the modern mind to accept that emotions can be converted into physical substances, but ayurveda teaches that emotions "crystallize" in the connective tissue. These "crystals" can be quite irritating, and can cause stiffness and inflammatory diseases in much the same way that toxic IPODs can harm the tissues. This theory is an extension of the concept that the physical body is a manifestation of more subtle levels of energy (see Chapter 28).

Emotional crystals must be removed or melted for there to be significant improvement in the physical state of patients with connective tissue disorders. Confronting emotional pain is necessary for their removal, and limited crying is thought of as promoting melting and elimination of these crystals.

In modern medicine, emotions are known to have a profound effect on the appetite and the digestive system as well as on sleep. Unresolved emotions are a common cause of psychogenic health problems, and psychosomatic medicine is based on this connection. An understanding of emotions can, therefore, be very useful in bringing them to the surface and releasing them, so that the body can return to a calmer, healthier state.

In Ayurvedic terms, emotions are classified primarily according to their qualities (AIR, FIRE, & EARTH), and their character (POSITIVE, ACTIVE, and NEGATIVE) as described in Chapters 4 & 24).

THRILLS OF THE RACE
EMOTIONS

Many scholars have attempted to organize, define, identify and explain emotions, yet considerable controversy and ambiguity remains. It is not the intent of this book to revisit that maze of difficult emotional terminology, but there are certain aspects of emotions (Table 19-1) about which most experts can agree.

The effect of emotions on the physical body via the nervous and endocrine systems cannot be minimized. In Ayurvedic thinking, emotional influences extend outside the neuro-hormonal systems into the subtle energy system (see Chapter 28) and beyond.

Emotions often involve several of the characteristics mentioned in Table 19-1. Ayurveda holds that any unique combination of those characteristics forms a unique energy pattern at the mind level in a similar way that a collection of wires and charges forms an unique energy pattern. Those mental energy patterns can be negative, positive, or neutral. If emotions are seen as patterns of energy, then the release of energy from these patterns can result in emotional changes. The advanced Yogic/Ayurvedic techniques described in Chapter 28 can help in this energy release process.

Negative emotions tend to occur when certain of these mental energy patterns are combined with the small-self-centered aspects of an individual's consciousness (see Part Four). Positive emotions occur when there is some connection with the Greater-Self-centered aspects of existence.

The wrong use of consciousness energy is a cause of difficult emotions. This means giving too much of our attention to the finite and transient aspects of life rather than to the eternal and internal.

TABLE 19-1: CHARACTERISTICS OF EMOTIONS

EMOTIONS ARE OFTEN:

1. Intense

2. Personal

3. Subjective

4. Exciting or Frightening

5. About Events that are NOT Routine

6. A response to a Strong Physical Stimulus

7. A Perception of Significant Change in a Personal Situation

8. Reflection of the Effects of Pain or Pleasure

9. Complex

10. Ingrained Response Patterns

11. Occur in Clusters with Other Emotions

12. Dependent on Personal Awareness

13. Dependent on Circumstances

14. Superficial or Deep

15. Associated with Instability

16. Short-lasting

17. Involve a Recurrent Activity or Issue

18. Related to a Social Situation

An awareness of the Aspects of Emotions (Table 19-1) may help an in. gain perspective on emotional swings. *Awareness* of emotions is key. The a. to see an emotional response from a distance makes controlling it possible.

In that process, one realizes the nature of one's own emotional response *after* the response has occurred. One observes the *aftermath* of an emotional response and concludes, "Well, I guess I responded with _____ (emotion) to that situation. Maybe next time, I can *foresee my response*, and respond differently."

Later, when the emotion is again triggered, an awareness of the *trigger*, and an awareness of the automatic *response* occurs *during* (rather than after) the emotional reaction. A person becomes aware of the emotional or reactive nature of his or her behavior *while he is doing it!* Even with this awareness, it is often too late to stop the reaction, and the same consequences follow imparting the same lesson.

Finally, a trigger is observed just *prior* to its outward emotional response. At this point, it is often possible to modify the response before any damage is done.

When experience with repeated emotional responses develops into more positive and less damaging reactions, "spiritual growth" occurs. This education and growth is one of the purposes for our existence on the planet. We are here to learn from our emotional mistakes. Some of us learn to observe and control ourselves faster than others.

Different types of emotions are associated with the different *quality* types of people. AIR types tend to be nervous, and they often have fearful or spiritual emotions. FIRE types are more prone to triumphant or angry emotions, and EARTH quality people often have loving or indifferent emotional characteristics (See Chapters 4, & 24.) If we are aware of these tendencies up front, we can often predict or explain their occurrence, and make helpful modifications based on acceptance rather than on blame.

WINDING EMOTIONAL HIGHWAY
THE EMOTIONAL JOURNEY

Dealing with the emotional experiences in life is like driving a series of roads with sharp curves and slippery surfaces. Figure 19-1 illustrates the path we often negotiate between some of the major types of positive and negative emotions. There are many ways to map out emotions. In this example, the more positive and constructive emotions are on the right side of the road, and the negative and destructive emotions are on the left.

Much of the time, we find that we are swerving from one emotion toward its opposite. At other times, we seem to stay on one side of the emotional highway. As we drive down the same emotional roads again and again, our responses to the passion road hazards often remain the same until an *awareness* of our responses results in better choices.

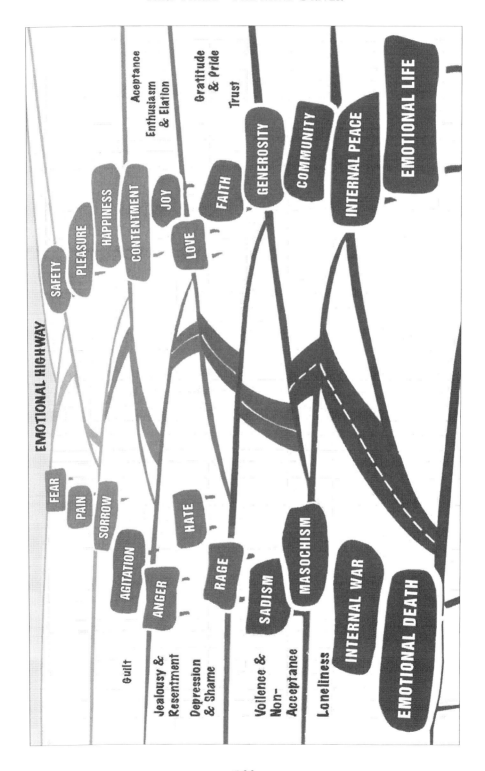

With each swing back and forth along this emotional freeway, a person's physical health is affected in much the same way that a motor vehicle is worn down by driving recklessly over difficult terrain. Suspense strains the muscular suspension, heart breaks wear down the immune brakes, and emotional tirades expose us to road rage.

We often bounce from one emotion to another like a car bouncing off the side rails on opposite sides of a highway. But the emotional highway is often circular. We start at the beginning and run the gamut of emotions only to find ourselves again dealing with some of the same basic emotional issues we have encountered before. We can choose to look at this repetition as a frustrating proof of the misery of life, or as a series of moving violations that remind us that there is still something to be learned on that emotional subject.

If this emotional racetrack is, indeed, circular, then the end of the race only comes when the vehicle breaks down, crashes, or when one successfully negotiates the hazards and claims a peaceful prize at the finish. According to yoga philosophy, even when an individual's race is done, s/he has the opportunity to enter another future event via reincarnation. This time around, the spirit has gained emotional experience, and can better warn the driver of the hazards to come.

Eventually, the good driver learns to stay on the right side of the road—the side where a sense of safety brings positive emotions. When that is accomplished, the journey along the highway brings peace and contentment.

SPEEDING OR CRUISING
DANGER vs. SAFETY

Danger is exciting. Safety is boring. Since Western culture cannot tolerate boredom, danger is the obvious option. The obvious question is "What's wrong with being a bit bored?"

The answer is that inactivity or boredom does not satisfy the mind. The mind demands *activity* and pushes us toward stimulating and dangerous behavior. In contrast, the spirit/soul/consciousness aspect of our being thrives on peace and quiet. The idea that peace and quiet are boring is mind self-preservation propaganda that comes from the fact that the mind is not needed if there is no activity. This mind fear leads to a culture that is based on selling mind-stimulating activities and accesories.

Once the active, dangerous road is selected, many of the activities and accessories become necessary to deal with the consequences of dangerous living. The cycle of stimulation and activity becomes self-sustaining, addictive and difficult to break. After a while, we may really *need* to hang glide, rock climb, go to horror movies, and gamble in Vegas.

NERVES OF STEEL BEHIND THE WHEEL
FEAR vs. CONFIDENCE

When danger is present, fear is usually the result. The primary fear is fear of the ultimate danger—death. If one has no fear of death, then one becomes completely confident, and enjoys a feeling of ultimate safety, security and longevity.

Of course, fear of death is an ingrained and natural part of life. According to some yoga philosophies, going beyond the fear of death and accepting death gracefully is one of our ultimate challenges. It is one of the most important *suma cum laude* graduations we can experience. The problem is that it is difficult to accept something about which we know very little. We don't know what happens after death, nor can we ever know until it happens to us personally. We must find an alternative to knowing the answer to this crucial question.

One solution is to create any number of stories that answer the after-death puzzle. Whatever that story is, it's *an answer* that removes some of the fearful mystery. We will go to "Heaven" where there is no danger. We thereby create a belief or a "faith" that the death transition is *not* something to be feared.

The yogic concept of reincarnation helps reduce the death fear, because death is not considered a final end. One can choose to believe that subsequent lives will follow during which a person may choose to study life challenges or to blow off self-evaluation once again and watch wrestling or Judge Judy.

Yoga and ayurveda teach that fear must be overcome by dealing with it directly. Many of the anesthetic, avoidance, and diversion techniques that people develop are used to avoid dealing with their immediate fears. Accepting fear as a part of life is difficult, but there are practices in yoga that assist in helping people accept their fears.

One method is to recognize that fear is usually a reflection of an increase in the AIR quality. With that understood, using techniques to decrease the AIR quality can be helpful. According to ayurveda, some element of excessive AIR quality is also associated with pain. Pleasure can be associated with any of the qualities.

Tempting fate and surviving is another way that we approach our fears. We can deal with fear vicariously by viewing enactments of fear from a known position of safety. Watching horror movies and other fantasy depictions of violence is one way we can "survive" our fears. But this exposure brings further agitation to the mind that demands even more fear-survival experiences.

POTHOLES OR FRESH ASPHALT
PAIN vs. PLEASURE

Most of the time, we want to be driving on the pleasant side of the road to feel safe and confident. But life continually brings events that push us over to the dangerous or painful side.

Don't like being bored? Just wait a while and trouble will find you. The question is:

How do we deal with the troubles that inevitably come?!

Do we anesthetize them away, sweep them under some activity rug, or do we look at them for the lessons they are, and change ourselves for the better?

Even if we run away from pain and trouble by building a financial fortress or health haven to shelter us, that will not protect us from the ultimate fear. We are all *supposed* to die. True immortality does not concern itself with the physical body. The body will surely lose its Life Force Energy, and we will certainly have to face that unknown moment no matter how hard we try to avoid it.

Instead of facing the "painful" reality of death and its painful sub-realities, we do whatever we can to find pleasure. Finding activities that increase the pleasure neurotransmitters helps us forget those fears. It's an intoxication process that can be helpful if it leads us toward a greater understanding. It is harmful if we forget the learning process, and become fixed on pleasure for its own sake.

It is often useful to think of pleasures that occur as unexpected gifts, or as evidence of some universal benevolence.

Another process that removes both painful death fears as well as pleasure obsessions, is to remove the concept that there is always significant pain associated with the actual death transition. The painful part of the death experience is the *fear* leading up to it! FDR was right.

We are able to get into our cars and travel because we have put the fear of a fatal traffic accident behind us. With this attitude, we can take pleasure in the ride to the ultimate spiritual ballpark.

WINNING OR LOSING THE RACE
HAPPINESS vs. SORROW

You can get to an uplifting spiritual ballpark only by driving on the safety/confidence side of the emotional highway. By driving down the positive side, you get pleasant neurotransmitters and you arrive at a major league paradise. Drive down the negative side, and you will feel over-stimulated, tense, worried, and you'll wind up in an emotional ghetto.

As far as the body-vehicle is concerned, the smooth road is best. Good health is associated with happiness, while bad health comes more frequently when a person spends his or her time in negative emotions. AIR and EARTH qualities are most closely associated with happiness and contentment.

Deep sorrow is more commonly associated with the EARTH quality. EARTH-types naturally tend toward sadness, but on the positive side, they can be happy and content as well. An awareness of these quality associations often precedes the ability to make changes in emotional state.

HEAVY TRAFFIC OR THE OPEN ROAD
AGITATION vs. CONTENTMENT

Some people love to drive in mid-town Manhattan. Other people enjoy cruising out to the lake. One activity is stimulating while the other is relatively quiet and calming.

As we drive in and out of these different environments, our bodies respond with different levels of neurochemical and electrical intensity. Constant stimulation and flirting with danger lead to agitation. During the agitated state, muscles tighten, coronary arteries constrict, the jaw clenches, and breathing becomes tight. Mind agitation raises the output of adrenalin from the adrenals and the brain, and the senses are awakened.

Agitation is associated with the AIR and FIRE qualities in Ayurvedic thinking. For this reason, activities that balance an AIR or FIRE quality excess can be help-ful. Eventually, running one's vehicle at full throttle takes its toll on the engine. Few Wall Street kings live to be a hundred.

Eventually, we all need to slow down for a while and take a rest on a quiet mental beach.

Contentment, an EARTH quality, is much more difficult to find. We are often taught that "more is better." But accepting "less" (objects, ego-strokes, activity, etc.) is actually "more" soothing to the body. You don't need all your thumbs to count the number of 100-year-old multi-millionaires.

Like the stagecoach driver who controls the horse team, the mind controls the use of the senses and action organs. The mind can be allowed to whip them to a continuous gallop if the Spirit-Passenger does not demand that it slow down to a pleasant cruising speed.

Each individual has such a Spirit/Consciousness with a certain strength of character, and each has a mind with a sensory-indulgent purpose. The life-long clash between the two is one of the great struggles of human existence. The daily outcome of that struggle results in an individual's choice of activity. That choice results in setting a target level for pleasurable neurotransmitters. Each individual's neurotransmitter "need" determines his/her behavior.

This neurotransmitter thermostat is individually set for their own comfort and safety. Those comfort concepts come from the individual's environment, and from what they feel deep down in their spiritual selves. The changing need for different neurotransmitter levels drives the mind either toward the stimulating or toward the quieting. Ayurveda and yoga recommend the quiet, spiritual, and contentment options. The result is a happy, healthy lifestyle.

TRAFFIC TEMPERS OR JOY RIDING
ANGER vs. JOY

When one hits a good-sized pothole that has been created by difficult life events, one often responds with anger. Intense, angry responses are usually the reflex result of a sudden loss of control of emotions, especially in situations that are urgent, provoked, offensive, malicious, or unjustified.

Anger's intensity makes it difficult to sustain for extended periods of time, but if angry emotions do remain, the strain on the physical system can be significant. It would be like continuously driving recklessly down the freeway. Sooner or later, there *will* be a wreck!

An angry response may also be an outlet for other difficult, pent-up emotions. While it is not good for the body to repress strong emotions, emotional release through anger has only limited value, according to ayurveda. Hitting a punching bag may help to some degree, but unless there is a mental awareness concerning the nature of the anger, its triggers, its effects, and its lessons, the punching bag will soon be worn out without true resolution of the anger.

The FIRE quality is in excess when anger is present. An awareness of this tendency can be helpful in avoiding the known triggers of FIERY behavior.

The AIR quality of joy, on the other hand, is like riding carefree in the back seat of a convertible, soaking up the scenery. Joy is the label given to more intense forms of pleasure and happiness. The energy of joy is high, but its quality is certainly different from the energy of anger. There is safety in joy, and peril in anger.

Some yoga philosophies caution against *attachment* to joy in non-spiritual things. Joy should be experienced and appreciated, but not expected. As mentioned, joy often alternates with sorrow, and each should be view as a means to spiritual growth.

✳

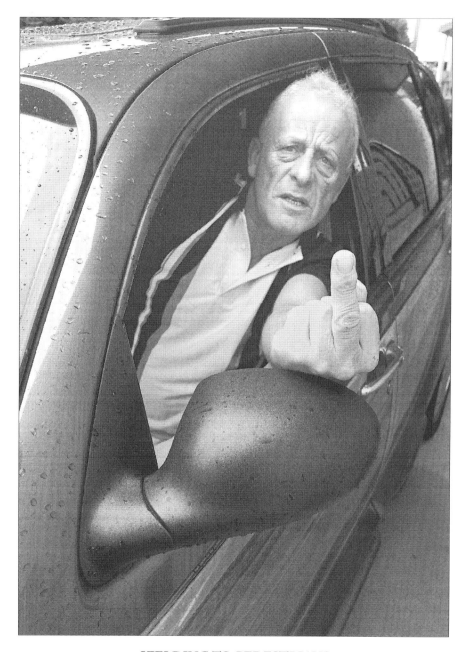

YIELDING TO PEDESTRIANS
GREED vs. COMPASSION

Greed may be a consequence of insecurity and unhappiness. The idea that there is a limit to resources, and that there is not be enough for everyone forms the basis of greed.

Greed is the desire for more than is necessary. Once the necessities have been obtained, toys become the focus of attention. Since there is no limit to the number of toys one can have, there is no limit to the desire for more of them. Acquiring becomes a diversionary activity that can cover up deeper pain.

Greed is primarily an EARTH quality, so those who are primarily EARTH quality by nature tend to struggle more with greed. Achievement and power, which are primarily FIRE qualities, can also result in greedy behavior.

Compassion, on the positive side, is also primarily an EARTH quality that involves recognition of the suffering of others. Usually, that suffering is recognized as substantial and undeserved. Compassion also implies a willingness to help, and to become personally involved. Many times it comes from recognition of the humanity of the person who is suffering. It also suggests the underlying equality of the person who is being helped and the one doing the helping.

Compassion is one of the cornerstones of yoga philosophy. The channeling of all types of positive and negative energy toward helping others has been described as an important therapeutic tool in ayurveda.

HATE MAIL & LOVE LETTERS
HATE vs. LOVE

When our anger gets personal and prolonged, we move into hatred.

Instead of focusing on an action or two, we become overwhelmed by the entire person or process that is associated with a difficult situation. Soon, the object of our hatred is seen as fundamentally evil, without any redeeming qualities. It becomes a threat, its existence feels unjustified, and we want to be as far away from the hated object as possible. We give up on helping, and see the elimination of the object as the only just solution.

While an object of hatred may seem worthy of disdain, our hatred provokes us into greater defensive behavior. The tension this creates can eat away at us, and the resulting stress on the body may result in psychogenic illness.

According to Ayurvedic thinking, hatred is a FIRE quality. It may be fanned by the winds of the AIR quality, or fueled by the oil of the EARTH quality, but it is first and foremost a reflection of the qualities that constitute FIRE. If we are aware of this fact, we can use that knowledge to stop feeding the flames, and to cool the anger with the methods that are used to balance excess FIRE in the system.

In contrast to hate, love is an emotional state that most living beings actively seek. An exact definition of love is difficult, and it has been the subject of endless essays, poetry, novels, movies, songs, and TV advertisements. This definition is one of the characteristics that separate philosophies from each other. Some hold that love cannot be described as easily as it can be felt.

Love of another being is usually distinguished from love for an inanimate object. Love, lust, and sex are considered to be separate entities, although they can certainly overlap and coexist.

There are endless descriptions and classifications of love. One type is *erotic* love, which is connected with biological sex drives. Physical attraction, touching, caressing, sexual intercourse, and other intimate sensual behaviors arising from basic biological drives characterize the erotic aspect of love.

Fraternal love is the non-physical affection felt by close friends or relatives. It consists of a deeply positive attitude toward the loved person that includes an overall appreciation of the individual as an intrinsically good person. There is often a sense of gratitude for the relationship, and an appreciation of the non-physical aspects of someone's personality. There is a concern for the well being of the loved one, and their negative aspects are often downplayed. The resulting relationships are often of long duration.

Romantic love has many of the characteristics of fraternal and erotic love. In addition, behavior that includes prolonged eye contact, close companionship, extended time together, developing similar likes and dislikes, and emotional support are also noted. There is also a desire to fuse with the beloved, and a wish to know and be known in intimate ways by one's love partner.

The romantic love relationship is often marked by a high degree of consideration and concern for the well being of the partner. Once a deeper involvement is established, a person's feelings of self-worth and well being become closely associated with the lover.

Agape is another classification of love. This is the divine type of love that goes beyond self-interest. It is the type of love that a God-like being has for those in his/her creation. It is universal. Everyone and everything is worthy of caring and affection. There are no judgments or discriminations made concerning the worth of an individual. All are equal. All are reflections of the divine.

In ayurvedic and yogic philosophy, the term "love" is most often used to describe the agape type of love. For the yoga practitioner, this pure love is the bridge between the inner and outer worlds. It is the highest food of the soul. It is described as a light that emanates from the heart and removes all differences, separations and self-interest.

Pure love is distinguished from conditional love. In the latter, as in any business transaction, there is an expectation of a return for the love given. Conditional love has a motive. Unconditional love, on the other hand, has no expectation of return. In its purest form, love is given anonymously.

Unconditional love also includes an acceptance of the negative aspects a person brings to the table. It applies to everyone, and is without lust. There is also a sense of affection for all of humanity as an expression of the divine spirit/soul.

On a less metaphysical level, the different ayurvedic qualities have associations with the different types of love. Physical love is more closely associated with the EARTH quality, passionate love with the FIRE quality, and spiritual love with the AIR quality. While there is often considerable overlap of the three, the type of love experienced in a relationship can be influenced by the amount of AIR, FIRE, and EARTH qualities that are present. Changes can be made by balancing these qualities.

In addition to being an emotion, love is also considered to be a state of consciousness. When one is thinking, acting, appreciating, and feeling with the above-described attributes, then one is said to exist in a state of pure love. In Ayurvedic philosophical tradition, there is no greater goal.

ROAD RAGE VS. PICKING UP HITCHHIKERS
RAGE vs. FAITH

When anger has built up to the point that it becomes unrestrained, then the intensity of that emotion vents in the form of rage. The loss of control of a situation, or the lack of sufficient understanding of circumstances, may lead a person to seek to correct a perceived injustice by means of violent behavior.

Life is full of challenges that can lead to anger and rage. That's the whole point! How do we *respond* to enraging (and other) challenges? If we respond by creating more anger and rage (or other difficult emotions), then we have created something that will have negative effects on our mental, spiritual and physical health. The challenge is to react to a negative with a neutral or positive response.

Don't get even, get even-tempered.

According to yoga and ayurveda, we can progress up the emotional evolutionary ladder by responding to hatred, rage, and pain with love.

This "love your enemy" idea does not only apply to physical responses. It means occupying a positive mental space in your own head and truly believing in the positives that are hidden in difficult people and situations. Staying in an open and accepting emotional state despite adversity is the basis of a healthier spiritual, emotional, and physical lifestyle.

"Staying in the positive" in the face of unjustified adversity requires faith. In this case, faith means that a loving response to adversity will not leave you ultimately vulnerable. Creating faithless emotional defenses may seem like a natural short-term response to emotional trauma, but in the long term, being overly defensive does not work. If one survives adversity only to live a life in angry negatives, then the spiritual battle has been lost.

According to reincarnation philosophy, physical survival is not all-important. The progress that the mind and spirit make toward living a positive life is of more concern. Emotional/spiritual learning carries forward to the next set of life-classes.

When you stop over-defending your physical and emotional bodies, it means that you understand and accept that your spiritual aspect is more important. Many of the great saints sacrificed their physical bodies for spiritual advancement. We are here to learn proper priorities, and to respond with sympathy and understanding in the face of confusion and pain.

Is this risky?

True faith is among the more risky lifestyles we can try. When Jesus urged giving up everything (petty), what did he promise? Gaining everything (worthwhile)! The spiritual can only be obtained by risking that letting go of *attachment* to the transient will bring lasting non-transient rewards in the undefined hereafter.

We are here to learn how to drive. If we can stay on the correct side of the road, especially when it's difficult, we have a much better chance of reaching our destination. Having faith doesn't mean completely letting go of the wheel and closing our eyes. It does mean living in the present moment with an open heart, and letting go of the implications of the past and future. The past and future will always be there. We have to trust that proper driving will serve to get us to our destination even when the immediate evidence says it won't.

Faith is the transition that takes us from mind to spirit. Faith is letting go of the mind and its ego, attachments, and desires. For eternal concerns, the mind just isn't that helpful. We need to let go of the mind and take a leap of faith.

COURTESY & CUTOFFS ON THE FREEWAY
GENEROSITY vs. SADISM

When internal angry emotions reach an increased level of intensity and cruelty, sadistic acts can be the result. Oftentimes, the difficult internal feelings involved are guilt, fear, frustration, confusion, and self-hatred.

By controlling, frustrating, confusing, or enslaving others, the sadist restores his or her lost power and covers over his or her negative feelings. Sadistic behavior is often an act of revenge for the humiliation of injured pride. As with other emotions, sadism may also be the result of unresolved emotional energy. That energy usually has a FIRE-like quality to it, so sadism may be approached using the Ayurvedic techniques that balance an excess of the FIRE quality.

Generosity, on the other hand, often comes from a feeling of physical, psychological, or spiritual abundance. This is what allows the monetarily disadvantaged but spiritually secure to be generous toward others, including the more well-to-do. The emotionally and spiritually secure usually feel under control, satisfied, safe, and clear in their understanding of their own life situation. Those with balanced AIR and EARTH qualities in their lives tend to be more generous.

Of course, there are many types of generosity. According to yoga philosophy, generosity, without expectation of reward, is the goal. Anonymity in giving removes much of the ego from the process, and makes the gift pure and free from the spiritually encumbering desire for recognition.

Gifts from the heart transmit loving kindness that can be limitless in number and depth.

DRIVING ICY ROADS VS. TAKING THE TRAIN
MASOCHISM vs. COMMUNITY

When anger, hatred or other painful feelings have no acceptable external outlet, physical or mental self-injury can be the result. Such pain can actually be "enjoyed" or used to obtain needed attention from others. The stimulation of self-inflicted pain can result in sexual excitement as well.

Masochism can also be used to divert attention from another source of pain that is even more difficult to face. It can be a way of paying for crimes that have been committed or imagined. This anger at oneself is a reflection of an excess of the FIRE quality.

Masochistic behavior is a form of self-isolation. A person identifies him/herself as unworthy in general, and unworthy of being with others in specific. As with other states of misery, a comfort zone of *familiarity* can be established in masochism.

In contrast, an attitude of equality, sharing, and acceptance of common goals can lead a person to seek out the physical, emotional, and even spiritual company of others. The intent can be anything from group fun-seeking to support for physical, emotional, psychological, or spiritual advancement.

The sharing of property, feelings, and/or goals creates a *community* of intentions. This sensation is calming and reassuring, and often provides a significant sense of safety. A comforting sense of selflessness is often found in community settings, and a willingness to serve other members of the group often results in elevated self-image. Mutual support often results in a higher level of achievement for the individual as well as for the group. The EARTH quality is often dominant in this situation.

NAGGING DOUBTS VS. LIFETIME WARRANTY
INTERNAL CONFLICT vs. INTERNAL PEACE

The mind and nervous system are naturally agitated when we spend time in unresolved emotional states. Although adjustments can be made to make chronic negative behavior more tolerable, continued negative behavior degrades the emotional, moral, and physical fiber of an individual.

A sense that there is something internal that is "eating away" at one's happiness may develop, and emotional inner turmoil may result. This can easily be translated into physical health problems. Such internal conflicts can be the result of any quality disorder, but the more self-assured FIRE types are less likely to be internally conflicted. The vacillating AIR types will tend to have more difficulty with self-doubt.

Staying on the positive side of the emotional highway relieves agitation. It may be "boring," but internal peace is required for emotional and spiritual growth.

A life that is marked by creativity and satisfaction is often the result. Those who are dominated by the EARTH quality tend to be more peaceful.

NEGATIVE JOB EVALUATION
FAILURE vs. SUCCESS

Failure is a relative term. If you don't believe that, ask any of your relatives. They'll gladly tell you whether or not you're a failure. No matter what other people think, what *you* think and feel about yourself determines whether or not you have failed. If you think of yourself as a failure, your lack of self-respect may well lead you to neglect your health.

The problem is that we sometimes adopt many of the bizarre expectations that others have for us. We adopt the definitions of "success" that we are given by the people who surround us early in childhood. Parents, relatives, teachers, siblings, and friends all behave in ways that tell us what earns their respect and affection. Because we have a physiological need for attention and affection, we quickly learn to follow those expectations.

The formative environment into which we are born is often thought to be a matter of chance. It's like standing on the street corner, waving for a cab, and not knowing if a beat up clunker or a shiny new limo will come by and stop for us. Some philosophies hold that *specific* taxis are dispatched to meet the educational needs of specific spiritual travelers. If you need a little pampering, dispatch sends you a Town Car. If you are a little too full of yourself, then dispatch sends you a minivan that smells bad.

Either way, we are raised to believe that certain results are expected if we are to be considered a "success." If we are raised to expect little from ourselves, it's fairly easy to feel successful. If we expect everything of ourselves, we will likely "fail." *We are human, not gods.* If we could already do everything, we wouldn't need to be here on Earth getting an education. We'd be looking down from above and laughing at the freshman class!

The culture into which we are born also determines our expectations for behavior, and our definition of success. Some cultures stress education, while others stress family, money, work, religion, or combinations of these and other endeavors.

One problem is that we are often raised with expectations that we achieve some type of "greatness." Greatness is defined as something out of the ordinary, immense, exceptional, significant, powerful, pleasing, influential, impressive, important, awesome, wonderful, etc., etc. It's a daunting task.

In modern culture, we are given these goals for a reason. Great achievements usually require great expenditures. Great expenditures mean great commerce, so the business community and its commercially funded media are always ready to pump us full of suggestions on how to *buy* our way to greatness.

Good commerce often means selling something that is completely unnecessary for survival, self-improvement, or the welfare of others. If nobody wanted to appear rich, there would be no need to build a Mercedes Kompressor SLK-DVD-S-Class-Convertible-Trump-mobile. If no one felt the need to look as fancy as Stuff Daddy, "Bling" would be no thing.

The advertising industry teaches us that expecting "less" of ourselves is a sign of weakness and inferiority. From a different point of view, it is difficult to be any "less" than a Paris Hilton, no matter how much "more" she might have. It all depends on what you have been trained to believe is "more." In yoga philosophy, *less crap* is more. In ayurveda, the drive toward success is a FIRE quality.

Putting aside the junky things we have been taught to value, and replacing them with generous living behaviors that reflect a sense of Greater Self-worth (see Part Four) is a lesson we are all here to learn. Small self-ish distractions are the daily quizzes that most of us fail.

When we say "no" to Madison Avenue, Hollywood, and Wall Street, we can be truly successful without their expensive trappings. Anyone can give of himself. Even a paralyzed Superman can work for the benefit of others once a difficult wake up call stops him from jumping through status hoops.

Are there goals and behaviors that are true and absolute for everyone?

Most philosophies agree on a few attributes that are needed for every spirit-passenger to feel comfortable (see Part Four). Each of us is here to adopt those character traits. We are *spiritual* beings. Ultimately, we are here searching for our spiritual cure.

Once we instruct our cab driver to drive down Giving Road, we become a major "success." At that moment, we are also on our way to Lover's Lane.

TRAFFIC COURT VS. THE WINNER'S CIRCLE
SHAME vs. PRIDE

When a person judges him/herself guilty of violating behavioral norms, then guilt and shame may set in. Whether it's harming another person, neglecting something important, failing to be responsible, or just pain old human incompetence, shame happens when one is aware of his/her failure to live up to expected standards.

Fear of being thought of in a negative way, offending others, or fear of punishment are also important in generating shameful feelings. Embarrassment for what is imagined to be undeserved success may also be operating. Shame is associated more with the EARTH quality, but can be a part of any type of mind.

This negative self-judgment may have a positive side in that guilt may help prevent a repetition of future failures. It may also generate appropriate apologies, explanations, confessions, restitutions, and learning.

In contrast, pride is an emotion that is usually generated by a positive self-judgment toward past and present activities. Getting credit for something, belonging to a group, overcoming difficulty, developing positive character traits, defining individuality, and/or receiving praise from others can all result in prideful feelings. Pride is associated with the FIRE quality and its tendency toward comparison.

Pride is a pleasurable emotion that comes from having an attribute that feels valuable, and from believing that one is a good person who has performed good acts. Positive feedback from others is often involved, and comparison of one's worth to others may also be operating.

The propriety of prideful emotions may vary, and the correctness of prideful feelings is a function of the degree of credit taken. Taking too much credit or appearing exclusive makes the trait egotistical. Such excessive pride is described as one of the Seven Deadly Sins in the Christian tradition, but pride in selfless works is less spiritually hazardous.

The Yogic/Ayurvedic teachings on pride are that it tends to fortify egocentrism and detracts from a person's awareness that the source of everything is more spiritual than personal. Pride is a quality that is dominated primarily by FIRE, and secondarily by the EARTH quality.

FOOL OR COOL
ANXIETY vs. CALM

When fear becomes intense, generalized, or incapacitating, then a state of anxiety is said to exist. Fear of object loss, control loss, and negative outcomes help generate an anxious state of tense energy. Change is often involved in the creation of anxious fears. Anticipation of upcoming events that hold real or imagined unpleasant sensations, associations, or outcomes are also factors in creating anxiety.

Unpleasant physical or emotional sensations will often trigger anxiety responses. Anxiety results when questions of personal vulnerability are raised, especially when the events of concern are critical to "essential" life functions. The nervous system is usually keyed up in the anxious state, which tends to be dramatic and marked by increased defensive alertness. In Ayurvedic terms, anxiety is associated with the AIR quality, and can be treated using the techniques for balancing excessive AIR in the diet, mind, and environment.

A calm mind, on the other hand, is marked by a lack of arousal, and by neurotransmitter levels that are weighted toward increased levels of calming endorphins. Pleasant sensations and associations are dominant due to a lack of fear and feelings of safety. There is a sense that current events present no critical threat to well being, so there is little need for drama or action in this secure situation.

There can be different levels of alertness in the calm state. An energized but calm

set of conditions can reflect confidence and experience with challenging situations. This state is quite different from a fatigued state of "calm" in which a lack of concern may be due to inattention or indifference. Calm has an EARTH-like quality.

Many times we can choose between the calm or the anxious state. The calm state is often thought of as "boring" whereas stimulating situations that may also result in anxiety are thought of as "exciting." Driving down the emotional highway to the left of center can be very exciting, but it can lead to deadly or injurious results. Many teenagers and insecure drivers need to flirt with danger and anxiety in order to confirm that they are alive and powerful. Many others already know they are alive, and that tense, emotional living hurts the body, mind, and spirit.

ON FIRE or WITHOUT DESIRE
ELATION vs. DEPRESSION

As with many other confusing psychological terms, the word "depression" needs definition. It has been variously described as a mood, a symptom, a syndrome, and a disease. No matter what the definition, depression seems to stem from a defective functioning of the mind's ego reinforcing mechanisms.

In depression, the normal response to difficult circumstances changes from a short-term adjustment to a disabling, long-term condition. There is an prolongation of the normal "working through" process, and a loss of the ability to adjust to life's normal upsetting events, or to changes in routine. Interpersonal or social difficulties, repeated failures, economic problems, and genetic predisposition are often cited as causing depression.

Depression is also characterized by being stuck in a negative outlook on life. There is a loss of distinction between *some* things being problems, to *all* things being problems. There is also a failure of the selective mental filtering system that isolates problem areas. *All* areas are seen as problems, and a negative worldview is the result.

The normal process of transferring psychic energy from a failed enterprise to something else does not occur. Instead, that psychic energy is put in a negative *internal* psychic place (introjection). The physical withdrawal that often occurs with depression is thought to be a way that psychic energy is conserved rather than being spent on very difficult mental subjects.

Physically, depression can manifest as withdrawal, low energy, hopelessness, pessimism, inability to experience pleasure, gloom, appetite disturbances, agitation, introversion, sexual dysfunction, work problems, and other findings of unhappiness.

The depressed person becomes unproductive, and time seems to pass slowly.

A preoccupation with the unresolved past often occurs, and the depressed person often becomes less able to form healthy attachments to people, causes, or things. Their voices becomes more monotone, slower, and softer. Posture can be slumped showing indecision and fatigue.

Difficulties in memory, concentrating, reasoning, calculating, doing complex mental tasks, and indecisiveness can also occur. Hypochondria, chronic pain, obsessive or repetitive behavior, irritability, or prolonged rumination can be noted. When self-esteem is decreased, or if guilt or anger is turned inward, suicidal thoughts and actions can manifest as the result of depression.

Depression can occur on its own, or it can be the result of any of the other emotional disorders mentioned above. The bottom line is that a depressed person is less able to enjoy life.

There has been great interest in the role that hormones and chemical neurotransmitters play in depression. The effects of norepinephrine and serotonin have been of particular interest, and manipulation of these body chemicals has spawned the recent development of modern anti-depressant pharmacopoeia. Adrenal, thyroid, and growth hormone activity are also considered important in depression.

In Ayurvedic thinking, the causes of depression can be varied. Depression based on fear is an AIR-type depression, while anger and attachment are from excess FIRE and EARTH qualities respectively. Most depression is ultimately a disorder of excessive EARTH quality. For this reason, approaching depression using the basic treatments for excessive EARTH quality problems is helpful (see Chapter 16).

In contrast to depression, *elation* (euphoria, mania) is an AIR-dominated state of high energy and good spirits. In this condition, there is often hyperactivity, creativity, and good natured, humorous activity. Generosity, joking, singing, and extra talking are often seen in this emotional state.

In its more extreme manifestation, elation becomes excessive and is called *mania*. In this condition, the mood is elevated and expansive. Self-esteem is often inflated to grandiose levels, and dramatic or flamboyant behavior is seen. Flight of ideas, distractibility, and a diminished need for sleep are often noted. Risky behavior resulting from inflated self-esteem and grandiose thinking can result in reckless driving, sexual indiscretions, and/or binge buying or celebrating. A rebound depression can result in fatigue, self-harming, and physical illness. Elation and mania reflect an increased AIR quality.

Movement back and forth from manic to depressive behavior is the basis of bipolar disease. Effective treatments for this condition are available in modern medicine. In ayurvedic medicine, brahmi, jatmamsi and bringaraj are used along with other techniques (see Chapter 16) to stabilize neurotransmitter function.

LEANING ON THE HORN
PHYSICAL EMOTIONAL PURGING

Since the body and mind are closely related, it is not surprising that emotions not only affect the body, but are released through the body as well.

In Ayurvedic thinking there are eight ways that the body manifests significant emotional release:

Stiffness	Weeping
Trembling	Voice cracking
Sweating	Goose flesh
Color change	Fainting

These activities are typical of excesses of the AIR quality. When we see these signs of emotional release, either in ourselves or in others, we should be aware of the need for emotional support, and for AIR imbalance treatments. Suppression of these releases is not usually recommended, because they reflect an unacceptable buildup of emotional tension.

Emotional energy can also be released through positive and creative outlets. Music, art, drama, dance, and other constructive activities are expressions of emotional energy that is channeled into controlled and productive activity. (See Chapter 22).

When painful emotions and other difficult thoughts cannot be constructively released in these or in other ways, then other means of dealing with the emotional pain must be employed. Anesthetics and Diversions are often used, but positive release can be learned through breathing, quality awareness, and counseling.

TABLE 19-2: **EMOTIONAL QUALITIES**

EMOTION	QUALITY
Terror	AIR
Security	EARTH
Fear	AIR
Confidence	FIRE
Pain	AIR
Pleasure	EARTH
Happiness	AIR, EARTH
Sorrow	EARTH
Agitation	AIR
Contentment	EARTH
Anger	FIRE
Joy	AIR, EARTH
Greed	EARTH
Compassion	EARTH, AIR
Lust	FIRE, EARTH
Hate	FIRE
Love	EARTH
Rage	FIR
Faith	EARTH, AIR
Generosity	AIR
Sadism	FIRE
Masochism	FIRE
Community	AIR, EARTH
Internal Conflict	AIR
Internal Peace	EARTH, AIR
Failure	AIR
Success	FIRE
Shame	EARTH
Pride	FIRE
Anxiety	AIR
Calm	EARTH
Elation	AIR, FIRE
Depression	EARTH

CHAPTER
20:
DRIVING
UNDER
THE
INFLUENCE (Anesthetic
Defenses)

ESCAPE IN A CLOUD

… So I pull my cab up in front of their old house on Ocean Avenue and honk. No one comes out. After a few more minutes of honking, some radio chatter, and two cigarettes, I get my butt out of the cab and head for the front door of the dump where Mark and Marcy have been living for God-knows how long.

I'm thinkin' "Shithead is probably stoned again." So I open the always-unlocked front door and head up the trash-littered stairway. It only takes a few steps to bring the unmistakable skunk smell of weed to my nose, and the music and smoke at the top of the stairs confirm my initial hit. "Well, at least there's the possibility of a contact high from this fare." Not bad.

After knocking for three or four minutes and no one answers, I open the door. Mark is standing there just getting ready to open it himself. The room is only a little less smoky than Steven's eyes. He lifts his open palm up to his shoulder in greeting, and turns without a word back toward the double bed in the open front living room.

He looks old. He's in his sixties now, but he looks much more like seventies than sixties. His face is totally wrinkled, and his long, straight, grey hair is tied back in a pony tail that sways behind his shoulders as he walks toward his brass dope pipe by the big brass bed.

Not much has changed about Steven over the years, except for the numerous lines that now crisscross his face. His forehead lines look like one of those groups of five lines people use to keep track of things as they add them up; four vertical lines up and down between his eyebrows, and one line across them.

The apartment is unbelievably small and narrow. There are just three open rooms in a row in the whole thing. The room by the street is the bedroom/living room with the bed pushed up against the street-side window. At the foot of the bed is an old, faded pink floral couch with one of the few sitting spaces that isn't piled high with junk. The walls are covered with yellowing political protest posters, slogans and political cartoons from his sixties revolutionary days.

Junk is everywhere—papers mostly. Piles of papers completely cover the wooden bureau on one side of the room. Under the bureau, more stacks of political papers are leaning precariously to one side, or falling over into piles. Dust is everywhere. Tie-dyed sheets are tacked up over the windows and pulled back to the sides of the dirty glass letting in grey light from the rainy, wintry day.

Next to the bureau sits a small desk with an outdated computer. The monitor is on and a video game sits suspended on the screen.

Mark's kid, Sam, comes into the room. Sam also has long hippy hair, and the beautiful face of a young teenager not yet ravaged by self-abuse. I remember when I first met Sam and thought how beautiful he was even after I realized that he was actually a boy.

So he sits down on the chair in front of the computer and begins to play. It's some generic video killing game. Bad guys appear on the brightly colored screen, and Sam deftly blows them away to the cheerful "ding-dong" chimes the machine makes after it duplicates the explosive sound of a gun firing.

So Mark lays back against the pillows propped up at the head of the bed. His long frame is stretched out toward the foot of the bed. He picks up his brass dope pipe, lights it and offers it to me. I take a polite hit and gave it back. Gotta stay semi-functional.

Then Mark begins to cough. The "chronic" is what marijuana smokers call the dry, deep, forceful and painful cough that comes from years of smoking harsh weed. All kinds of techniques have evolved for dealing with the harshness of marijuana smoke; everything from time-tested water pipes to freezing the stuff with dry ice. Some of those things work, but they take an effort that most stoned people really can't handle.

Mark begins another long coughing jag. One after another, the coughing spasms rock his body. Then, he heaves and shudders, his face turns pale, and then frikin' blue! Thoughts of 911 calls and CPR come mind, but then Mark gives one last cough, straightens up on the bed, and takes a big breath. His color begins to return as he spits something red from his mouth into a Kleenex.

"Dude, that was a bad one," Mark wheezes. "I guess I'd better get my ass over to the damn clinic tomorrow." Mark picks up his half empty beer bottle and drains it.

"That's *today*, dude!" (I was getting a little pissed.) "That's why I'm here, man! To take you!"

"Cool. Today, huh?" Mark lifts himself slowly from the pillows clutching the back of his neck. Chronic neck pain has kept Mark crippled up, and the medical marijuana, which he now smokes "legally" and continuously, keeps him mostly immobilized. "I'll be there in a minute," he says, and slowly wanders off in the direction of the bathroom lighting a cigarette on the way.

So I figure I deserve *something* for babysitting this old hippy, so I wander over to the fridge. The kitchen's fairly clean and tidy since it's Marcy's thing, but all the fridge has to offer is some leftover mac and cheese that's starting to look a little green and hairy. The diet coke, however, makes its way into my hands. I've nearly finished it by the time Mark walks out of the can, zipping himself up as he emerges.

We make our way down to the cab where Steven re-tunes my radio to 104.1 FM; Berkeley Free Radio. BFR is a low-wattage pirate station that operates without an FCC license. It symbolizes the fading rebellion that was the People's Republic of Berkeley. Santa Cruz and Berkeley are sister cities, both being way to the left of Mao Tse-Tung. I remember a lot about those lost revolutionary days. I guess that's part of why I like picking Steven up for his weekly trip to the clinic.

Lung cancer...

Bad luck, dude...

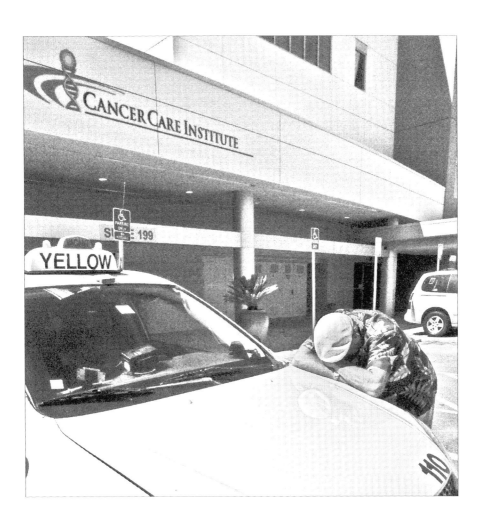

DRIVING UNDER THE INFLUENCE
ANESTHETIC DEFENSES

Pain is the problem. One way to approach pain is to cover it up with an anesthetic—any substance that reduces sensitivity to pain. Anesthetics are a fast and easy way to reduce the pain that always comes with life on this planet.

The alternatives to anesthesia are usually more difficult. They require effort, patience, delay of gratification, and self-discipline. Anesthetics can be found at the corner food and drug store. Some anesthetics, like alcohol, food, sex, and television are very socially acceptable, and are even promoted as evidence of success.

While most anesthetics have long-term down sides, their major advantage is that most of them act quickly in the short term to remove pain.

The essence of the addictive choice is that;

> *The added pain of working out a primary pain problem is greater than the addict thinks s/he can tolerate.*

There is already too much pain. Why add on the pain of dealing with it? Just do something *easy* to, once again, quickly kill or numb it!

CHANGING JOB ASSIGNMENTS
MIND STATE ALTERATION

In addition to the need to reduce painful input, there are times when the mind finds itself in a monotonous state that causes it to demand something different.

The mind thrives on change, so any state of inactivity triggers the anxiety that the mind will not be needed. If everything is going along routinely, then the mind has little to do. It is like a cab driver sitting motionless in congested traffic. If the cab is not moving, and no fares are being collected, then there may be no need for a driver! The bored mind-driver worries that he or she could be laid off. Maybe even eliminated!

Sensing this threat, the mind searches for something else to do. It is completely contrary to its nature to be inactive, quiet and content. Therefore, creating a change, *any change,* becomes an important activity for the inactive mind. In daily life, this can translate into the use of mind-altering substances and diversionary activities.

592

GETTING HIGH ON THE JOB
MIND DRUGS

Whether it's pain or boredom, there comes a time when the mind takes action to induce a change. One way is to create a change is to play with its engine chemistry. Put a little nitro in the tank and rev up that engine!

The chemistry of the brain/mind engine is the chemistry of neurotransmitters. The amateur anesthesiologist soon begins experimenting with what drains our dopamine, ups our epi, enlivens our endorphins, and stimulates serotonin.

We are looking to relieve discomfort. Once that is achieved, we might as well go for all-out pleasure! Sensory input can be amplified with stimulants and hallucinogens that give a glimpse of what it feels like to drive in the Daytona 500. Of course, once we get a taste, we need another helping. It is just so much easier to (pretend to) be super right now, than to do all the hard work it takes to be the real deal.

We choose the quick and easy way. Why not?

The problem is that our amplified experiences are mostly fake. When we come back down, we *know* they are fake, and the pain of that knowledge is added to our original pain. We feel like we're still stuck in a difficult and boring world. More and more juice is then needed to cover over that added pain.

HAPPY HOUR
ALCOHOL ANESTHESIA

Since ancient times, the mind altering (and mind-numbing) qualities of alcohol have been cultivated, promoted, and accepted. Life can be hard! And naturally derived alcohol does the anesthetic job!

At first, alcohol is a stimulant. The mind-driver likes this little boost in the energy level and wants more. As more alcohol is consumed, however, it has an increasingly depressant effect that helps to numb painful anxious thoughts or physically painful sensations. Inhibitions are often decreased, and laughter often replaces fear.

As the toxic phase of alcohol use begins, it brings its own sense of illness including nausea, vomiting, headache, hangover—and even death!

No matter.

The original anesthetic mission has been accomplished. Sensations have been numbed, and the mind is no longer watching the "My Life Sucks!" channel. Instead it switches to the "I Feel Relaxed" channel for a while. Of course, a little later, the mind is watching the "I Feel Like Crap!" channel. This may not be the greatest, but feeling physically bad is often more tolerable than dealing with the serious emotional difficulties one might be having on the job or in the home.

Alcohol use is socially acceptable. We go to "happy hour" to change our sad mind-channels and to remove boredom. Alcohol itself is an acceptable topic of conversation. It is given hundreds of different taste variations so that it can be viewed as something other than the same ethanol anesthetic. It is given brand names like "Budweiser" or "Blatz" in much the same way that other common painkillers are called "Bayer" or "Bufferin," "Paxil" or "Prozac."

It also does not matter to the short-term oriented, pain-phobic mind that the long-term health effects of alcohol can be ruinous. The mental problems are here NOW! The long-term oriented conscience knows that there needs to be a better way, but that would take "painful" work. The mind rarely chooses to add short-term pain.

Painful self-discipline (from the consciousness) is what the mind must be trained to accept.

A life spent sorting pain mail in the mental post office is difficult, and it may seem necessary to anesthetize on occasion. But when the occasions become dysfunctionally frequent, a change needs to be made in post office policy.

DOUGHNUTS IN THE BREAK ROOM
FOOD ANESTHESIA

Although it is not traditionally thought of as an anesthetic, food often has the short-term effect of lessening pain.

From the moment that our fetal supply of nutrition ends with the cutting of the umbilical cord, an internal hunger-pain is born. Babies don't laugh to indicate hunger. They cry because hunger registers as pain. Pain is soothed at the earliest age by food, and we learn that food is the treatment for pain before we learn anything else.

When we experience pain later in life, our primary response often remains the same; we treat pain with food. Food helps ease our survival fears. If we are fed, we also know that the odds of survival are greater. We feel less fear pain.

Eating brings a feeling of safety that is the essence of pleasure. When we feel safe, we are happy. When we are very safe, we feel pleasure. Since food is a necessity, it's hard to make its use into a negative addiction. Instead, food is accepted, encouraged, and made into an art. Food is one of the basic aspects of any culture, and interest in food is a sign of good health. Having luxurious food is a measure of success. How often do we hear someone proclaim, "I hate food! I'd rather be fasting!"

As the antidote to one of our primary life pains, food becomes a primary pleasure. We soon learn that food pleasure releases internal electrical and chemical sensations of safety and security. The postal-mind employees are happy and work well when there are doughnuts in the break room. They are surly and inefficient when hunger pains develop. It may be hard to sort pain mail all day long, but if the doughnuts and pastries are fresh and plentiful, you *can* make it through the day.

We soon develop the ability to excel at using this chemical pain antidote even when we don't really need it to survive. Somehow, doughnuts and candy are constantly present. Whenever we need less pain and more pleasure, we can always reach into that big white medicine cabinet known as "The Refrigerator."

Food is usually linked with the EARTH quality. Of course, the type of food used will determine the qualities that are affected. Heating/spicy foods will increase the FIRE quality, cooling ones will increase AIR and EARTH qualities.

In Ayurvedic thinking, food is linked with love. It is well known that humans (as well as many other animals) need love as well as food in order to thrive. Children deprived of affection grow poorly, and "maternal deprivation syndrome" is a well-known medical entity that has documented the physical need for affection.

When love is absent, it is often replaced by food. Perhaps food stimulates the same neurochemical/neuroelectrical centers that love does. Feeding oneself is also a statement of self-love. If self-love is absent, then food can provide the needed replacement. Obesity may result. Most treatments for obesity (Chapter 16) fail in part because they do not provide a source of love to replace food that is withheld.

REEFER MADNESS
MARIJUANA ANESTHESIA

Another fast and easy way to change mind channels or reduce pain levels is to smoke weed. Reefer alters those nasty sensory perceptions, removes inhibitions, relaxes the body, and stimulates or calms the mind. It makes many people giggle and laugh. Exactly how this happens is unclear, but what is clear is that, like any other mind-altering substances, marijuana can be used to avoid dealing with reality.

Marijuana's medicinal value has been the subject of considerable controversy. Ayurveda agrees that it can be useful for nausea, glaucoma, depression, anxiety, IBS, insomnia, and some somatic pains, but it also stimulates both the AIR and FIRE qualities. For this reason, many inflammatory, infectious, and mental conditions can be worsened by chronic marijuana use. In addition, it can be hard on the lungs and the heart.

Like any mood elevator, marijuana can be habit-forming. Like any intoxicant, perception alteration can be a problem. Working with dangerous postal machinery can be made hazardous by marijuana use. Its negative effect on memory has also been a concern, but I don't remember why.

SMOKING EXHAUST
TOBACCO ANESTHESIA

Smoking tobacco is another common anesthetic. The many toxins in tobacco smoke make smoking a cigarette like putting your lips around a delivery van's tailpipe! Carbon monoxide is one of the deadly gases that are produced from the combustion of gasoline in an internal combustion engine and in cigarettes. It binds with the oxygen carrying hemoglobin in the blood and renders the blood incapable of carrying oxygen to the body's vital organs. A person chronically inhaling carbon monoxide slowly suffocates.

One would never purposely inhale this nasty gas unless its anesthetic effects on the consciousness were actually desired. If one wanted to silence the mind for a while, one might certainly start up the postal delivery van in a closed garage, pucker up, and wait for the anesthetic gas to do its work.

With its oxygen supply reduced, the brain-post-office that houses the mind's message sorting operation, is deprived of its energy utilities. Soon, mind-operations inside the brain slow to a crawl. However, if the postal employees inside are already overwhelmed with pain messages, the slowdown might provide a temporary "cigarette break" from dealing with all those painful reality messages!

The tailpipe smoke itself wreaks havoc on the physical post office building. Side effects of tobacco anesthesia can include headache, insomnia, sore throat, fatigue, agitated dreams, erectile dysfunction, heart attacks, strokes, lung cancer, bladder irritation, kidney dysfunction, liver disease, wrinkled skin, and breast cancer. And let's not forget bad breath and stained teeth.

But none of that matters! The mind-workers are happy *for the moment!* No pain mail can be sorted with the room full of smoke. But with the ventilation system shut down, a new problem arises. No one can breathe! The mind-worker is functioning in a stifling building in which the toilet doesn't work, the phones are dead, and the paint-skin is peeling off the walls.

After using cigarette smoke long enough, things in the body-post office don't ever run well. The sorting room routines deteriorate. The employees get depressed from working in a building that is falling apart. It sends them the message that "people who work in a place this bad must not be worth much." That painful message generates additional need for even more anesthesia. More and more employees need to participate in tailpipe sucking.

Soon, another problem appears. The workers suck on the tailpipe so often that their lips begin to stick to it. They're physically stuck! Physical cravings cause the body to *require* a continued supply of tailpipes. Tobacco addiction is one of the more difficult habits to break. The smoking employees soon progress from their *mental* needs (for which they started smoking) to *physical* needs. They wait, in apprehensive pain, for the tobacco truck to bring them physical and mental relief.

The fact that their lips are wrapped around a little paper tailpipe has been explained away in a cloud of advertising images. Fortunately, the image of the smoker is becoming as tarnished as their lungs, breath, and skin.

The postal workers know it's a bad idea to suck on cigarette tailpipes, BUT CONSEQUENCES WILL BE *IN THE FUTURE!* When they step outside to suck on the mail truck's tail pipe, the future is far enough away that it does not affect their real time need for escape from pain.

But then, the future arrives. The body/building collapses in the form of debilitating physical diseases such as emphysema, stroke, cancer, and coronary disease. A terrible new physical pain arrives to cover over the original mental pain. This new collapse pain is so severe that the psychological pain messages that were there in the beginning are completely lost in the rubble! In that sense, the original pain has been eliminated—by worse pain, or severe illness. But it's not a total loss. The mind can now focus on fighting whatever person, institution or agency it has made responsible for the disability it has inflicted on its own body.

Tobacco smoking increases the FIRE and AIR qualities. EARTH-type people can tolerate the effects of smoking a bit more easily, but the smoke injury to the arteries further aggravates the EARTH congestion problems.

THE VACUUM TUBE
TELEVISION ANESTHESIA

After a long day at the post office dealing with pain messages, it's sometimes soothing to come home, take your brain out of your skull, and toss it into the mind-numbing abyss that is television.

TV is about the unusual and the stimulating. The news, for example, rarely reports things that function smoothly or normally. TV programmers are not interested in the simple achievements of daily life such as cheerfully getting out of bed and going to a difficult work situation. Nor are they interested in the quiet spiritual discoveries that are made as a result of awareness, kindness, sensitivity and affection. Quiet activities don't stimulate the mind, and they don't sell Budweiser Beer.

TV is largely a diversionary escape from the boring or difficult everyday world to an active world of fantasy, adventure, sports and consumerism.

Although it can be a very helpful and informative tool, television is often just another way to keep the mind occupied and away from uncomfortable or painful challenges. All you have to do is sit there! You don't even need to stay awake because the effect of TV is to put your worries to bed. The common practice of falling asleep in front of the tube achieves that goal.

If you happen to stay awake, you can substitute TV's adventurous, exotic, or humorous diversions for the painful reality of mail sorting. You can vicariously experience something more "interesting" that what you yourself do with your time and your life.

Watching the tube also gets you in on the TV conversations that go on everywhere. If your own life is too empty or difficult to discuss, you can always talk about the bizarre lives of the characters that populate the sitcoms, soaps and reality shows.

The down side is that it may leave you without a life of your own. That may be OK in the short term if your life lacks interest, but it doesn't fix anything. Like anything else, if television is used to avoid difficult or painful issues, it can leave you with an internal tension that requires even more anesthesia.

TV can increase any of the AIR, FIRE, or EARTH qualities, depending on whether the shows are active, angry, calming, or combinations of the three.

LIVING IN THE MALL
SHOPPING ANESTHESIA

Once we have exposed ourselves to the stimulation of television, we cannot escape its consumer messages.

"You are what you own" is one basic message that is sent. Focusing on physical possessions can help dull the pain of difficulties in emotional, career, or relationship areas to name a just few. It is much easier to let the mind drag you toward the latest sparkling bauble than it is to work on your problems. It's openly called "Retail Therapy!"

Another consumer message that we buy is "You should have THIS." Of course, "THIS" turns out to be whatever the corporate world is trying to sell. "THIS" always changes, because if it didn't, you might already have it, and there would be no new selling involved. Buying and selling keeps the mind busy.

Focusing on the material keeps the mind from noticing that there are long-term issues to face. Once objects are obtained, they require upkeep. The upkeep process also results in mind busy-ness that diverts attention from painful problems.

The shopping process stimulates the AIR quality, the status acquisition process reinforces the FIRE quality, while the accumulation of solid objects makes the EARTH-lings feel happy.

WORKAHOLIC SUPERVISOR
WORK ANESTHESIA

Another way to divert attention from difficulty is to plunge into a work routine. Most of us are already working, so a consuming work immersion program is a prefabricated way to stay too busy to deal with painful and difficult issues.

People often relate to each other on the basis of their jobs, so increased social interaction can be a side benefit of excessive working. Rewards for extra work can also be found in the form of promotions, achievements, and recognition. Positive strokes that are difficult to find in one's personal life can be found through hard work. Another benefit is that more money is available for other diversions or anesthetics.

A sense of identity can be provided by work immersion. If someone asks about your identity, the answer is "I'm a doctor" or "I'm an insurance broker." An unemployed situation feels insufficient. We are trained to believe that "we are what we do" when, in fact, that is only a small part. What we "are" is quite different from what we "do" in yoga philosophy. Work obsession is primarily a FIRE quality.

Yoga teaches that building resources is a proper and consistent stage in life (known as "Artha"). When done with limits, working and achievement are positive ways of spending time. It is when we become obsessed or consumed with "success" that we fail to remember to deal with the more important emotional/spiritual aspects of our lives.

"ADULT" MAIL
SEXUAL ANESTHESIA

Once basic survival needs such as food, shelter, and possessions have been satisfied, the mind can turn its attention from survival fears to the search for pleasure. The sexual pleasure instinct provides a sensual activity for pain killing anesthesia.

In the developed world, sex is rarely a survival issue. Most of us don't need extra children to do chores on the farm or in the family business. Except for the risk of sexually transmitted diseases, sex is thought to be a physically healthy practice. In fact, the image of being sexy is sold as a desirable validation of one's vitality.

In Ayurvedic thinking, excessive sex can weaken the immune system, sap a person's strength, and leave vital organs such as the heart more vulnerable to disease. The risks are different for men than for women. The loss of semen is seen as a depleting act, with sexual energy intended for direction toward spiritual goals.

Sexual strength varies with a person's quality type. AIR quality types tend to be more delicate sexually and can enjoy less frequent sex (twice a month) without becoming depleted. FIRE types are stronger and can be sexual once a week without being stressed. EARTH types can have sex several times a week because of their naturally greater endurance.

Sex is a basic physiologic source of pleasure and involves simultaneous stimulation of all of the senses. Sexual stimulation releases neurochemical and neuroelectric energy that makes the mind feel less pain—anesthetized. It would be like the post office receiving a flood of intoxicating, perfumed department store flyers. The sexual orgasmic rush is powerfully sensual, and can overwhelm many painful thoughts and sensations. As such, sex can be used like any other drug to divert attention from painful issues and to replace the pain with pleasure. Regrettably, the pain sources remain intact, and once the sexual anesthesia has climaxed, the problems return.

The social consequences of using sex for anesthesia can create additional problems. Sex is associated with various aspects of interpersonal relationships. Clarity about the meaning of sex for each partner is often lacking, and difficult emotions are often created from the use of sex for anesthetic rather than for giving and loving purposes. These interpersonal difficulties are avoided by the use of masturbation anesthesia. The diversionary sensory effects of sexual stimulation can be obtained without involving the complicating issues another person may bring to a sexual situation.

The use of sex as an anesthetic is often extended into fantasy and fetishes. As is often the case with other anesthetics, its repeated use requires an increased dose to obtain the same effect. The elaborate pornographic fantasies of others are even shared! When this happens, an escapist world is created which is stimulating to the mind and keeps its attention diverted from the original problems. Pornographic anesthesia is regarded as neurotic in ayurvedic thinking.

DRIVING OFF A CLIFF
SUICIDE ANESTHESIA

Of course, the ultimate form of killing the senses, thoughts, and emotions is killing the entire problem-plagued person. Without a physical body and brain, the mind and all its issues cease to be a problem. Or do they?

After the body is dead, how can we know if the spirit thinks, feels, or has psychological issues? While those with near-death or visionary experiences have communicated some tentative answers to these questions, the inability to confirm these observations leaves the answers to these questions to personal faith.

In ayurvedic/yogic philosophy, if the cab in which the spirit and mind are riding is totaled, the spirit still walks away. It may walk away bruised and battered, but it always walks away. The "surviving" spirit must still deal with the consequences of the actions of the mind it hired. This philosophy is called "Karma." Actions taken in one's lifetime have mental/spiritual effects and consequences that go on one's permanent driving record. These impressions remain when the spirit leaves one body, and are present when it returns to finish traffic school in another vehicle.

Destroying the body does not destroy the spirit. By definition, the spirit is that which endures beyond the body. A more extended discussion of the nature of "spirit" is given in Section Four.

Ayurvedic/yogic philosophy holds that actions during a lifetime create impressions on the spirit-passenger that remain after the body and mind are gone. These spiritual personality traits (known as "Samskaras") reappear when the spirit passenger hires a new cab and sets out on a new life's journey. Because of those impressions and tendencies, the spirit may return with the same problem behaviors and issues that it had while traveling in the previous vehicle, and may continue to seek the same destinations as before. The challenge of each new incarnation is learn *better* ways of driving.

This means that a person's problems and pains are *not* removed by suicide anesthesia. In fact, in some schools of ayurvedic/yogic philosophy, if we intentionally wreck the cab, we are sent to a special spiritual jail where we must hang out with other unhappy cab-wreckers for long periods of time. A purgatory-like state of isolation and limbo with its own type of pain may be the result of purposely running off the road.

Angry, frustrated, and violent FIRE types are the most susceptible to abruptly ending a painfully challenging road trip, but all quality types are vulnerable.

SPIN-OUT
NEGATIVE-SPIRAL BEHAVIOR

No matter what the cause, many difficult behaviors can become self-perpetuating. It's a lot like losing control of a speeding car in an icy spin-out and continuing to floor the accelerator! The *response* to the problem behavior *reinforces* the difficulty, and problem behavior just gets worse.

There are people who drink because they're ashamed to be alcoholics. Some people feel bad because they are sad, and others over-eat to kill the pain of being too fat. Lonely and insecure people may acquire more wealth so that they become more exclusive. People do hateful things to others because they themselves are hated, and people play games of chance because they can't control their lives. People who have no life of their own watch someone else's life-story on TV.

Once you hit a big, icy patch of life-difficulties, your mind-driver can completely lose control. If this leads to a disastrous physical or psychological crash, then every-thing comes to a stop, including (temporarily) dealing with other serious problems.

The mind-driver's response to a psychological crash is crucial. The mature driver does not waste time and effort complaining about what has happened; he or she simply deals with the situation. The mature mind has enough experience to distance itself from the situation and see the deeper lessons that the problem behavior illustrates. The mind can simply shake off a problem as a random oc-currence, or it can drive over to Joe's Bar and cover up the "pain" of the "mistake" with an anesthetic or two. But when anesthetic behaviors are added to existing problems, the total number of difficulties is increased. This increases the stress, which increases the need for anesthesia, which increases the stress, which demands anesthesia, etc.

The drunken mind driver gets back in his cab and winds up smashing yet an-other fender. This compounding of the error pushes the driver back toward Joe's Bar until a final event terminates the spinout. This may be anything from getting arrested to winding up in the hospital or morgue.

Hopefully, the spinout behavior can be stopped before an irreversible major crash occurs. More often, it doesn't stop, and some critical event is necessary for a person to realize the need to regain behavioral control. One difficult part of regaining control is accepting that being in *more* control is actually possible, but that *total* control is not. The Twelve Step programs and many religions are big on this concept.

It is important that the spirit-passenger direct the mind to avoid behavioral spin-outs. If one is constantly racing around beltless with Diana and Dodo, sooner or later, problems will arise. If, instead, one is driving Miss Daisy, steady progress is likely.

'GOT TO HAVE IT!
ADDICTION

One of the perils of negative spiral behavior is addiction. Since anesthesia is used to avoid rather than to address problems, once the anesthetic wears off, the unresolved problems remain and are often worsened. Because problems are worsened by the addiction themselves, increased anesthesia is often required. The anesthetic itself becomes both the source of the pain and its solution.

Volumes have been written on the nature of addiction. The addiction problem has been ascribed to everything from character flaws to a genetic biochemical necessity. It is not the intent of this book to review all of those descriptive efforts. Instead, the essentials of the Ayurvedic approach to addiction are described.

Addiction is an out-of-control effort to fill some *emptiness*. It doesn't really matter whether that emptiness represents a lack of love, acceptance, fame, or money. There is an expectation that something should be where no thing is. There is a misperception that there is a hole that needs filling.

The ayurvedic/yogic view is that *emptiness is not bad*. The hole does not need filling.

Ayurveda asks the addict to realize that the greatest thing in the universe—the biggest, most prevalent, and dominant aspect in all of creation is ... emptiness! It is vast and pure. It encompasses everything. Every thing, from elephants to diamonds, is made mostly of empty space - and is contained in empty space. Emptiness is King!

Accepting this concept is a huge philosophical leap for the Western mind.

The least is the most.

Ayurveda asks the addict to just exist for a while in the emptiness! Accept it. Sit quietly without effort, expectation, labeling, or judgment. Empty and quiet the mind through regular mediation. (See Chapter 23.)

Next, it is important to practice *witnessing observation*. This is especially true for the detached observation of one's own emotions. Don't try to suppress them, just observe them running their course, just as a flower blooms, and then fades. *Don't identify* with the difficult feelings. Try to believe that what you truly are is much more than the conclusions of a stressed-out mind. Try not to think of your personal lapses as failures. No student gets it right every time, and many need to try repeatedly.

604

Part of the problem with making all of these mental adjustments is that the addictive mind is often too messed up to make them. Ayurveda offers the *Five Cleansings* technique to help relax and clear the mind. After this procedure, not only are many of the addictive toxins removed, but the cleared mind is better able to approach daily life with fresh attitudes.

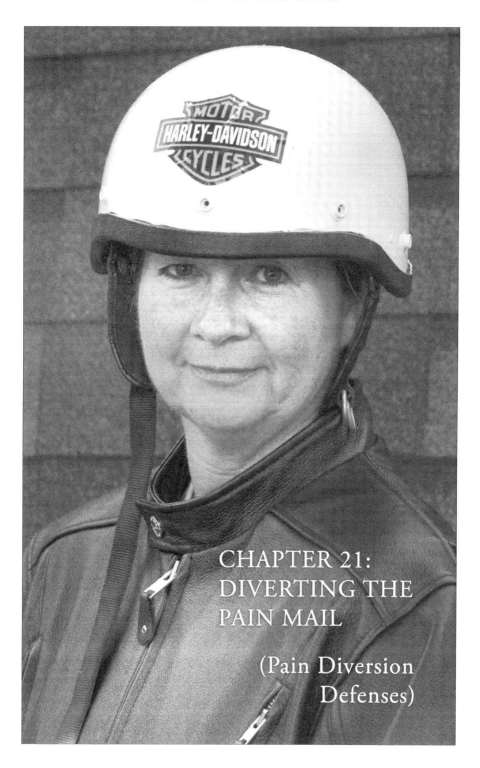

CHAPTER 21:
DIVERTING THE
PAIN MAIL

(Pain Diversion
Defenses)

LIVE TO RIDE, RIDE TO LIVE

"Hey, Regg!"

"Hey, What?"

"You got a phone call from Helen, Dude."

"Helen?"

"Yep."

"You're b-s-ing me, aren't you?"

"Nope."

"Well, I'll be damned!"

"I thought she dumped you a long time ago."

"No, she was in love with someone else, Margo. I dumped *her* two-timin' ass!"

"Sorry, guy."

"Yeah, well, so was I, but it worked out."

"You never did tell me the whole story about that one, Regg."

"Well, I'll tell you all about it sometime when I'm good and loaded. I'm 10-97,"

Yeah, Helen was hot! Five foot two, twinkly eyes of bright blue, with soft, henna-dyed hair. She had swaying hips, a coy little smile that radiated from her thin lips, and a wispy little voice that sounded like a cooing dove. She always wore a ruby necklace, small pierced ear studs, and usually, her cherished black leather vest. She was sexy. She was irresistible even at forty.

But, as it turned out, Helen was in love with Jessica.

Jessica was simply irresistible to Helen. Jess was a very sturdily built, sexy, black, 650-pound, vibrating Harley-Davidson "Soft tail" motorcycle. Helen had always wanted to be a biker chick, and now that she had saved the money to buy "Jessica," her dreams were coming true. She was both cool and hot at the same time.

She had named Jess after a warrior heroine from one of the Dune series movies. She loved to escape into those adventure movies. She'd have some wine or vodka or maybe even smoke a joint, settle into her futon couch in her darkened living room and dissolve into a fantasy world where she had limitless power, beauty and purpose.

On weekends, she rode with the meanest-looking men on the planet and held her own. She had a fringed leather vest covered with patches. "Ladies of Harley" and

607

"Harley Davidson of Santa Cruz" orange lettering jumped out of the black background on her jacket. She was even a member of the 'Polar Bear' winter riding Club. The day's weather forecast was important only because it determined whether or not she could be Helen Harley for the day.

She loved the damn Harley club. She once did a limited strip routine at a club meeting to advertise the leather clothes at the local Harley store, and was proud to be the HOG secretary-treasurer. She belonged. Her social group was her life. The inside of her house was almost completely covered with Harley toys, emblems and paraphernalia. Whenever her friends saw a Harley, or Harley paraphernalia, they would think of Helen and buy her yet another souvenir.

She even chose or rejected men based on whether or not they rode a Harley. When she married for the second time, it was a to a Harley rider, and the wedding procession was a thunderous, fifty-plus Harley motorcade! She had become her bike. It was great. She was the rebel her strict German mother never allowed her to be.

She rode her motorcycle to school and was delighted when the roar of the engine got the attention of the suits. She strode into work with wrap-around Harley sunglasses, Harley jacket, and Harley black leather chaps and boots. Heads always turned. "I'm getting in touch with my 'Dark Side,' she would explain.

Curiously, there was another side of Helen. She was a special needs elementary school teacher. She had spent her working career teaching the most difficult students a teacher could ever be asked to handle. And she was good at it. She had graduated Summa Cum Laude from some special ed school, and risen in the ranks at the County Board to Assistant Director of Special Education. But her work eventually became just one thing—a way to get money to spend on her beloved Jessica.

Helen was also an avid gardener. Her backyard was an oasis of color and fragrance in a neighborhood of junky cars, messy front yards, and windows covered with sheets instead of curtains. She could also cook almost anything from scratch.

Helen's mind was so busy, she would occupy it with complex computer games, or knock it unconscious with alcohol, and wild sex with various partners. It was that 'more than one partner' thing that put a quick end to our relationship! Fun is fun, but at that point, I needed something more.

Anyway, it certainly was a gas while it lasted, and it hurt like hell when it ended. Sometimes I think that the world's all about finding the fun and getting rid of the pain. It could be that …

"Hey, Reggie. I got some drivin' for you to do, my man."

… Speaking of the pain …

DIVERTING THE PAIN MAIL
PAIN DIVERSION DEFENSES

Covering up pain with an anesthetic is one way of dealing with it. Another method is to *change the pain into something else* or to *move the pain* to a more acceptable, less sensitive area. If too many pain messages are pummeling one area of the mind, then it makes sense to send those pain letters to another department that can handle them. This temporarily solves the problem, and allows the release of some of the anxious energy that comes from receiving painful input.

SENDING PAIN-MAIL TO THE WRONG ADDRESS
REFERRED PAIN

One basic example of pain rerouting is the phenomenon of referred physical pain. In this situation, an actual physical pain message that starts in one location is channeled to a pathway that normally comes from a different location. This gives the impression that the pain is really from somewhere else. For example, injury to the heart muscle is often experienced as pain in the left arm.

CONVENIENTLY MISFILING THE PAIN-MAIL
PROJECTION & DISPLACEMENT

In a similar manner, difficult thoughts or emotions need not be directly experienced. They can be avoided by sending them to the wrong place either consciously or subconsciously. If these difficult pain messages are sent out to another post office, there is no need to deal with them at all.

Typical *projection* misfiling includes statements such as "I'm not really the nasty one (false), *he* is!" or "I don't really hate him (false), he hates *me*!" and "I'm not persecuting him (false) he's bugging *me*!" Also, talking pointedly about someone else's problems rather than one's own problems is an example of avoiding issues by putting them on another person or object.

Of course, problems arise when the other postal minds in town keep getting nasty mail that isn't theirs. The misdirected mail is eventually returned, and additional painful complaints are filed. In addition, the problems that are projected or displaced are not faced and continue to grow. Extra suspiciousness, prejudices, hypervigilance, and collecting evidence of persistent "injustices" toward oneself are examples of this misguided compensation mechanism.

As with many other mental problems, this disorder usually represents an excess of the AIR quality, and AIR balancing treatments are used to help treat it.

HIDDEN PACKAGES
REPRESSION / SUPPRESSION

Rather than move unwanted emotional or thought problem-mail to some other post office, just hiding it in the back room can work temporary wonders.

When we are *aware* of hiding our unacceptable thoughts or behavior, it's called "suppression," and when we ignore it automatically, it's known as "repression." Either way, that nasty thought package stays in the back and is no longer an *immediate* problem. But it cannot be ignored forever. Continuing to ignore pressing issues allows them to eat away at us from the subconscious. This may cause any number of health problems, especially in the connective tissue.

Repression and suppression are typically EARTH disorders.

TAKING PACKAGES HOME
INTERNALIZATION / INTROJECTION

Rather than ignore a significant and difficult piece of thought or emotional mail, we can control it if we unconsciously make it a part of us. We can keep tabs on it by making it a part of our lives.

An example of this would be Helen the biker *overtly* becoming the "bad" person she was raised to believe she was. Her fear of actually being a bad person was removed by actually becoming a "bad" motorcycle gang member.

If we desire to be *closer* to a loved object or concept, internalizing it into our own persona fulfills that desire. It helps us avoid losing the object of our desires.

Another example would be unconsciously adopting the manners or habits of our parents or teachers, which could be positive or negative. Internalization is an EARTH quality.

F'GET ABOUT IT!
DISSOCIATION

If a situation is intolerable, it can simply be set aside mentally, and be completely ignored!

A person can even change his identity in order to avoid problems. People can totally or partially disappear from the difficult parts of their lives, and assume a new identity that is not bothered by the troublesome problem. Multiple personalities can also be created in order to skirt emotional issues.

The mind can separate parts of itself from the rest of its awareness as it does in hypnosis. It can also use amnesia to avoid dealing with a subject that is just too painful. Objects can be made to appear differently in the mind by removing them from their emotional connections. Hallucinations can even be the result. Auditory hallucinations are AIR-like in nature, visual hallucinations have FIRE qualities, and kinesthetic hallucinations tend to have EARTH-like qualities. The dissociation process itself is usually an AIR-quality disorder.

MICRO-MANAGING BOSS
CONTROLLING

Another diversionary response to circumstances that are difficult to control is to control everything else. Whatever out-of-control problem brings us difficulty or fear, we can get *some* measure of control by controlling *other* things.

Because the control of something *else* doesn't help with the primary problem, the problem persists or grows even greater, and the need to control (other things) grows with it.

Eastern philosophy recognizes that there are limits on the control of life events. Many people choose to believe that a divine consciousness controls events, or that the planets and stars are in charge. Such letting go of control (see Chapter 22) and "jumping into the abyss" of life events is an approach that helps relieve one of the burden of control.

Over-controlling is almost always a FIRE disorder.

SORTING THE SAME EXACT WAY EVERY TIME
OBSESSION / COMPULSION

When a little controlling doesn't quite suppress a problem, a lot of controlling sometimes does.

Deeper fears of the uncontrollable, undesired, and the unacceptable may lead to behaviors that provide an elaborate structure for control of those difficult thoughts, ideas, and images. Often, the focus of the obsessive-compulsive preoccupation is outside the person who becomes obsessed. The preoccupation progresses to behavior that becomes involuntary and often irrational.

Often, excessive rituals and rules are created to prevent a feeling of loss of control, and to bring order to the confusing and unacceptable. These excesses may lead to the isolation of the obsessed individual who finds it easier to practice their control activities alone.

OCD problems are usually a combination of excess FIRE and AIR qualities. Once again, the "Letting Go" process is needed (see Chapter 22).

NEVER GO IN THE DEAD LETTER OFFICE AT NIGHT!
PHOBIAS

When intense fears dominate a person's life, they are controlled by focusing them on a few specific objects or situations. These anxieties are often out of proportion with reality, and the perceived causes of the fears are over-emphasized as well. A deep-seated and misplaced guilt or anxiety may be the cause, and unresolved experiences or traumas can also create phobias.

The extreme depth of the fear usually leads to avoidance behaviors and serious constriction of normal life activities. Public places, where escape from the perceived threats might be difficult, are avoided. Fear of public humiliation is often included in the furtive behavior.

Other threatening environments such as closed spaces or heights are often avoided. Certain objects may be perceived as threats and are singled-out and avoided at all costs. If the feared objects or situations are not successfully avoided, then a panic reaction can result.

The safety of the home environment is often over-developed, and the intense fear can easily lead to a victim staying home continuously.

A person with a major phobia is often aware of the excessive and irrational nature of the fear and its resulting behavior, but is often unable to break away from the defense patterns that hold him.

This type of intense fear is almost always a reflection of an excess of the AIR quality.

ANALYZE IT TO DEATH!
INTELLECTUALIZATION

Emotions are different from generic thoughts, and must be experienced in the heart as well as the mind. Attempting to deal with these personal and sensitive aspects of life in an *analytical* way is like trying to grow flowers with drafting tools.

Approaching difficult emotions with intellectual thought is one way to avoid the emotional essence of a problem. For example, reading detailed psychology textbooks may impart plenty of sterile information about an emotional subject, but a movie, play, or piece of music may be a more emotion-sensitive approach.

It is important to let oneself *feel* without thinking too much. It is an art to be able to observe one's own feelings without intellectual judgments and labeling.

Intellectualization is a FIRE quality manifestation.

HIDING IN THE SUPPLY ROOM
EMOTIONAL ISOLATION

A similar way to avoid the anxiety of dealing with difficult mind issues is to separate oneself from feelings, emotions, relationships, and environments.

Difficulty interacting with others in relationships is avoided by simply not participating in open or honest interactions. Use of this defense technique often results in relationships that are described as impersonal, stiff, distant, compulsive, formal, strained and unsatisfying. This behavior may not be fully manifest outwardly, but the ability to appear warm and personal on the exterior may cover an inner wall that is often guarded by other defense techniques.

Life-situation difficulties can result in an isolation of emotions. Physical illness and untoward events may be too difficult to face without a wall of emotional separation. This type of diversion defense often results from a lack of self-acceptance.

Yogic and ayurvedic philosophies point to the basic problems of duality and separation thinking as causes of this type of defense (see Chapter 24). If one does not accept the basic unity of the personal/spiritual self with that of others, then that perceived separation produces fear, and emotional distance is created.

Isolation is primarily an excess of the AIR and EARTH qualities.

HIDING IN THE DAY CARE CENTER
REGRESSION

When protection or stability are removed, a way to avoid the anxiety, pain, or hostility that can follow is to return to an earlier time or behavior that provided a successful defense, means of expression, or gratification.

This return to an earlier pattern of response to stress is usually instinctual, primitive, and inappropriate for the person's age. This regressive behavior seeks gratification of needs that are not being met. The regression may be triggered by a sensory-linked childhood memory, and may result in a behavioral return to that earlier point in mental time. The feeling of a safer childhood situation is thereby revived. Regression is most often a combination of disturbed AIR and EARTH qualities.

STUCK IN A NOWHERE JOB
DEPRESSION

There is always a bit of confusion about the term "depression." It can either be a symptom of other problems, or it can be so consuming that it becomes a problem in and of itself. This mental state involves unhealthy excessive feelings of low self-esteem, worthlessness, and pessimism. It results in sadness, gloom, listlessness, and a 'stuck' feeling.

Feelings of helplessness can be reinforced by real or perceived failures, and can emerge as a result of a deficiency of normal self-supporting mental skills.

Depression can also be the result of simple psychological stress, or from an absence of the capacity to adjust to difficult life situations. Normal depression is seen when losses and difficulties occur, but when they persist beyond an expected recovery time, the depression may become self-sustaining.

If a person is severely subjugated in a situation, then depression can result. If no appropriate outlet for anger is available, the only acceptable response may be to turn that anger inward against oneself.

After a period of time in a depressed state, everything becomes a problem. The ability to be selective with responses to different problem areas is lost. Once this depressed state has persisted for a period of time, brain neurotransmitter levels may adjust in a way that keeps the gloomy cloud in place. In that situation, antidepressant drugs and herbs are often used to induce a change in the weather.

Depression is primarily an excess of the EARTH quality, but it may be initiated by imbalances in AIR or FIRE qualities as well.

MAKING EXCUSES
RATIONALIZATION

There are two types of rationalization. In one type, explanations are created that account for behavior that is irrational, unacceptable, or otherwise hard to explain. In other cases, explanations are created for events that occur for no apparent reason.

Assigning explanations to random behavior, thoughts, feelings and emotions helps remove them from the unexplainable category, and puts them into the scientific and logical arena where control is possible.

The excuses for irrational or unacceptable thoughts, emotions, and actions can be real or imagined, logical or illogical, and are often designed to avoid a painful/truthful explanation by providing a plausible (but incorrect) clarification.

The FIRE or AIR qualities usually dominates the rationalization process.

THE BEST DEFENSE IS A GOOD OFFENSE
REACTION FORMATION

It is easier to avoid our mental/emotional problem issues if we pretend that our problems are our strengths.

Some thoughts, feelings, and situations are not only too difficult to accept, they are also too difficult to avoid using other diversion or anesthetic techniques. In this situation, the mind pretends that the situation is completely opposite from reality.

The mind simply replaces a pointedly negative situation with one that is excessively positive. For example, a deep-seated negative or sadistic urge can be replaced by excessive outward kindness or charity.

This type of diversion behavior is most typical of the FIRE quality, but the scattered approach of those with an AIR quality excess will also yield this response.

CALLING IN SICK - AGAIN!
HYPOCHONDRIA

Another means of escape from a source of pain is to create a physical illness that diverts attention from it.

Illness preoccupation removes us from concern with mental difficulties. Physical illness is more socially acceptable than mental difficulties, and can easily elicit sympathetic attention from others. People are much more comfortable providing advice for straight-forward medical conditions than they are with complex psychological or emotional issues.

Self-created illness can be a form of self-punishment for a perceived flaw. With

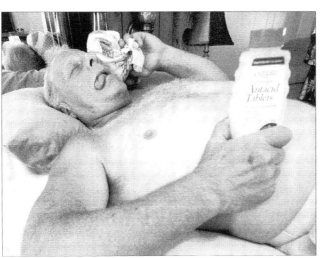

such an imagined illness, extra attention, and a diversion from guilt over destructive wishes are obtained.

Displacing mental concerns to the *physical* body may be a result of a preoccupation with the body itself. Problematic biological drives can be redirected to a less embarrassing body area. Symptoms can be either vague or specific, and sensations are often unrealistically interpreted as abnormal. Reassurance that all is well rarely provides any relief.

Hypochondria is most commonly a result of an excess of the AIR quality.

JAMMING UP THE SORTING MACHINE
PSYCHOGENIC PHYSICAL ILLNESS

Another method of slowing the flow of psychological pain messages is to toss so much mental junk into the sorting machine that it *physically* stops parts of the body from functioning. If one becomes physically sick, the illness takes priority over issues of unhappiness or responsibility.

When extra attention is given to fixing the *physical* aspect, less attention is given to the *psychological* problems overflowing at the mental sorting desk. A lot of unquestioning attention can also be obtained in support of physical illness. In contrast to the shame that is unfairly associated with mental illness, it is cruel to criticize someone who can't breathe, walk, eat, etc.

Sympathy is generated, and this soothes the pain. This attention can be a good substitute for unavailable pleasures until the true source of the illness is discovered by others (or oneself). At that point, disapproval reactions may arise.

Baseline psychological pain messages are not processed during acute physical illness, but they must be processed later, or be avoided by developing further illness. Of course, if we injure the body badly enough, we may lose the ability to use it later on for positive growth responses and pleasure.

All quality types are good at this diversion.

ROLLING THE FUZZY DICE
GAMBLING

Whether playing bingo at church, the lottery, office pools, or betting on cards and sporting events, many people engage in some form of gambling with money. When the process becomes all-consuming, it becomes an addiction as well as a diversion from the psycholgical stresses of life.

Unlike many addictions that seek some form of anesthesia *from* pain, the high likelihood of losing at gambling indicates a subconscious desire *for* pain and self ruin. Some psychologists describe this addiction as an expression of the need for punishment through losing. Gambling has been associated with the loss of a parent by death, separation, divorce or desertion. It is a known outlet for stress and anxiety.

Gambling can become so consuming in a person's life that it negatively impacts family, job, and other personal areas. The gambler's relationships often become just a means of supporting his/her habit. The turmoil that gambling generates also generates plenty of attention, albeit negative.

Primary psychological issues can be covered over by a gambling preoccupation, and money is viewed as both the cause and the solution for life's problems. Forgery, fraud, embezzlement, and tax evasion often become additional complications, that can increase the distance of gambler from the true source of his/her pain.

The winning side of the gambling experience is often enticing enough to sustain a player through significant periods of losing. The winning experience includes a perceived supernatural ability on the part of the gambler to beat the odds. In so doing, there is a triumph over the uncontrolled. Fate has been outwitted by the gambler's intelligence, and any inability to control life has been momentarily reversed. At the winning moment, life is clearly good, and the "winner" can view him/herself as being touched by the divine.

All Ayurvedic quality types are prone to this diversion/addiction. AIR-types need to transform their fears and anxieties, FIRE-types need to deal with anger and control issues, and EARTH-types often need to approach the melancholy and inertia in their lives.

PULLING THE FIRE ALARM
CRISIS CREATION

Creating a crisis of any type will slow or stop the flow of *chronic* pain for at least a short time. If our problems are great, we can easily manufacture thoughts, stories and situations that are greater. The emotional turmoil that is created then requires the immediate attention of others as well. Nagging problem thoughts, emotions, and beliefs are temporarily forgotten.

Of course, adding a crisis to existing problems solves nothing in the long term, and only increases the need for further diversion or anesthesia.

This type of behavior is most typical of the AIR and FIRE types, and must be resolved accordingly.

WRECKING THE OFFICE PARTY
ANTI-SOCIAL BEHAVIOR

One behavior that can divert attention from personal pain is to make trouble for others as well as for oneself.

Criminal activity is often the result of being raised in a subculture in which nasty behavior is more commonly accepted. Abusive home circumstances, gang environments, and deprived inner city situations are just a few examples where stealing, fighting, arson, rape and murder more commonly occur. These can distract the mind from the pain of an impoverished or hopeless situation.

Less violent but persistently reckless and disruptive behavior such as lying, cheating, forgery, promiscuity, workplace irresponsibility, and resisting authority are other examples of an inability to deal with difficult social relationships.

The consequences of this type of behavior often leads to the creation of a whole new set of personal problems with the law that can effectively cover over the original psychosocial difficulties.

High FIRE quality is the usual cause of this disorder due to unresolved anger and control issues. Following a FIRE-reducing program helps to restore social awareness and balance.

RISKY BUSINESS
DANGEROUS DIVERSIONS

Tempting fate works in several ways to deal with difficult mental issues.

First, it is a way of generating adrenalin anesthesia. The rush of doing something dangerous completely wipes out lesser concerns, because it calls on the mind's number one priority—survival. The focus of attention is diverted from inner issues to immediate outer needs.

The outcome of flirting with danger can be good or bad. If one does poorly with a dangerous behavior, then the injurious consequences become the primary concern drawing attention away from the original difficult mental issues. If things go well, and one survives the danger, then increased self-esteem is the result. In addition, there is usually a restful letdown period afterward which acts as an additional anesthetic.

Sooner or later, the avoided issues will resurface, and more and more danger will be required to hide from the problems.

Enduring danger has a way of affirming life. Surviving the physical danger experience suggests that other (emotional) dangers can also be overcome.

The strength and confidence of FIRE-type personalities may lead them toward dangerous diversions. AIR-types may also fly off in dangerous directions.

GOING POSTAL
VIOLENCE

If internal pain gets too intense, it may lead to an explosion. Smoldering internal fury over a perceived threat, or a natural aggressive impulse may be released by a sudden provocation, or by the use of drugs or alcohol.

Violence can be the result of an inability to manage a chronically irritating situation, or from a sudden lost of self-esteem. The target of violence is not necessarily the real source of the irritation. Emotional violence, as opposed to physical destruction, is more insideous and deep-reaching..

In ayurvedic thinking, violence is almost always associated with an excess of the FIRE quality. Since FIRE quality individuals are much more prone to violence, an awareness of their outward physical features can be a very helpful warning to those they confront not to test their forceful tendencies.

CRASHING YOUR OWN DELIVERY VAN
SELF-INJURY & MASOCHISM

When the pain of life issues becomes too great to bear, and when externalizing the pain through other diversions is ineffective, externalizing the pain in the form of self-injury can serve to refocus the pain away from its true source.

Self-injury can take many different forms including doing physical damage (e.g. self-cutting) to unconsciously sabotaging one's own efforts in other areas.

Usually, feelings of humiliation, self-pity, and abuse accompany this type of passive-aggressive behavior. The attention that is obtained from being injured is also a factor.

This problem is more likely to occur among those with excessive EARTH or AIR qualities.

PAIN-MAIL HOLDING ROOM
PROCRASTINATION

A very common method of diverting attention from painful every day problems is to decide that they can be handled at a later time when they will be easier to manage. This leaves the pseudo-impression that the problem is resolved. In terms of the present moment, it *is* resolved, but internally, it is clear that the difficulty will return.

Of course, this approach simply leaves a bigger pile of pain mail to manage. As the pile gets bigger and bigger, it becomes easier to conclude that it cannot be managed in the present, and should be put off yet again.

There are several reasons why this negative spiral approach simply generates increased internal pressure, anxiety, and pain. We'll deal with those in another section later. EARTH types are the most prone to procrastination.

"OH, WAS THAT IN MY JOB DESCRIPTION?"
PASSIVE-AGGRESSIVE BEHAVIOR

Yet another way to avoid pain is to control difficult situations through strategic inaction, even if it means creating additional problems in the process.

Anger can be expressed by refusing to deal with important issues when others are depending on you. Sabotaging of another's plans with inaction can indirectly expresses negative emotions without being obvious or forthright.

Aggressive (controlling) passivity can be subtle, and take the form of disinterest, indifference, foot-dragging, or withdrawal. Obstructing other people's work can manifest as needless inefficiency, lack of initiative, superficial efforts, "errors" of omission, or over-literal "misinterpretations."

Passive obstructive behavior is yet another way of getting attention.

A combination of FIRE and EARTH disturbance is most commonly responsible for this behavior.

SURE! WHAT THE HELL!
IMPULSIVENESS

When chronic, painful tensions build to an intolerable level, small provocations, or sudden opportunities can trigger impulsive behavior that relieves the stress and gratifies the desire for pleasure. Drugs, and loaded social/emotional situations can easily ignite impulsive behavior.

Since the impulsive acts themselves often go well beyond what are considered to be the social norms, the results can be harmful to others, or to the one committing the impulsive act. Although negative, regretful feelings often follow an impulsive action, the initial excitement and the shift away from a bad mood or situation may be too difficult to resist.

Those with high levels of the AIR quality are the most prone to be impulsive, but FIRE types can run a close second.

DAY-DREAMING ON THE JOB
FANTASY ESCAPISM

Another way to avoid painful reality is to escape into imagination and fantasy.

While this is much more common among children than it is among adults, many older people still find comfort in soap operas, movies, science fiction, and other dream worlds. Real-life situations that involve too much intimacy, conflict, or tension can be manipulated or taken less seriously by transforming them into exaggerated fantasies.

A limited amount of fantasy and escape is necessary for most of us, but when it replaces too much of the real world, physical and mental health problems can occur. Directly facing our real-world problems and creating pleasure and excitement outside of fantasy is an ogoing challenge.

Both the AIR and EARTH types specialize in fantasy. FIRE types tend to be more practical.

OFF IN HIS OWN POST CARD WORLD
SCHIZOPHRENIA

Thoughts and emotions can become so difficult and confusing that a completely different, other-worldly existence may need to be created to place them in order.

This new world need not have the same rules that make reality so difficult. Social problems can be resolved with different (and often bizarre) social rules. Serious behavioral disturbances can result, and emotions that are not appropriate for the situation can become the norm. These can include withdrawal, abandoning social conventions, and offensive or threatening behavior.

Normal associations of people and objects can change. Emotional disturbances and distancing become common. Communications often fail to follow the old rules, so a new system is adopted. Thoughts, activities, expressions, speech, and associations can become fragmented, unintelligible, and devoid of meaning. Bizarre symbolism and hallucinations can become the currency of connection.

With the mind freed of normal rules, sensations can take on different meanings, and hallucinations of all types are possible. In addition, sensory sensitivity is often markedly increased, making the escapee vulnerable to being overwhelmed by sensory stimuli. This can result in withdrawal from the sensory world or an inability to inhibit responses to stimulation.

Perceptual confusion can occur, and difficulty determining whether experiences are coming from the "outside" world or from a person's mind are common. Imagined external controlling forces often find their way into the new mental world.

A loss of the normal separation of one's identity from the outer world (ego) can also take place. One can believe that he or she is actually someone or something else, or that his or her thoughts belong to another person.

The normal interconnection of thoughts can be disrupted, and the mind can jump around without apparent logic. Inconsistency can also manifest as an extreme ambivalence of attitude, or a jumping from normal to abnormal thinking and behavior.

Clearly, it is difficult to function in the physical world when living in a very different mental place, and returning to the real world can be difficult. Loss of connection with reality can easily lead to loss of health care habits. From there, all types of physical illnesses are possible.

Just as the modern medical world recognizes the need for strong medications and therapies for this extreme condition, Ayurveda recognizes the need for stronger herbal medications and procedures to cleanse the mind for reality programming.

Schizophrenia is primarily a disorder of AIR quality excess, and this type is most commonly associated with auditory hallucinations. FIRE excess is often a factor when visual hallucinations are seen, and an EARTH excess problems manifest when kinesthetic hallucinations occur.

LEGAL HOLIDAYS
PLEASURE DIVERSION

Avoiding painful life issues through *excessive* pleasure-seeking can be a serious detriment to one's health.

We are constantly urged to "live for today" and to mortgage our futures for immediate gratification. This now-oriented approach comes from the fear of a lack of future opportunities to have fun. There is an absence of faith in the future. We fear that we "will die without having lived."

The yogic concept of reincarnation reduces this urgency. Fulfillment will come, but it may take more than one lifetime. Christianity and Islam also promise future satisfaction in another world in exchange for temperance in this one.

On the other hand, yoga philosophy also urges us to live "in the present moment." If, as a result, one gives himself permission for profuse self-pleasuring, then all sorts of excesses in diet, sex, drugs, and other unhealthy behaviors become possible.

In either case, moderation in self-pleasuring is urged for the benefit of one's health and the development of self-discipline. Excessive pleasure seeking is primarily a sign of excess EARTH quality, but the AIR and FIRE qualities are far from immune.

TABLE 21-1: **DIVERSION QUALITIES**

DIVERSION	QUALITY
Referred Pain	AIR
Projection & Displacement	AIR
Repression/Suppression	EARTH
Internalization/Introjection	EARTH
Dissociation	AIR
Hallucinations	AIR, FIRE, EARTH
Controlling	FIRE
Obsession/Compulsion	FIRE, AIR
Phobia	AIR
Intellectualization	FIRE
Emotional Isolation	AIR, EARTH
Regression	EARTH, AIR
Depression	EARTH
Rationalization	FIRE
Reaction Formation	FIRE, AIR
Hypochondria	AIR
Physical Psychogenic Illness	AIR, FIRE, EARTH
Gambling	EARTH, FIRE, AIR
Crisis Creation	AIR, FIRE
Anti-social Behavior	FIRE
Danger	FIRE
Violence	FIRE
Self-injury & Masochism	FIRE, AIR
Procrastination	EARTH
Passive-Aggressive Behavior	EARTH
Impulsiveness	AIR, FIRE
Fantasy Escapism	AIR, EARTH
Schizophrenia	AIR
Pleasure Diversion	EARTH, FIRE, AIR
Escape Sleeping	EARTH

NIGHT SHIFT
ESCAPE SLEEPING

For a few precious hours, life's problems seem to go away when one falls asleep. Even though it is obvious that the problems will reappear on waking, it remains a tempting way to avoid dealing with mental pain.

Escape sleeping can take the form of sleeping through important meetings, difficult confrontations, or life in general. Extra naps and early bedtimes are also useful to avoid other stressful realities.

The sleep defense is rarely helpful since problem resolution activity, rather than avoidance, is the key solution for stress disorders. The exception would be for an excess of the hyperactive AIR quality, for which extra sleep is often recommended.

Excessive sleeping is an EARTH quality disorder, so early rising is suggested in addition to rebalancing with LiFE-rich foods and anti-depressant herbs.

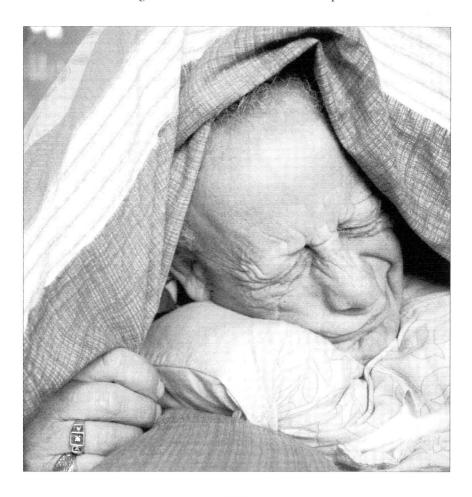

CHAPTER 22:
CONSTRUCTIVE DEFENSES

I TOLD YOU LIFE IS HARD

From the beginning, I had to deal with my parent's problems with alcohol and anger. Dad would start drinking as soon as our small dry goods store closed up for the day at five-thirty. After dinner was done, he'd drink into the night. We'd find him the next morning on the couch or living room rug.

Then Mom would throw her usual silent fit in front of everyone - huffing and snorting all morning long as she tossed the pots loudly onto the stove or into the sink. But not a word! – all the way through dinner. Then, the same painful, drunken, bitching scene would start all over again through that evening, the next evening, and beyond.

After I got out of there, I thought I was home free. Then I got married.

My husband turned out to be even worse than my parents! How could that happen?! *And why did it happen to me?!!* Hadn't I had already paid my dues surviving my childhood?!

And I was doing so well, too. I was working at Mt. Zion Hospital up in the city, and making really good money, and I felt really good about myself! I was doing great.

Then I met Stan on the tennis court in Orinda. I had decided to take lessons, and he was the tennis pro. He was so overwhelmed by my statuesque body, my long legs, and my irresistible smile that he pursued me relentlessly, despite my nearly complete lack of tennis ability.

And I was taken with his energy and intelligence. He was smart enough to graduate from law school, but decided to go into real estate. He was also a professional athlete. He had been a minor league baseball player, and would have made it to the majors, so he said, if he had agreed to cut his hair and shave his moustache. Once he blew that decision, he went on to the tennis world and became a superior student of the John-McEnroe-School-of-Obnoxious-Arguing.

We had fun for a year before we got pregnant, and decided to get married. As soon as we tied the knot, he changed! 100%. He became a complete tyrant. I wasn't able to do anything to his satisfaction, and he spent every spare waking moment controlling and criticizing what I did.

I wasn't allowed to drive when he was in the car. I wasn't allowed to touch the car radio or the air conditioner. He refused to wear a seat belt, or to put one on our son, Seth, when they drove together without me. And he drove like an absolute maniac!

No artwork was allowed in our home. I cooked dinner, he took his share and ate alone in his room. He began lowering all the window shades in the house and turned off the heat in the winter. He slept for long stretches of time, and made our son sleep with him in his room on a mattress on the floor.

He made life-changing decisions without my input, and moved us down to Santa Cruz so that I had to quit my job and become totally dependent on him. Then, when our son was old enough to play baseball, he moved us down south to the desert for the winters so Seth could play baseball all year long. Stan decided that Seth was going to be the Tiger Woods of baseball, and that Stan would be his teacher-father. He made Seth practice with him everyday for hours. He kept him out of school for a whole year so he could practice without the distraction of schoolwork. Santa Cruz County did nothing to check up on Seth. I tried to keep education in Seth's life with educational field trips, but Stan killed that too.

I didn't leave Stan because I couldn't believe this was the same person I'd married. Sometimes, I still can't believe it.

Stan's real estate empire grew large, and he leveraged all our credit to keep it growing. He even ran up debt on his aging mother's credit cards that he never repaid. He was always in court suing someone, or on the phone planning the lies he and his real estate partners would tell in court. He was smart, and he knew that the courts would do nothing about the lies. Perjury had gone out as a crime with the Clinton administration.

He yelled and cursed at me constantly, and taught our son to behave the same way. On two occasions, he hit me, and the cops made him move out for a short time. I actually called up Dr. Laura on the radio and told her my story. She said my husband was sick, and that he should "get a life." She also said I should move out. I would have long ago, but I was afraid I'd lose my son if I left.

Stan made that loss happen when I did get up the guts to leave. He even admitted using his money and influence with a County Supervisor to get the judge in our divorce case to give *him* custody of our son. My incompetent lawyer let him get away with it. After I left, Stan tried to starve me into an unfair settlement. Luckily, my family and friends helped me get through it, and helped me keep a connection with Seth.

I hid the pain of my situation with food, money, alcohol, weed and downers for the longest time. I left town whenever I could to stay with my sister in Salinas. I would have slipped into extended abuse if I hadn't run into Monica. She showed me a positive way to deal with the pain of my circumstances. It turned out that there's a whole different view of the world that can help manage those pains without the damaging side effects that my drugs and alcohol had.

Doing what she suggested wasn't easy, and it took a long time and a lot of help, but it worked for me. I learned to be the observer of my own behavior. To make a long story short, I was eventually able to see myself making a mistake before I actually made it! Huge.

The other thing I was able to do was to learn how to give things away. I did things for people. First, I did people favors for the strokes it got me. Later on, I gave myself the strokes. Finally, helping others for no reason just became a fulfilling way of life.

Speaking of helping others, I think I'll check up on that long-suffering hack out there.

"Hey, Reggie!. You there? … Reggie? …"

BETTER MENTAL MAIL MANAGEMENT
CONSTRUCTIVE DEFENSES

While anesthesia and diversion can work well temporarily as defense mechanisms, constructive activities build a positive behavior spiral that allows for growth and improvement, as well as pain reduction.

MAKING CAR PAYMENTS
DEALING WITH PAIN

"The best way out is always…through."

-Robert Frost

According to ayurvedic psychology, pain and its associated addictions and diversions are rarely cured if the problems that cause them are not faced directly. This means several things.

First, the *pain must be experienced*. It must be felt fully, and not anesthetized and/or avoided. This is called "Being with the Pain." This means looking deeply at its character and describing it without assigning it a label that dismisses it.

Second, *understanding* the pain is important. Think about why you have interpreted the experience as painful. Has it triggered an old fear alarm in your mental post office? Does it threaten your safety? Your ego?

Let the pain teach you. Let it make you aware of yourself, your situation and others. Observe yourself experiencing the pain. You may even be able to *thank* the pain for its positive aspects. You may want to remember that wherever there is pain, there is also pleasure. Masochists are adept at finding the pleasure in pain. The odds are good that pleasure will eventually arrive.

It is often helpful to review the basic facts about pain as outlined in Table 18-2 "About Pain."

Next, actually let the pain move into you. Let it hurt you a bit. Let it make you cry, or grieve. That is what pain is supposed to do. Keeping it out entirely is impossible.

Then, *let it go!*

Letting go of pain is extremely difficult. It's the challenge of many lifetimes. There are several ways to let go of pain. Many of the methods involve some sort of ceremony. This is commonly seen in funerals, where the pain of a lost loved-one is organized in a traditional way, and then put in a predictable place. Subsequent follow-up rituals are often needed, since letting go of difficult pain often requires repeated effort.

Letting go of a child at graduations or weddings are examples of a mixture of painful and pleasurable letting go. Ritual is important for difficult transitions.

TABLE 22-1: **CONSTRUCTIVE APPROACHES TO PAIN**

PAIN ASPECT	PAIN APPROACH
Life always comes with some pain.	Practice Acceptance.
Pain is universal.	Share Someone's Pain.
Someone always has greater pain.	Offer Help.
Pain is usually transient.	Let Time Pass.
Pain is often situational.	Change the Environment.
Pain and pleasure are connected.	Observe the Connections.
Pain and pleasure often alternate.	Wait, & Remember the Pleasure.
Pain is a mental conclusion.	Gradually Retrain the Mind.
Pain is non-acceptance by the mind.	Accept what you can.
Pain is often a result of self-interest.	Serve Others.
Attachment brings pain.	Ultimately Nothing is yours
Pain is confusing.	Study pain's circumstances.
Pain is a life-lesson.	Identify & Remember Lessons.
Pain is often a call to self-control.	Develop self-discipline.

Writing about pain, as people do in diaries and letters, is another way to externalize, organize, and clarify the situation. Another technique is to summarize one's pain on a piece of paper, and then create a private letting go ceremony in which they the paper is burned. This may seem superficial, but it helps focus on the need for change.

It is also important to recognize that you are not the first or only person to experience your particular type of pain. Pain is a universal part of human existence, and many people have similar problems. As humans, we share many painful experiences. Service to others in pain strengthens the sense of sharing, and eases the pain. When pain is shared, its effect is lessened.

It is not easy to accept the difficult. We fight so hard against adversity that we make ourselves completely miserable. We set pain-free expectations that are often far too high. No one is suggesting that all pain and misery are acceptable, but a lot of it actually is! People get by, and life does go on.

Mind problems are often created by a body that is *physically* out of balance. Clearing and rebalancing the mind is often necessary to break the cycle of addictive behavior. Mind active herbal medicines, and correcting AIR, FIRE, or EARTH quality imbalances are effective ways of dealing with difficulties. The *Five Cleansings* technique can also be used to temporarily clear pain.

Changing the environment is also an option. Physically remaining in a difficult situation is like stubbornly pushing a dead car uphill. It is important to get yourself on flatter ground before you resume the task of pushing life's load.

There are also many additional ayurvedic techniques that are helpful in clearing and rebalancing the mind. See Part Five on "Advanced Automotive Techniques."

STOPPING AT THE FITNESS CENTER
EFFORT OF MENTAL HEALTH CHANGE & MAINTENANCE

Making difficult changes takes effort. Great effort.

Oftentimes, it's extremely difficult to escape a negative behavior spiral. It's almost as if a gravitational behavior force has you trapped, like a bug going down a drain.

Sometimes, a life disaster to provides sufficient proof that change is needed immediately. It is only *after* one has actually had a heart attack, stroke, asthma attack, or another health crisis, that one starts behaving in a healthy manner. Yet even after such a motivating experience, the resolve to remain healthy often fades with time and the absence of reminders of the dangers of unhealthy behavior.

What is it that motivates us to make the difficult changes to get healthy and to stay that way? We are often very aware of the benefits of healthy living and the perils of wrong living, yet we cannot overcome our current behavior. We cannot do what must be done!

When asked what *can* be done to overcome this inertia, one yogic scholar replied, "Early in the morning, kick yourself!" Such a response smacks of the Nike shoe motto "Just Do It!" or the Nancy Reaganesque "Just Say No!" admonition. But there is a difference.

In order to "kick yourself," there must be an acceptance of the pain of the kick; the short-term pain for the long-term gain.

We are back to the problem of accepting pain. Accepting pain goes against every basic, animalistic instinct we have. That is exactly the point.

A measure of our personal evolution to a stage above the primitive
animal state is our ability to accept some pain.

Such behavior could reasonably be called "advanced," "mature," or "enlightened." Part of having a "higher" consciousness is an acceptance of enough pain that we can progress in our development as spiritual beings.

In this sense, the apt slogan is "No pain *acceptance*, No gain!"

Hopefully, we can understand the value of pain as a growth and education tool. The yogic concept of (painful) austerity ("tapas") is rooted in this need. In order for the mental metal to be forged, it must endure the heat.

Accepting the Buddhist notion that life's pain is actually necessary, lessens its perceived "painful" nature. Accepting pain leads to discipline and self-control. These, in turn, lead to an awareness of what is truly important. Hollywood and Madison Avenue will have to change their tune if the demand for continuous pleasure falls and we discover that *attachment* to pleasure leads to an absence of spiritual growth.

WAITING FOR THE DELIVERY VAN
PATIENCE

Another sign of maturity is the ability to wait for the good things that eventually come. Without patience, there is no delayed gratification, and without delayed gratification, there is little opportunity for mental or spiritual growth.

Patience comes from a sense of security, and from a faith that the time given up in waiting for something important will reap even greater dividends later. It is important to be able to know when there is an urgency to act, and when things can wait. This maturity comes only with time and experience.

Most spiritual philosophies affirm the value of patience and emphasize the importance of outgrowing immediate childish needs. Developing the maturity of patience increases self-esteem, and leads to better health. Patience is an EARTH quality.

GETTING READY FOR THE POSTAL HOLIDAY SEASON
ANTICIPATION

One kind of constructive diversionary mind busy-ness is the planning and anticipation of future events. Making preparations for all of life's daily activities usually promotes a successful outcome. This, in turn, leads to positive self-image and subsequent improvements in many areas of endeavor. A positive self-reinforcing behavior cycle is created.

Rejecting procrastination in favor of anticipation behavior is more difficult initially, but much less difficult overall. Anticipation is a FIRE quality.

The compulsive need to plan everything can, of course, be come excessive. Over-focusing on details may help obscure the big picture problems that may be much more painful than the details.

CONTINUOUS POSTAL HOLIDAY SEASON
BUSY MIND

When things get busy, the mind is usually happy because it thrives on activity. Problem issues also fade into the background when the need for intense mind activity arises. The mind must take care of the "necessities" first. For this reason, many people deal with their problem issues by staying busy with work or other daily life details. FIRE and AIR ary typical qualities of busy minds.

People often create work for themselves to avoid their issues. As defense mechanisms go, a busy mind is a fairly constructive way to avoid problems. Of course, it doesn't solve them. Many creative things can be accomplished by allowing the mind to run fast and long on one project or another.

A mind that is going a hundred miles an hour all the time is eventually going to crash. When it does, the problems that have been piling up during the busy-ness will resurface and will still require attention.

SPORTS MAIL
SUBLIMATION

The overt manifestation of some primal instincts is *not* acceptable in many social situations. Violence, sexual aggression, theft, and other behaviors with similar characteristics are normally forbidden. However, there are certain situations in which demonstrating natural urges is completely acceptable.

Sports, such as football, boxing, or ice hockey are examples of accepted violence. Aggression, competition, and violence in sports are deemed acceptable and even desirable. These urges can be released in a controlled manner through sports. Such sublimations can be major improvements over original nasty impulses. It is certainly preferable for an angry person to be a boxer instead of a murderer or rapist.

Ruining a business competitor is considered an acceptable transformation of a nasty impulse into a socially acceptable form. Being aggressive, and competitive in the everyday business world is considered a necessity.

Someone wanting a chronically sick family member to die can transform (sublimate) that feeling into a constructive career in the healing arts. Improved self-esteem can be the result, and the original guilt or anxiety can be removed by this constructive defense mechanism.

Not being able to express difficult behaviors or emotions can be a serious problem that can actually result in physical illness. In ayurvedic thinking, emotional re-pression can result in many physical problems, especially connective tissue dis-orders. Release of otherwise unacceptable feelings can, therefore, become quite therapeutic. All quality types are good at sublimation.

Intense positive or creative thoughts and emotions can also be released through other creative activities such as music, writing, dancing, and painting. This ex-plains the emotional nature of many great artists.

As with any other mental activity, using an energy outlet to avoid dealing with difficult issues can ultimately be counter-productive. For men, a sports interest is often substituted for a discussion of difficult or emotional life issues. Men can express their aggressive sides in sports and be supported in the effort. Yelling, screaming, cursing, and wearing outrageous clothing is also accepted in many sports situations.

Women can also express their intense emotions through sporting activities. In the past, women had to vent their unacceptable feelings by immersing them-selves in spending activities such as shopping and home decorating. Social gatherings and child rearing focusing are other constructive ways of avoiding life's difficulties.

No matter which positive transformations or substitutions are made, it is helpful if a person remains aware of the underlying pain motivations for his or her activities.

NON-PROFIT MAIL
ALTRUISM & CHARITY

Two activities that serve to occupy the mind and nourish the spirit are service and charity. Giving to others almost always brings positive energy to the giver. It diverts attention from one's own problems to those of others. At these times, it often becomes clear that one's personal problems are less serious than originally imagined, and often less serious than the problems of others.

In ayurvedic/yogic philosophy, it is important that there be no expectation of return benefit in exchange for a service provided. *Selfless* service is completely different from service with expectation of recognition or reward. Such expectations are considered to be more of a business transaction than true charity, although both are constructive ways of dealing with one's personal issues.

Like any other activity, charity work can be overdone if it is used as an escape from personal problems, or if responsibilities at home are ignored in the process of helping others.

A great yogic scholar was once asked to characterize the most important teaching of the Bhaghvad Gita (Hindu scripture). His two-word distillation of this lengthy philosophical work: "Selfless Service."

CHURCH MAIL
RELIGION

Another way to deal with the painful events that life brings is to accept the explanations for pain that are provided by many of the world's religions. For many people, religions and their philosophies provide an acceptable and constructive way of dealing with mental, emotional and moral challenges. Religion provides a forum for discussion of problems in a secure environment. It often provides the close structure, protection, and camaraderie that are required in many recovery programs.

Service to others is a common part of many religions, and yoga philosophy strongly emphasizes this as a stepping stone to self improvement.

Religions are sometimes narrow and exclusive. Many religious groups forget the basic principles of brother/sisterhood, and instead focus on their differences and ethnic disparities. This helps create a feeling of superiority, limiting the constructive aspects of the religion to its own group. Christians help Christians, Jews help Jews, Muslims help Muslims, and the rest can go to hell. Religions often require a commitment from a participant to accept more doctrine than the individual may need.

Each religion has a different take on spiritual issues, but one of the central concerns continues to be an explanation of pain and how to deal with it. While it is difficult to summarize the philosophical differences between religions on many subjects, a popular tee shirt has succinctly boiled down the outlook held by each religion on the "shit" that happens (pain).

Although yoga and ayurveda are not thought of as religions, they do provide a definite philosophy on proper moral lifestyle, as well as a holistic science for maintaining good physical, mental and spiritual health.

MUST-HAVE MERCEDES
WEALTH

Pain can also be covered over by the many distractions and counter-balancing pleasures that can be purchased with money.

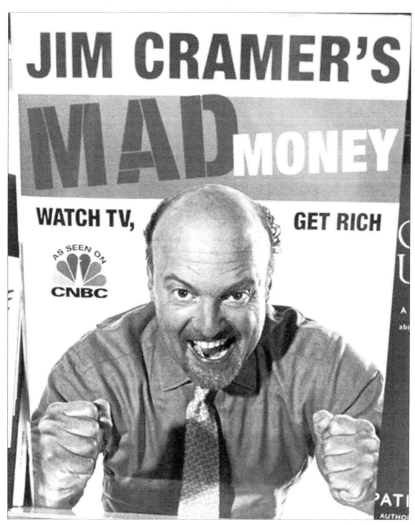

A problem occurs when the objects and activities that money buys fail to remove the original underlying pain. What often follows is an endless pursuit of additional objects and diversions followed by the accumulation of money itself.

As responses to pain go, building wealth can be quite constructive, especially if one remains aware of wealth's limited value. It is responsible behavior to generate resources for one's self and one's family. Building resources is a normal stage in life (known as "Artha") according to yoga philosophy.

Moving from necessity to opulence and self-indulgence is not a helpful development. There is a natural guilt that comes from greed and hoarding that can take its toll as both mental, physical and spiritual illness. Whether it's King Midas, King Abdullah, or Don King, excess accumulation can become a spiritual burden that can present obstacles as great as the eye of a needle.

YOUR BLUEBOOK VALUE
EXTERNAL VALIDATION

Many pain diversions and constructive responses are designed to reinforce a person's self-worth by generating praise or recognition from others. The process starts early in childhood when our actions are either rewarded with praise or discouraged by negativity. It continues for a lifetime, and beyond.

Instead of teaching that we are all inherently OK, our money-motivated-media sends the message that we're not OK, unless we purchase their sponsor's products. If we do, we'll find validation beyond our wildest dreams! If we don't, we'll wind up doing time on the Maury Povich show.

Although seeking *external* validation often leads to significant external achievements, it's no replacement for an innate *internal* sense of value. Most religions teach that the individual is *inherently* worthwhile. Most yoga philosophies agree.

But how can one believe in *de novo* validity when so much of the "evidence" in life speaks against it? Religions say it's a matter of "faith," a hope-filled conviction that something is true despite all the evidence to the contrary! Other belief systems teach that this "unworthiness" is simply a false currency backed by the transient and unsubstantial (e.g. Wall Street, Hollywood, Madison Avenue). A life that brings *spiritual* dividends is said to yield a sense of self-worth that is even greater. Remembering to check your *Karmic* bank balance can make all the difference!

Each individual is connected to the most powerful force there is—the Greater Collective Consciousness. If one can remember to "feel the force" of that connection, then one can call on billions of Yodas and yogis to give witness to the greatness in each one—of US.

PLANNED UNEMPLOYMENT
ASCETICISM

Since most pain involves the senses, reducing sensory input can reduce pain. For this reason, some choose to deal with pain by eliminating many sensory experiences. They remove themselves to a world of physical and/or emotional isolation. No experience, no pain.

The classic example is the yogic renunciate ("Sadhu") hiding from the pain of the world in a cave or jungle. Such caves can exist in the jungle of a big city. Hiding can be a constructive *temporary* defense for those who are confused or overwhelmed.

In yogic and ayurvedic thinking, removing oneself from worldly difficulties has a purifying effect, but it can be overdone. It is important to eventually learn to live in the world and not hide from it. That's why we're on Earth and not isolated on the moon; to learn from our painful and pleasurable interactions.

POST OFFICE JOKES
HUMOR

Humor allows us to deal directly with painful issues by focusing on their pleasurable aspects. Just as all pleasure has a painful downside, all pain has a pleasurable or funny upside. A joke focuses on the positive side. When comedians need a laugh, they "poke fun" at a difficult aspect of life such as divorce, communication difficulties between spouses, inefficiencies in society, racial differences, etc.

This is constructive in that it stops the mind from hitting a negative neurotransmitter-producing button and substitutes positive chemistry. It allows for the development of a less-stressed point of view on a subject, but it rarely results in a focused plan for working out the problem.

Humor also allows for the expression of feelings on uncomfortable personal subjects with less discomfort, because it relates *personal* issues to issues faced by society as a whole. Ayurvedic psychology considers one's personal pain as a reflection of the pain of the whole world. The human experience is one that we share with others. We are all connected. Therefore, most people can relate to personal pain issues. It is much easier to relate to those serious issues in joke form than it is to have serious discussions about them. Making a joke out of *everything* can be a counterproductive avoidance mechanism if it is overused without any reflection.

AVOIDING HARASSMENT URGES
SUPPRESSION

All animals have primal urges and responses, and the human animal is no exception. Suppression of primal behavior considered socially inappropriate is important for real-world success.

Although the suppression skill is basic to growing beyond infancy, it is one that many adults still lack in some areas. Suppressing the desire for food satisfaction is especially important when the opportunity to over-indulge arises. Holding back natural urges for sex, dominance, and violence is also necessary.

Suppression of anesthetic desires, such as alcohol and drug use, is crucial to confronting real-life problems. Suppression of the desire to use other unhealthy defense mechanisms and negative diversions, is also important.

Just as obviously, too much suppression of desires can lead to a failure to deal with key problems, and to a stifled personality. Ayurveda recommends non-suppression of natural urges whenever appropriate. Stifling a sneeze, cough, fart, laugh or tears for too long a time is felt to be unhealthy. According to ayurvedic tradition, suppressed emotions physically crystallize in the connective tissue, and can cause symptoms and disease.

OFFICE PARTY
CELEBRATION

Many cultures set aside time for celebration of milestones and other life events. There is certainly enough grief to go around, so it is important to celebrate the positive!

TABLE 22-2: **CONSTRUCTIVE PAIN DEFENSES**

1. Dealing Directly with Pain

2. Patience
3. Anticipation
4. Busy Creative Mind
5. Sublimation, constructive

6. Altruism & Charity
7. Religion
8. Wealth Building
9. External Validation
10. Asceticism

11. Humor
12. Suppression
13. Celebration
14. Education
15. Selfless Service

As opposed to hedonistic pleasure-seeking, celebration and honoring of life's positives is an important balancing activity. This is especially true when there is a spiritual connection to that which is being celebrated.

Christmas is a good example of recognizing the positive aspects of our world, and taking the opportunity to create joy, charity and understanding. Weddings, baptisms, graduations, and achievement recognitions are further examples of taking the opportunity to recognize the positive, and to release tension and anxiety in support of good things.

Of course, like all good things, celebrations can be perverted into an excuse for self-indulgence. Partying should be occasional, and not vocational.

CONTINUING EDUCATION COURSES
EDUCATION

For many of us, life is a long search for ways to deal effectively with pain. If only we could find a way to get rid of life's pain, we would be happy and healthy. As it happens, there is an effective way to make that happen:

Education transforms pain into understanding.

If pain prompts us to carefully study the situation that brought it, we will learn how to stop that pain from recurring. That added sense of control brings pleasure, and the subsequent absence of that same pain is pleasurable.

Life offers us many chances to discover responses that will work for us. It all depends on attitude. If our attitude is that pain is unfair, and that it makes life unlivable, then the odds are good that we will follow Pinocchio to the sensual circus and its anesthetic side shows.

But if our attitude is that *pain is an invitation to education*, then we will take the opportunity to gain understanding, and embark on our own quest for that which gives us inner peace, satisfaction, tranquility, and community. We must learn how to focus our minds on the circumstances of our pain, and open our hearts to the ways we can deal with it (Table 22-1).

Life's educational curriculum has many basic pre-requisite courses that must be completed so that individual consciousness can become unified with its greater counterpart (see Part Four) . One must have a purpose in life. Without one, life is like driving a cab without a destination. Once this purpose is in place, we can more effectively learn how to optimize our body-vehicle's performance, and how to manage our mind-driver's idiosyncrasies.

Education must ultimately focus on spiritual development. Our studies should lead to discovery, improved self-esteem, social interaction, building resources, and the advancement of society. It should relate in some way to the real world and not become an ivory tower escape.

CHAPTER 23:
TRANSFERRING TO
ANOTHER POST OFFICE
Behavior Pattern
Changes

I JUST CAN'T CONTROL MYSELF !

Even when I frikin' *know* that what I'm doing is just plain stupid and self-destructive, I *still* can't stop! Not just the shit that I'm flat-out addicted to, like smokes and beer. It's shit like the food that I can't stop eating whenever I'm pissed off or stressed-out.

I can actually see myself in slow motion headed for the fridge, or Mountain Mike's Pizza, knowing that all that extra, unneeded, bad food is just going to find its way to my butt and my arteries.

But, even knowing that, I can't say "no" to the taste of that sweet, heavy, friendly stuff, especially when my ex is bitching at me on the phone, or Margo is hassling me on the radio. I get so sick of the hassles in my stupid, boring, pointless life that I need something satisfying *right away*! I need something that will change the channels in my head! That's how I got into food, booze, and sex.

I watched my dad die of emphysema. I watched his shame at his own foolishness for having smoked himself into the ground when he knew all the time that it was killing him. And now, I'm doing the same damn thing! Of course, he had Mom on his back night and day. No one could blame him for needing some pleasure after putting up with that!

I guess that makes me a real son-of-a-bitch. I know that I shouldn't think about myself that way. I know that all the shit I've been through is why I'm always lookin' for some kinda boost - anything to get my mind off what I turned out to be. All the dreams that I had, and now, I'm still a frikin' hack, hauling people around two shifts a day.

My kids - they're grown and gone. They never call unless they need money. And now, I can't even give them that!

Margo tried to get me to quit smoking and the other stuff. She tried to show me some of her goofy yoga. I can see how it worked for her, how she got away from *her* addictions, but that shit's just too weird. I can't sit cross-legged and chant "OOOMMM." Not even for the five minutes a day she said would help me.

Whatever… nothing really changes … except …

TRANSFERRING TO ANOTHER POST OFFICE
BEHAVIOR PATTERN CHANGES

It has been postulated that any creature can respond to major difficulty by doing one of three basic things; it can *change*, it can *move*, or it can *die*.

While dying is always an option, it doesn't get us anywhere physically, mentally, or spiritually. The long and the short of dying as an option for dealing with psychic pain is that it doesn't work. The psyche returns in another incarnation with the same nasty baggage it previously had (see Chapter 20).

Moving to a new physical or social environment, on the other hand, can have major effects on the mind, the physical condition, and on spiritual health. Keeping good company is a cornerstone of many philosophies. The concepts of "Right Association" of Buddhism, the "Satsang" of Yoga and the "Good Fellowship" of Christianity are just some of the examples of this important principle.

We can change our interpersonal community relatively simply by changing jobs, going on vacations or spiritual retreats, or getting a divorce from a difficult relationship. But these changes may not heal the inner causes of pain that follow us wherever we go.

People who are unhappy in their work environment must use all kinds of gymnastics to make up for that fact. If they could find an inspirational job, most of the food, booze, pills, herbs, and other diversions or anesthetics they use would be unnecessary.

It is important to *want* to get out of bed in the morning! It's ideal if you can't wait to get back to your area of work interest. If you don't see an interesting future in your job, then it is important to begin making plans to do what you really want to do with your life. If you are just marking time at work so that you can get home to your real interests, then see if there is a way to combine your vocation with your avocation.

You don't need to drop everything for a pipe dream. Get some feedback on your dreams from someone you trust. Work toward something special and interesting.

Regrettably, most people believe that they have no choice about changing jobs. If that's what you believe, that's the way it will be. As a physician, I know that there are dozens of patients for whom I wanted to take out my prescription pad and write:

"Rx: New Job"

For the better part of sixty years, we spend one third of our time on the planet working! What could be more healthy than making those years tolerable if not enjoyable? Taking time away from a difficult job is important. I *have* written many prescriptions for desperately needed vacations:

> "Rx: Take two weeks vacation
> & call me the next morning."

The excuse for this consistently successful therapy *not* being accepted is that we feel the need to spend our necessary vacation time keeping up with the competition or earning extra money for toys we don't need. We trade our health for toys! Vacations with a tangential focus on the meaning of it all are a good idea! Life can be hard. We need to rest. Another taboo prescription I would *like* to write is:

> "Rx: Divorce the: Son of a / Bitch"

There is nothing sacred about a relationship that ruins one's physical, mental and/or spiritual health. It doesn't matter what minister, priest, rabbi, or guru has sanctified a deeply flawed relationship. There is no point in holding onto misery for the sake of tradition or insecurity. It's unhealthy. Period.

My personal observation is that most marriages function fairly well for about a dozen years. After that, some space is usually needed if it hasn't already been created within the relationship. Some species (like penguins) mate for one season. Others mate for life. The human relationship is good for a dozen. Anything extra is a bonus!

It must be said that this estimate is not the traditional yogic/ayurvedic point of view. Duty, commitment, responsibility, and respect are hallmarks of most relationships in those systems. While it is true that relationships should not be thrown away lightly, there may come a point when the mental and physical health of the participants is being ruined rather than nurtured. This is often the result of fear-based over-attachment.

Other needed changes in behavior and environment are more specific to the individual. There are, however, some general principles that apply.

SUMMONED TO THE SUPERVISOR'S OFFICE
FACING THE PAIN

An initial approach to behavior change should include some understanding of the pain factors that are motivating anesthetic or avoidance defenses.

Although some voices in ayurveda believe that pain should NOT be "labeled," it is important to understand a problem so that effective change can be created. If pain is buried in a hidden mental cubbyhole, it cannot be identified, faced, confronted, owned, shared, transformed, and then, let go.

This is a monumentally difficult process. Chapter 22 on Constructive Defense Mechanisms begins with a review of the nature of pain and some of the approaches to facing it.

In Ayurvedic thinking, pain is looked upon as a wake up call. When painful mistakes lead us to the Supervisor's office, it may be the result of random circumstances, or the unavoidable consequences of our behavior. Either way, the Supervisor can be viewed as a mirror for our behavior problems that won't go away. That mirror may be covered by the hazy film of our personal illusions, so our first job is to clean away those illusions and games.

We must become our *own* supervisors. In the same way that a supervisor at work observes what we do, *we must observe our own actions*. We must learn to be both the observer and the one being observed. When we can watch our own actions from a distance in this way, we can begin to understand, and then to control what we do.

411
GETTING INFORMATION

When a problem occurs, its resolution is often aided by obtaining additional information. Without full information, logical and systematic approaches to problem resolution are difficult at best.

In most any problem situation, *when you don't know what to do, get more information*! Resources for information are plentiful. The internet, libraries, help lines from the phone book, friends, clergy, and counselors are examples of information resources.

The difficulty is finding the motivation to start looking for information. If an outside source of motivation is part of the treatment scenario, that often suffices. If no outside pressure is being applied, then a declaration to another person of one's intent to learn more about a problem can provide a gentle external stimulus.

911
COUNSELING

When the post-office-mind becomes overwhelmed, we can use Fed Ex to help with the flood of pain messages we receive. In a similar way, counseling helps us cope when our mental post office is overloaded. Whether it's a trusted friend, counselor, clergy, social worker, or shrink, getting help is usually beneficial.

It's not easy to make the call for help. Psychologists can be expensive, and using one means that we can't handle the problem by ourselves. We may put off calling for help until the pile of pain mail has reached our necks, but whenever we do call for help, we should remember not to take it personally. Sometimes, pain-mail just piles up.

It's also hard to know whether to call Fed Ex, UPS, or Airborne Express. Finding the right counselor or psychologist is difficult. When choosing this type of help, it is important to know that the counselor is a properly trained, professional who is responsive and reliable. He or she should be both sympathetic and directing. The counselor should also have a spiritual side that is respectful of, if not similar to, one's own spiritual inclination. It is not uncommon for counselors to bail out on issues of "personal faith," yet these are the issues that are often the most central, and the most important in therapy.

MYTHICAL MAGIC BULLETS
EFFORTLESS CHANGES

When one is in acute pain, it's natural to want the pain to end quickly. The greater the pain, the greater the desire for rapid relief. Ideally, a pain remedy works like magic, and with the speed of a bullet!

There are a few such magic mental pain-killing bullets available. Most take the form of strong psychoactive drugs and narcotic painkillers. Street drugs can work fairly fast too. Alcohol and tobacco are a little slower, but they still work fairly rapidly.

But if relief comes instantly and easily, then no *effort* is required in the process. For most people, the *process* of working to fully understand and fix a problem promotes learning and behavior changes that are longer-lasting.

If instant relief is used, then the experience of pain is missed. A unique principle of several Eastern philosophies is that *some pain is meant to be experienced,* and should not to be avoided, nor removed too rapidly. It is the process of "being with the pain" that provides the insight into its cause and purpose, and, hopefully, generates some new response that prevents its recurrence (see Pavlov).

Chronic conditions are often created over long periods of time. The idea that it should only take a magical moment to fix something that has been broken for a while reflects a misunderstanding of the repair process. A worn-out engine cannot be repaired in five minutes. In the human mind, difficult behaviors become ingrained over many years. It is unreasonable to expect them to be *fixed* just by taking pills. Mind issue resolutions require lots of thinking, feeling, and experimenting with alternative behaviors and routines.

POSTMEN & DoGs
DELAY of GRATIFICATION

Time is often needed for mental digestion and resolution of difficulties. Sometimes, there is just no substitute. One of the most helpful behavior skills that provides this necessary time is a *Delay of Gratification* (DoG).

Infants have no concept of delaying the gratification of their immediate needs. If they need something, they scream for it immediately! As children get older, they learn to accept longer and longer periods of waiting before they get their needs met. Those who learn this lesson early tend to be able to use that skill well later on.

Even dogs know about DoG. They can "stay" and wait because they know that if they do, they will be rewarded *in the future.*

Most adults develop the ability to plan into the future, and to leave the resolution of their needs and desires for later times. But needs and desires can be

intense, and many cannot be put off into the future. Problematic diversions and anesthetics can result. Learning delayed gratification is a standard part of the curriculum in the School of Life.

What are some conditions that allow for good DoG training?

1. The belief (faith) that the future will provide some relief from pain or discomfort.

2. The ability to deal with the immediate painful situation by choosing constructive rather than destructive responses.

3. A structured environment that promotes the creation of consistent delayed rewards.

4. The ability to perceive personal procrastination as it occurs.

5. A sense of self-assurance and self-worth that allow for close examination and acceptance of pain.

It is difficult to practice all of these DoG skills at the very moment a temptation presents itself. That is why DoG training classes must be repeated frequently, but once learned, a DoG can be man's best friend.

QUALITY SERVICE
QUALITIES & TRANSFORMATIONS

There are many different aspects to the Ayurvedic approach to mind transformations. As usual, a person's AIR, FIRE and EARTH qualities exert a major influence on their mental tendencies, their types and frequency of problems, and their ability to make changes.

The same principles of quality rebalancing that are used for excesses of these qualities in the body also apply for mind imbalances. AIR minds need to be grounded, FIRE minds need to be cooled, and EARTH minds need to be stimulated.

Psychological and neurological problems occur with greater frequency with AIR quality disorders. Agitation, hypersensitivity, reactivity, impulsivity, and instability are some hallmarks of AIR type mind disorders. Unrealistic perceptions, imagination, and even delusions are usually associated with an excess of this quality.

It can be difficult for AIR types to settle down enough to begin behavior pattern changes. Their expectations tend to be high, they may expect immediate results or magical transformations. Disappointment is common when success does not follow quickly, and changing support systems is more likely to occur. AIR types need reassurance, support, and patience.

For transformation, AIR types need to do a few practical things at a time. They need to develop consistency and routine. Action, rather than thought, is more important, but they need to be approached gently.

FIRE types usually have only a moderate number of psychological problems. They can easily be anti-social, and can lack good self-control. Anger, aggression, and hostility are common FIRE problems, and blaming others is more common than self-deprecation. FIRE-types often display a self-assurance that conceals low self-confidence. This false self-confidence often creates a barrier for transformation, and FIRE types often blame others for their own difficulties, including those who are trying to help them. Their expectations for success often lead them to be impatient with the transformation process. They often doubt the need for treatment or the validity of what is done for them. Tact and diplomacy are required when dealing with FIRE types, but once they are committed to a course of action, they do it religiously.

EARTH types appear to be more satisfied, but tend to have deeper-seated psychological problems. They tend toward withdrawal, and inactivity that reflects clouding of the mind. Motivation is often low, and dependency high. There is a perceived need to possess things despite significant inertia.

That inertia often requires EARTH types to be stimulated into action. In order to inspire them to act, stimulation may need to take the form of a severe shock. They may just accept their problems rather than muster the energy to resolve them. A more stern and less sympathetic approach is often needed to get them going in a healthy direction. EARTH types can be slow to make changes, and may need repeated prodding to continue their healing. Once momentum is gained, however, it tends to be sustained.

All the techniques in the ayurvedic repertoire can be used to help balance the mind. The images one takes in via TV and the environment are important. Aroma can be especially helpful as can meditation and yoga postures. Diet and herbal medications remain important therapies.

DRIVER'S LUNCH BREAK
MENTAL DIGESTION

The process of contemplating, feeling, understanding, accepting, and letting go of an experience is called *mental digestion*. It is discussed in the sections above on pain.

In the same way that the gastrointestinal digestive process is the effective way to deal with food, "mental digestion" is the most effective way to deal with unresolved emotional experiences. If well-digested by the power of discrimination, long-term benefit is obtained.

Using anesthetics and diversions is like taking a mental antacid. The mental digestion problem may be temporarily calmed, but its cause is still there, and no long-term resolution is obtained.

Mental digestion is hard work. It is one of the most difficult types of work that we are called on to do. It is easy to give ourselves an anesthetic purgative, but we will have missed the nutrition that comes with letting our emotional enzymes, and acceptance acids do their work on the experience-foods that make up our lives.

TAKING OUT THE TRASH
KICKING ANESTHESIA

One of the hardest endeavors is to break the cycle of pain and anesthesia. The main reason this is difficult is that it involves a major change in the approach to pain itself. Remember:

When an anesthetic wears off, the pain returns.

The only alternative to repeated addiction is to *accept some level of pain* in the beginning, and digest it.

It is not the intent of this book to replace the extensive body of work on the approaches to the addiction/anesthesia problem. Instead, some of the basic elements of the approach to the subject are given along with the ayurvedic therapies.

First of all, some level of *awareness* of the psychological, physiological, and genetic problems that push a person to anesthesia is necessary. If you don't know you have a problem, you're unlikely to change. Most people are already aware of their addictions, but deny their seriousness until a consequence seriously *impacts others* in their lives. It's only when someone gets fired, divorced, injured, sick, suicidal or impoverished that they are forced to admit the problem. Until then, a plethora of mind games can be played to avoid the admission of addiction.

Once a person is admits that there is a problem, it is often necessary to identify it. As mentioned, labeling mental issues is often discouraged in ayurveda, since the process leads to pigeonholing pain rather than facing it.

On the other hand, a clear sense of what is going on is essential. Often, it is necessary to have an outside observer provide a point of view on what is happening. Some serious professional study of the dynamics of the addiction, and the specifics of the individual situation usually helps in developing the needed understanding and perspective for changing behavior.

Understanding the *history* of the behavior is also helpful. If one sees how anesthetic habits are a response to difficult situations, then the self-blame can be more easily eliminated. An understanding of the *triggers* that cause the need for anesthesia can be recognized and avoided or modified.

Once this realization happens, a *commitment to change* is required. Often this only comes when one hits rock bottom. The wiser and more intelligent among us are able to change before disaster strikes, but most of us require a kick in the cortex.

Confronting and identifying the issues involved in our addictions is an important and difficult step. The AIR-quality fears that develop as a result of pain should be examined, and the process of accepting those fears should be developed. AIR-balancing treatments can be used.

Fear of being out of *control* also needs to be examined, and distrust of self and others often come up as pertinent FIRE-imbalance issues. Dealing with our intense FIRE-quality feelings, and the way we act on those feelings, is an important phase of the understanding process.

The assumptions that we make that lead to confusion should also be revisited. The judgments and comparisons we make about ourselves and others should also find their way into our awareness for review.

Once progress has been made in these areas, it is important to take some big risks. The first is to risk a commitment to change. Change is very difficult, especially if the addictive rut is deep and long-term. No underestimation should be made of the difficulty. For this reason, it is very important to have some type of support for the effort. It is important to choose a support person or group carefully. Rely on someone you trust to recommend someone who has proven helpful.

Once you have obtained support, it is often helpful for there to be some type of semi-public disclosure of your addiction problem. It need not be broadcast on the evening news, but admitting your problem if asked has the effect of raising the issue from an evil addiction to a worthy attempt to fight a problem that many others also face.

Avoid unrealistic expectations of a speedy recovery. Chronic illness often requires a long term cure, so expecting a rapid resolution can lead to disappointment and giving up the effort. Avoid an "all or nothing" attitude about your recovery. You are meant to recover at your own pace.

It is important to be aware of some of the pitfalls of kicking anesthesia including a reemergence of denial, dissociation, escape into activity, diversion, and just simply giving up. It is also important not to try to fix all areas at once. Fix things one at a time. Take small risks. Be aware of self-criticism, guilt, and comparison with the situations of others.

It is also important to recognize that kicking anesthesia is a process that often consists of taking two steps forward and one step back. Be kind to yourself. Take a break (not a relapse) from the hard work of recovery every now and then. Acknowledge the need to take care of yourself.

If you are using an alternative temporary anesthetic or diversion while you work on losing your present one, remain aware that you may be shifting habits and not confronting your problems.

It is also helpful to have a positive short-term, tangible reward, and a long-term tangible prize at the end. Keeping a daily calendar of progress is often helpful as well (see Chapter 30).

Changing your daily routine and environment can be important too. Being around addicts can easily lead to relapse. Establishing a regular pattern of behavior helps reduce the time spent in uncertainty and insecurity.

Maintain your self-esteem. This includes truly living your beliefs and believing in truthful living. What you think of yourself matters much more than anyone else's opinion or response to you.

An ayurvedic approach to problems that removes some of the associated guilt is to partially "blame" the genetic *quality* of the person with the addiction. For example, an AIR quality person may be vulnerable to developing an AIR-like mind that is inconsistent, spacey, unpredictable, etc. If you find yourself in one of those states, accept that the problem is too much AIR quality. Then, ask where you acquired that extra AIR quality? If it's your genetic nature, then there is no personal blame, since that is a quality that you inherited.

If you can identify an *outside* source of the quality excess, then you can blame the quality itself (e.g. "Too much AIR quality) for the problem, and remove some of the personal responsibility and guilt. Acceptance of the effects of excess qualities is better than feeling inherently bad.

There are also herbs for individual substance abuses. See the Disease listing section of the book in Chapter 16.

It's also important to accept emptiness, quiet, and "boredom." The feelings of emptiness that often lead to addiction can be changed if one realizes that the greatest and most pervasive thing in the universe is emptiness. Physically, we are mostly empty space. Mentally and spiritually, the same is sometimes true.

Accepting the imperfections of life is another important step. It is useful for the addict to surrender in some way to a higher power and to see his or her small-self as part of the Greater-Self (see Part Four). According to Ayurvedic philosophy, an individual's pain is shared by the whole world.

UNDER THE RUG
DIVERSION AWARENESS

Many of the same problems posed by anesthetic defenses are posed by mental diversion activities. They can be as serious and as deep-rooted as many of the addiction/ anesthetics used to deal with pain.

While most people are aware of their addictions, many are unaware of the more subtle diversions they use to avoid dealing with their problems. Counseling, reading, and the observations of friends are often the sources of the awareness that are required to deal with diversion problems.

Many people use combinations of several diversions and addictions to avoid their issues. When a full awareness of the defenses that are being used is obtained, a program to eliminate or reduce them can be created. From there, acceptance of the underlying pain is possible.

It is helpful not to become judgmental about secrecy and hiding. If we were able to use better ways to respond to stresses, we'd have already used them. Most of us don't even recognize what we're doing, and have no experience with other ways of coping. Some just don't have the energy that constructive defenses require.

CLUB MED vs. the DA'S OFFICE
MEDITATION or DIVERSION / ANESTHESIA

One consistent alternative for dealing with mental pain is to use meditation instead of diversion or anesthesia. Quieting the mind with a healthy technique such as meditation has the advantage of avoiding guilt, and reinforcing self-respect. With meditation there is no anesthetic hangover, and little effort once a person's daily practice has been established (see Chapters 8, 16, and 27).

Breath control, focused imaging, phrase repetition (Chapter 28), and thought observation take only a few minutes. They can be done while riding as a passenger in a vehicle, in a waiting area, or during any lull in attention-requiring activity.

It is not even necessary to sit quietly and close your eyes. Meditation can simply be the observation of your own situation and actions. For long-term improvements, meditation is always better than medication. Even lawyers know that Club Meditation beats visiting the addictive D/A's office.

CLEANING THE POST OFFICE EVERY DAY
AYURVEDIC MENTAL HEALTH TECHNIQUES

If no one cleans up every day, the mental post office becomes a mess of thoughts, worries and emotions. Only a clean and tidy mental post office can function well. The mental maintenance team in the yogic/ayurvedic system is an eight-member cleaning crew known as "Ashtanga Yoga.". Through this process of daily routine, behavior restraints, body postures, breathing practices, sensory reduction, breath focus, repetitive phrase use, and quieting the mind, the stress we feel minimizes and contentment maximizes (see Chapter 23).

In order for the cleaning crew to do its work, certain preparations are required.

There must be cleaning supplies available. In yoga /ayurveda, this takes the form of behavior restraints and observances (Chapter 15) .

It is nearly impossible to clean an office without some kind of physical broom, and *physical* cleanliness is important for mind development. It sets an example of order and caring that the mental processes imitates.

We also need a dustpan to collect and to throw away those unnecessary thoughts and objects that clutter our lives. We can become preoccupied, overwhelmed and distracted from important things in our lives by the amount of junk we collect. Both physical and mental *austerity* are therefore recommended in yoga and ayurveda.

A RELAXING GAME OF EIGHT BALL
EIGHT-PART YOGA PRACTICES

One of the main goals of yoga and ayurveda is to quiet the mind. When the mind-driver is given a rest, the body-vehicle is given a rest.

Quieting the mind is the essential goal of the eight-step technique of Ashtanga Yoga. Yoga is not a means to develop an attractive "yoga butt.' It's purpose is to develop a body that is healthy enough to *sit still* without discomforting distractions. When distractions and sensory input are reduced, the mind has less to play with, and it eventually quiets itself. This allows many natural, healthy processes to occur, including mental relaxation.

Doing all eight parts of the yoga discipline is a challenge even for the most dedicated students. Luckily, once the breathing practices have been incorporated into a daily routine, the mind relaxing effects have started to have an effect.

YOUR MIND IS WHAT IT EATS
MIND FOOD

In the same way that junk food can ruin the body, junk thoughts can pollute the mind. Remember, the mind loves stimulation, action, and intrigue. It abhors peace, quiet, and contentment. Knowing this, the merchants of the world make sure that we are bombarded with thoughts and ideas that involve anything and everything contrary to serenity, silence, and acceptance.

If we are content, we don't need to buy anything.

As a result, we live in a world in which entrepreneurs will do anything to slip a sales pitch in between the action scenes. These action scenes routinely include violence, lying, sex, cheating, denigration, pursuit and destruction. They are then sugar coated with fake laughter from a machine, or with sardonic one-liners from the terminator.

After enough immersion, we become brain-washed by these negative activities.

We learn to accept stimulating trash because we have become addicted to stimulation. After that, it is no surprise that we should feel agitated and anxious. We have allowed ourselves to be filled with negative, stimulating tensions.

That is why many intelligent people escape from their rat-race treadmill jobs to go to the beach and let the peaceful sun, sand, water and air cleanse their minds of their Hollywood and Madison Avenue rubbish.

When the mind is peaceful, the body becomes healthy. It has been shown that physical illness can be greatly helped by laughter. Conversely, watching trash TV will have its negative effect no matter how desensitized one has become.

EMPLOYEE REHAB
MENTAL QUALITY
REBALANCING

Just as the body has different ratios of the AIR, FIRE, and EARTH qualities, the mind has its own proportions of the same characteristics. When any of these are found in excess, mind imbalance will result.

In general, too much AIR quality in the mind tends to bring nervousness. Too much FIRE brings aggression, and extra EARTH quality results in lassitude.

Correcting these quality excesses can be done using balancing foods, herbal medicines, and activities as outlined in the preceding chapters. Further correction can be obtained by using the methods outlined in Part Five on "Advanced Ayurvedic Techniques."

Primary mental rebalancing, however, is accomplished by modifying the mental intake as described in Chapters 18 and 23. Environmental changes and practicing yogic breathing and meditation are key to making mental modifications.

SPRING CLEANING
FIVE CLEANSINGS TECHNIQUE

The Ayurvedic methods for removing toxins and excess qualities in physical disorders also works well for mental problems. The mind can accumulate an excess of the AIR, FIRE or EARTH qualities, causing mental fatigue and poor mind function in the same way that working in an office that is to cold, hot, or damp can cause physical symptoms.

The specifics of the *Five Cleansings* technique are described later in Chapter 23.

HOUSEHOLD CLEANSERS
MIND IMPROVEMENT HERBS

There are certain herbal medications that are especially useful for clearing the brain and the mind such as gotu kola and ginko biloba for memory, and St. John's Wort for depression. Marijuana is another plant product that alters the mind, and psychedelic mushrooms and cocaine-producing coca leaf are other examples.

Anything that changes the balance of the AIR, FIRE, or EARTH qualities will have some mind-altering effect. In Ayurvedic medicine, herbs that are specifically used for their mind-balancing effects include brahmi, jatamamsi, shankapushpi, saraswati, valerian, and vacha.

Foods and spices that have mind-calming properties include sweets, nutmeg, hot milk, garlic, licorice, heavy meats, nuts, and dairy. Foods and spices that are stimulating to the mind include fresh vegetable juices, green tea, and ginger.

DRIVING TO YOSEMITE
NATURE THERAPY

When looking for a mental or physical cure, drive to the country and observe nature's splendor. The trend toward using "natural" medicines should begin with spending time in a natural setting. Just being there is therapeutic.

Most natural environments have qualities that are healthy for most subtypes. AIR-types, who are often over-stimulated, are usually comforted by the calm and quiet of a lake or woods. It's difficult for them to sit still and enjoy nature because their innate tendency is to be moving, changing and doing. Being in an environment which is slow, peaceful, and passive is balancing to AIR-types, and their stress will be lessened by placing themselves in an environment which forces them to slow down. AIR-types tend to be cool and dry, so they should choose places in nature that are warm and moist. Tropical settings work well.

FIRE-types are often concerned with achievement, status and production. For them, being in nature offers little in the way of ego reinforcement, and many fireballs consider it a waste of time. Flowers and trees are rarely impressed by thousand dollar suits or chauffeured limos. To see oneself as a small part of a larger natural creation is an important humbling experience that is beneficial for FIRE-types. It calms and balances their naturally aggressive nature, and reinforces their creativity.

Because FIRE-types tend to be hot and oily, they are wise to choose places in nature that are cool. A vacation in the desert would be a mistake for FIRE-types which may leave them irritated and angry. For balance, the cool ocean, high mountains, and northern climes work well.

EARTH-types are already fairly content. For them, sitting and admiring nature can aggravate their natural passive and immobile qualities. They should choose aspects of nature that involve movement such as ocean waves, rivers, and wind. Stimulating activities such as walking, horseback riding and biking, are important ways for EARTH-types to change their world.

Nature is an important part of what we are, but civilization tends to distance us from it. If a tree sapling is raised in the city, it often struggles, but if it is nurtured in the country where it belongs, it thrives. As natural creatures, we also need to be where we can relax and thrive.

POST OFFICE DÉCOR
SOUNDS, COLORS, GEMS, OPTICS

Using subtle energies can also create change. While not magic bullets by any means, the use of sound, color, and optical patterns (called "Yantras") can affect the mind in positive ways over time. In the Ayurvedic tradition, even gemstones, used in the appropriate ways, have a positive mental effect. These subjects are discussed in greater detail in Chapter 28.

JOGGING TO WORK
EXERCISE

Unless it creates undue pain, there is little doubt that exercise is good for the mind. The advantages of increased circulation to the organs, including the brain, have been well documented.

The physical discomfort that may be present when one is actually doing the exercise often ends when the exercise stops, and a state of relative comfort follows. At that time, the release of pleasurable neurotransmitters can be appreciated. Regular exercise is a form of self-discipline, and yields the benefits of confidence and mental control.

Excessive exercise is occasionally a problem for the already hyper AIR types, but it's almost always good for sedentary EARTH types. A moderate amount is good for FIRE people who may tend to overachieve in this area as well as others.

One should not over exercise. Ayurveda recommends exercising to half one's capacity, or to the point of light sweating.

HEALTHY VENDING MACHINES
MIND-HEALING FOOD

When the AIR, FIRE, and EARTH qualities are out of balance, the mind takes on those excess qualities and becomes unbalanced. If the proper foods are used to correct those quality imbalances, then the mind is also improved.

A spacey, unfocused mind is typical of an AIR excess, so heavy, oily, and sweet foods are used to bring the mind back to earth. Light, dry, and raw food should be avoided.

An irritated, angry or violent mind reflects an excess of the FIRE quality, and heating foods that are spicy-hot, salty, sour, or fermented should be avoided. Bitter and sweet foods should be taken to help restore clarity and patience.

If the mind is weighed down and foggy with excess EARTH qualities, then eating light, dry, spicy, and bitter foods will help much more than drowning one's sorrows in EARTH-heavy ice cream. Light, dry, and spicy foods are recommended.

RENT
MONEY

Money worries are a common cause of stress. Most people have enough money for the survival basics, but perceived deficiencies leave them with the stressful feeling of insufficient funds. Many go into debt in order to satisfy imagined needs or expectations, and the debt itself becomes an added mental stress.

Credit counselors are available, and many correctly treat credit abusers as addicts. Those who actually do have trouble makings ends meet for the basics need immediate outside help. Financial advisors can be useful resources, but many place their own interests ahead of their client's.

One can become preoccupied with money accumulation to the point that it becomes all-consuming. This preoccupation can be a diversion that overshadows other difficult issues.

Modern self-worth is often measured monetarily, and the dollar-oriented media is adept at brainwashing people to believe that cash is king. Of course, once this golden goal has been selected, it is easy to believe that one never has enough. A mindless Midas addiction to gold can spiral out of control.

Breaking this FIRE and EARTH-dominated illness is achieved by facing diverted pain problems, and by rediscovering the Universal Unity that hoarding and greed obscure. Preoccupation with portfolios must be rolled-over into a karmic bank account filled with kindness instead of cash.

COWORKERS
RELATIONSHIPS & ASSOCIATIONS

Much of what we are here on Earth to learn involves our relationships with others. Starting as children and moving through school, work, love, family, and community, we must constantly make decisions on how to behave and communicate with the other people.

If we have been given good communication and relationships skills, we often do much better in life. But learning these skills is not easy, and the process is often left to chance. The establishment of routine psychology and sociology courses that focus on these practical skills is still a long way off in most schools.

Parents do most of the (unconscious) modeling of relationship dynamics that they learned from their own clueless parents. It is often a hit or miss process. Observing another family's different social dynamic is often the eye-opener that makes one aware of other relationship options.

Many younger people receive their relationship instruction from the boob tube via situation "comedies," soaps, movies, movie star gossip shows, and the news. Because positive or peaceful behavior is not stimulating, negative behavior is often displayed in order to draw the interest of viewers to the unusual. Violence, tragedy, greed, sex, and bad-mouthing may be interesting, but they give youngsters the wrong tools for dealing with relationships. These interactive mistakes are even salted with artificial laughter to convince the viewer that these dysfunctional interactions are good.

There is very little that is more important than learning positive, functional interaction skills. In the School-of-Life on this planet, the "three Rs" are "Reality, Relationships, and Re-discovering (the divine)."

CLOSING UP THE POST OFFICE
MEDITATION

Just as a post office needs to close at night and be cleaned up for the next day's activities, the mind needs to quiet so that stress and tension can dissipate. Sleep helps with this process, but even during sleep, the mind remains busy on a subconscious level. When mental activity is extensive and no rest occurs, many physical and mental problems can arise. Meditation is a method of deeply relaxing the mind, as well as the body. When this relaxation takes place, the physical and mental aspects return to their natural, unstressed condition in the same way that a plant grows better if it is not artificially bent over and stressed.

Meditation is simply a gentle *focusing and re-focusing of awareness, and the observation of one's own thoughts and circumstances.* It is this "witnessing awareness" that allows us to gain perspective on our stressful thoughts and activities, and leads us from bad habits toward better health.

Meditation involves gradually and gently developing the ability to concentrate. When most things (including thought) are concentrated, they tend to become more powerful. When more power is available, activities can be completed more easily, and with greater skill and depth. The senses operate with more power as a result of meditation. Not only can the senses be better controlled with the meditation, they can also be enhanced once the meditation is done.

Meditation also provides a sense of connection with many other aspects of our world and beyond. In yogic/ayurvedic philosophy, there is one Greater Consciousness of which individual consciousness is a part. Meditation helps connect us with that Greater Self.

Because meditation requires developing quiet and inactivity, many people view it as a boring process that produces little. That's exactly the point. The purpose is to reduce the activity and production that stimulate and stress the mind. When we stop feeding the mind activity, it begins to relax.

In point of fact, the results of meditation can be interesting, productive, and sensual, as well as curative for many ailments. But the process does require considerable time, effort, and patience. An initial faith that the investment in quiet non-activity will pay off down the road is required. It's another form of delayed gratification.

There are many techniques of meditation, but most of them involve a few basic elements. The first is to find a regular place for meditation that is quiet and without sensory distractions such as noise and bright light. If quiet, repetitive background music lessens both external distractions and internal thinking, then it can be useful, but eventually, silence is best. Some meditators use ear plugs and blindfolds.

The mind and breath are closely connected, so quieting and focusing the mind is accomplished by lengthening and following the breath. Various patterns of observing and controlling the breath ("Kriyas") are used with attention given to the length of inspiration, expiration, and the pauses in between. Nose and mouth breathing are also varied, as are the "locks" ("Bandhas") that are used to focus and strengthen the subtle energy movements that occur during meditation.

It is important to find a favorite object on which to focus attention. It can be a phrase, a peaceful object, a geometric design, a sound, a light, an affirmation, or the image of an inspirational teacher. Anything that is quiet, positive, and consistent. Repetition is then used to develop concentration and focus. The repetition can be silent, or quietly spoken.

Many meditators start with multiple subjects of focus and observation. When the interest in one thought subject fades, another thought appears and is observed. Eventually, fewer and fewer subjects are observed until a single object of attention becomes dominant.

Objects of internal visualization can also be chosen for their balancing qualities. If increased AIR quality is required, then the sky and clouds can be chosen for visualization. A candle flame can be chosen if some FIRE quality is needed, or a calm ocean, lake, stream, or mountain can be used if EARTH-like stability is needed.

Whichever object is chosen for focus and concentration, the technique always involves the *observation of one's inner dialogue.* When you close your eyes, thoughts and feelings immediately appear. Remember, *you are not just your thoughts and feelings.* Observe them just as you would observe clouds floating by on a pleasant afternoon or branches floating down a river. They appear, you notice them, and then they move on.

Observe yourself thinking "I must do that errand" simply as a thought that floats into your consciousness. Observe it, and then watch as it floats away, and a new thought appears in the sky of your consciousness or in the river of your thoughts. No judgments are necessary. You need not tell yourself to "stop thinking about that." That would be like telling yourself to "stop thinking about a pink elephant." Simply *observe* the thought and watch it gradually fade away.

If you find yourself becoming frustrated and struggling to focus despite changing objects of attention, let go of your effort and stop the meditation for the moment. You can return to it later. After unpressured repeated efforts, success will come.

Start with just a small amount of time in the meditation effort, and extend the time gradually. Five minutes in the beginning is fine! Twenty to thirty minutes is usually required for deeper relaxations, and multiples of 20 minutes can be added as the practice grows. A gentle bell timer, or an hourglass can be a useful measure of the time spent, as long as measuring remains important.

Mind-altering substances are usually discouraged. One of the advantages and attractions of meditation is that it can be used to decrease reliance on external sedatives and stimulants. The positive calming energy that medita-tion creates actually brings its own "high." This high is better than substance induced highs in that there is usually no rebound "low" that follows.

Make yourself comfortable. Sitting with a straight back allows for proper movement of energy up the spinal area, but it is more important not to be distracted by any discomfort involved in positioning oneself for meditation. Sitting is important, but sitting *comfortably* (in a chair if necessary) is more important. Preparing for sitting by doing stretching and breathing exercises is always good. Comfortable clothing is also a less distracting.

It's also a good idea to do something to stabilize your hands. The hands frequently tend to fidget, so putting them into a relaxing position on the knees or clasped together helps keep them still. Keep the eyes closed. This helps reduce external input, and redirects the focus of attention inward. The tongue can be stabilized with its tip touching the roof of the mouth behind the front teeth. The feet and legs are usually crossed in a non-painful semi-lotus position. If sitting in a chair, the feet are usually touching to complete the subtle energy circuit in the lower extremities.

Sitting still and "doing nothing" is not easy, so it's important to remember that "doing nothing" is still doing something. The mind always rebels against inactivity, and has been likened to a monkey that is constantly jumping around. Teaching the "monkey-mind" to be quiet is the goal of mediation.

During meditation, thoughts, images, feelings, and sensations arise. It is virtually impossible to eliminate all of these. Instead, be content with *observing* them, and moving from one observation to another - as long as you, the observer of the process, remain aware of what is happening. Move gently back and forth between thoughts, breath observation, phrase repetition, and your object of concentration.

When you catch yourself obsessing about some difficult issue in your life, gently observe, "There I go again, thinking about . . . . ," and move to the observation of your breath. After a few breaths, another thought will float into your consciousness. Don't try to push the thought away. Simply observe the new thought, examine it, watch it float through your awareness, and bring yourself back to the breath, or to your repeated phrase, or your object of concentration. Stay with each as long as needed, and accept the next thought as it arrives.

Some methods of meditation recommend labeling the thoughts as they float into view. Other meditation teachers stress avoiding any such labeling, especially if that process shortens the deep examination and "being with" the thought or feeling.

Eventually, the empty time in between thoughts will begin to lengthen. Thought waves slow down. This space between inhalation and exhalation, and between thoughts holds the peaceful benefit of meditation. The goal is to spend more and more time in that quiet, empty space.

Keep the benefits of meditation in mind as a motivating goal. Remind yourself that peace, joy, and health are among those benefits. Clearer thinking, reduced tension, anxiety, stress, cholesterol, heart disease, and addictions are also among the benefits of regular practice. An increase in love, spontaneity, awareness and a sense of meaning and purpose have all been described as benefits of meditation.

There are other quieting mental activities that come close to meditation, but they lack the focus and reduction in mental activity that are the hallmarks of the meditative process. With daydreaming, there is an involvement with thoughts that is different from the detached observation that is more typical of meditation. Self-hypnosis involves a loss of attention and perspective on the whole process. Prayer can be a form of meditation as long as the element of *detached observation* of the process is present.

Timing is important. It is helpful if some open-ended time can be scheduled after the meditation. Attempting to meditate with the pressure of upcoming events is distracting. Most meditation techniques recommend avoiding meditation right after meals, but a hungry stomach can also be distracting. Again, it is also helpful to prepare for meditation by doing yoga postures, breathing exercises, and phrase repetition before sitting to meditate.

As with any other learning effort, practice is essential. Repetition brings success, so do your meditation practice as regularly as possible at a consistent time of day or night. Regular practice and consistency are necessary, but it is important to *relax* into the effort. Enjoy it!

One problem with meditation is that it is difficult to start and stay with the process if mental turmoil is already present. To deal with this, sit down briefly at your designated place, close your eyes and observe your thoughts. Don't expect any success at meditation initially. Examine your emotions, then get up and forget about meditating. The next day at the appointed time, do the same thing. Eventually, you will be able to bring yourself to focus on something else; your focus object, phrase, breath, etc.

There are many techniques of meditation. If one method proves too difficult, try another. Most religions have ways of looking inward for a spiritual connection. These can be strict or relaxed, quiet or active. An Ayurvedic approach to meditation involves matching the mental quality needs with the type of meditation. A heavy EARTH-type mind might need more stimulating meditation, while a hyper AIR-type does better with very deep and quiet work.

Some meditation techniques are active and involve looking for truths Other approaches are passive, and the mind is allowed to simply reflect on the issues at hand. As you explore, it is important to notice the recurring issues to which you are attached, and your resistance to letting them move out of the mind. Try not to dwell on preoccupations, but instead, gently move your thoughts to positive areas.

Meditation on the subtle energy movements through the energy channels and major energy centers is a common focus during the advanced observation process. Devotion to a form of divinity is also typical.

There are often difficulties along the meditation path. When the meditation going gets tough, bring your attention back to your breath, your repeated phrase, or your visualized object. Sleepiness, boredom, restlessness, doubt, fear, procrastination, self-judgment, pride, attachment, and avoidance of reality often occur as a part of the meditation effort. Don't be discouraged. These common problems clear away with practice, but it takes effort, and occasionally, a consultation with an experienced mediator.

A meditation teacher should understand the sharing nature of meditation, and should not require financial remuneration or pledges of loyalty. Meditation groups can also be a source of support in the effort.

Whatever the difficulties, the meditation should ultimately be relaxing. The idea is to *reduce* tension in the mind by having it do less and less. When this happens, a transformation of consciousness occurs, and one can often visualize and participate in blissful states. It can be the ultimate, gentle, relaxing, curative high without rebound depression.

Ultimately, the state of meditative observation extends to activity in everyday life. You begin to notice, *in advance*, how situations approach you. From your observer's perspective, you begin to see things coming rather than being surprised by events. You begin to see the big picture while you are doing the small details. You learn to observe yourself in the present moment without dwelling on the future and the past.

Finally, the effect of meditation on *health* cannot be overestimated. Many of the mystic healers in our folklore used meditative techniques for healing the sick, and modern studies have shown the validity of the mind-body connection for maintaining health.

When the mind is quieted in meditation, a de-stressing occurs. This allows for a healthier body, and for better health decision making. By establishing feelings of connectedness, restoring body alignment and balance, creating spaces for the release of emotions, and by helping to break unhealthy habits, meditation is suggested as the ultimate medicine for all in need of a healthier life.

REMOVING POST OFFICE CLUTTER
AUSTERITY

The yogic/ayurvedic principle of "Austerity" is meant to encourage restraint of desires for the unnecessary, rather than creating a total renunciation of the social and material world. Simplification and focus are the goals, but the material world remains one of life's realities and teaching tools.

Clutter is often created to conceal painful issues. When there are fewer confusing objects and minor issues to consider, dealing with the ones that remain is easier and more effective. Removing life-activity clutter forces us to deal with these painful subjects, and offers time to focus on the spiritual.

BEACH TIME
ISOLATION & REFLECTION

Just as austerity helps remove the clutter associated with physical objects, physical isolation further removes one from physical and mental distractions. It serves to highlight the important areas that remain.

Physical isolation from mental diversion can be extremely difficult for many of us who have become addicted to activity. When it is practiced, isolation should be supervised by an occasional monitoring visit.

The best vacations from mental stress are often the simple ones that awaken an awareness of the calming quiet that flourishes in nature. Repeated reflection on natural patterns and truths brings an ordering and healing effect.

MAINTENANCE CHECKLISTS
DISCIPLINE & DAILY ROUTINE

Just as austerity and isolation allow for an uncluttered approach to mental challenges, a methodical lifestyle promotes healthy mental habits (see Chapter 8).

The methods and benefits of establishing a daily physical routine have been described in Chapter 8. If daily activities include regular mental routines, such as prayer, quiet time, TV limits, meditation, or walking in nature, then the mind will become quieter yet stronger.

The use of checklists for regular activities is helpful, and calendars are helpful for charting one's practice goals and progress (see Chapter 30).

SKIPPING LUNCH BREAK
FASTING

The mind often becomes clouded and heavy, especially for those with an undue build-up of excess EARTH quality. When such a fog envelops the mind, fasting can be a useful way to clear it.

The absence of food starts a series of metabolic events that results in the release of epinephrine. This stimulant wakes up the brain, and the mind becomes clarified. Once awakened, the mind is able to work on its issues.

The difficulty with fasting is finding the discipline to endure the "pain" of hunger. Essentially, discipline boils down to *accepting short-term discomfort in return for long-term benefit*. Discipline is a central sign of maturity, as well as a key to success in life. Dumb luck helps. Self-discipline is critical.

The first and most basic area of discipline is the ability to control our food choices. Fasting is the ultimate test of our self-control because eating is the most basic activity we do after breathing. If we *can* control our eating, we have a

shot at controlling other things. If we can't control our mos
tory desires, then we are unlikely to be able to control other impo
Controlling one's food intake can also be the key to building self-
self-discipline.

Therefore, according to ayurveda, most everyone should practice short periods of fasting from time to time.

But isn't fasting a little extreme? Not at all. The human species was designed for fasting. As ancient hunter-gatherers, intermittent periods without food were common. With the exception of the weak, the very old, the very young, those with blood sugar imbalances and some FIRE types, most can benefit from a one day fast. We can skip breakfast, "suffer" through no lunch, and restrain ourselves modestly at dinner where we can celebrate the beginnings of self-discipline.

Fasting also kindles the fire that promotes good digestion. Good digestion, in turn, promotes good energy and health. Good health and energy promote further self-discipline, and a positive cycle of growth and strengthening follows.

Start with a vegetable or fruit juice fast at first. Instead of skipping breakfast and lunch entirely, have a small amount of fresh, life-force containing juice instead of dead bacon and heavy pancakes. You will feel lighter and more energized. Don't let this new energy make you more anxious. Use the extra energy to do something creative or useful that you have planned in advance.

Increase your fasting ability as you are able. Do it for the whole day—maybe two!

If done correctly, fasting can be a way of getting high! As the blood sugar goes down, cortisol (the "well-being hormone") levels go up. Energizing adrenalin also goes up! Heart rate goes up! Endorphins kick in, and you wake up feeling good! Sometimes, less can be more. Sometimes, a little hunger … is good! Of course, this can be abused in the same way any mind-altering activity can be abused. Anorexia or bulimia can be the result when the need to get high or preserve a distorted self-image occurs.

For many of us, food is love. It brings us back to the loving comfort of our primal source of physical and emotional nourishment; Mom. If we have enough love from others or from ourselves, then we don't need as much food. But if we run short on love, we can always run home to Mama Frigidaire.

FORWARDING ADDRESSES
EMOTIONAL SUBLIMATION

Difficult thoughts and socially unacceptable emotions can be successfully managed when transformed into the acceptable. Primal urges can be tamed by moving their energies to other activities, both positive and negative.

671

Hunger for sex is a natural part of human existence, but when it is transformed into an anesthetic or diversion from painful issues, it can become an addiction with only transient pleasing benefits. In spiritual terms, sex can become a distraction from achieving the goals of reducing ego, attachment, and desire.

In yogic practice, sexual energy is best channeled toward a spiritual focus. An opening of the heart is one goal of this "tantra" practice in which erotic energies are transformed into divine (agape) love and intimacy. The melding of sexual passion with interpersonal *com*passion is one way that this practice has been described.

One goal of tantra is the transformation of emotions toward the discovery of higher aspects of consciousness; turning emotional energy into spiritual ascension. The techniques for the management of these energies is the subject of considerable literary discussion. One example is for a sexual couple to visualize themselves as deities, merging their divinity in sex that is meditative and inwardly directed, rather than sensually focused.

The use of sex for emotional rechanneling may be a worthwhile practice as long as it is based on sound spiritual foundations and aspirations, and not on self-indulgence. Glimpses of the ultimate union of all spirit can be obtained if the former is the true goal.

FAVORITE RAP CD COLLECTION
OUR BASIC NEGATIVE STORIES

Mental, emotional, and spiritual healing requires that we push the "eject" button on the negative thought recordings that we play in our heads day and night.

Everyone has a favorite downer disk to insert into his/her internal CD player, but there are a few best sellers that we need to drag to the trash ASAP. Most of these stories stem from the concepts of separateness, comparison, and judgment. Yoga and ayurveda teach that these ideas of separateness are ultimately false in the spiritual sense. If we do feel separate, we are also likely to feel alone. If we feel alone, we may then conclude that we are not worthy of love, companionship, or validation.

Separateness also leads to comparison and judgment. We compare ourselves to others and come to illusory conclusions. The "I'm not good enough" recording has been played over and over in our heads from an early age, and the idea that we are "not worthy" of positive things is another sound bite that we play. Ayurveda discourages both. Turning off the TV helps.

Our attempts to explain our problem outcomes can result in the false conclusions that "I didn't do it right" or "I'm not good enough." Making "mistakes" is part of the learning process. In that sense, mistakes are acceptable and even necessary for true education to occur. Some philosophies hold that all our experiences, including the difficult ones, contain the lessons we are here to learn for our spiritual advancement.

A negative view of the world's abundance is also bad for one'
believes that "there isn't enough" (opportunity, objects, affect
around, then one will continue to be stuck in a negative, lim
that brings physical and emotional illness. Developing a faith t
fact, an infinite abundance of resources in the infinite universe is a challenge
that advanced life-classes attempt to teach.

We are always turning on our CD players and listening to the oldies. Stories
about past problems haunt us, and we need to eject them. Similarly, fears
about the future rob us of the joy of the present moment.

When we buy into lyrics that tell us that the world and everyone in it are just a
bunch of random chemical reactions, we miss the whole spiritual advancement
point of being here. The idea that the body, mind, and spirit are disconnected
needs to dumped into the trash along with other wrong-headed tunes such as
"*What's Love Got to Do With It*?" Love IS it!

The sterile concept that nothing is eternal, omniscient, or omnipotent is
another sour tune that does little to help us in our efforts at spiritual evolution.
If we believe that we just disappear when our bodies die, then we have flunked
life's advanced level courses.

TIRE CHAIN REMOVAL
DESIRE, EGO & ATTACHMENT

Yoga philosophy teaches that ego, attachment, and desire are three of the main
obstacles to pain reduction, contentment, and realization of what is ultimately
important. Eventually, these chains have to come off.

Ego creates a false sense of separateness from others. "I am…Arab, you are…
Jew." While there are differences between us on many physical levels, there
are also important similarities that ego negates.

Ego can easily generate a primal, survival-directed selfishness. Egocentric actions
become lonely, and dramatic, and we forget about sharing. Ego deprives us of
true love, health, and the sense of community we are seeking. It thrives on negative thoughts, words, and deeds.

Ego can help us avoid dangers in the world, but it can also lead us to behaviors
that are counterproductive. Ego keeps us tied to our individual small-selves, and
away from the Greater-Self of higher community consciousness. Ego binds us to
the physical, and limits our efforts to find the spiritual. It implants the false
subconscious notion that "I may live *physically* forever!"

After ego has been established, "I" becomes "I want." In order to fortify
itself, negative ego creates desire. The objects of desire can be physical, mental,

_motional, or spiritual. The objects of desire reinforce one's separateness, and define one's (separate) character traits.

Yoga teaches that most achievements that come from desire are transient. Few people can name the past emperors of Rome. Fame and fortune fade, but moral actions and awareness last, according to yoga philosophy. Desire for those lasting, cosmic attributes is beneficial, while the desire for more mundane objects and attributes clouds, confuses, and brings pain to the mind and obscures the spirit.

But the most binding chains are those found at the intersection of Madison Avenue and Attachment Boulevard. Our natural, primal fear of death creates a strong *attachment* to all of life's inconsequential objects and stories. Because our lives are transient, we will eventually lose *all* of our possessions. It's a game we cannot "win" and playing it with a "win/lose" attitude just creates mental pain.

We are here to experience desire, ego, and attachment, and we are expected to grow beyond them.

GRIDLOCK HAPPENS
ACCEPTANCE

Pain is a part of life. One of the purposes of human incarnation, according to yoga philosophy, is to learn to go beyond preoccupation with pleasure and pain.

What we learn on our life's journey varies from individual to individual according to his or her spiritual needs. Different passengers in different taxis are destined for different grad schools where, among other things, they will all study the meaning of pain and pleasure.

At some point, mental acceptance is necessary for the resolution of pain. If the mind is always saying "this pain is unfair" or "this pain cannot be happening" or "I can't handle the pain," then the mind will continue to search for ways to anesthetize or to hide it.

Acceptance is contrary to the basic nature of the mind. It would be like hiring a taxi driver to sit stuck in traffic all day. Pretty soon, the driver will do something dumb. Taxi driver-minds that can accept the realities of worldly traffic usually have fewer ulcers than those who rail against life's difficulties.

It is difficult to know when to accept things and when to work hard to change them. Knowing the difference between the changeable and the unchangeable is often just a matter of observation of the effect of repeated efforts and the passing of time itself.

ROLLING ON DOWN THE HIGHWAY
JOURNEY AS DESTINATION

The question of where we are headed in our lives is one that surfaces repeatedly in most internal inquiries and philosophical discussions. The purposes of life are as variously defined as the many philosophies that enliven our libraries.

The yogic/ayurvedic point of view is that we are here to face the spiritual issues that we have yet to understood or master. If we continue to avoid our difficult spiritual problems we have failed. If we don't venture out on a spiritual road trip, we will have fallen short. We *must* get out on the spiritual highway!

For most of us, that adventure involves overcoming various fears including fear of poverty, loss of control, and death. It is recognized that this is a supremely difficult task that may require considerable repetition and many lifetimes.

Most people don't have the patience for a lengthy journey. They choose to discount the concept of a multi-lifetime purpose, and decide that success is measured in easily attainable, transient physical things. Long-term spiritual achievements require a different level of patience.

In yoga philosophy, there is no heavenly parking lot beyond the horizon. Heaven is a blissful, present-day state of heart. Heavenly joys are manifest on the journey itself as each one of us encounters, confronts, and masters the road hazards that appear.

CRUISING THE STRIP
ENJOYING LIFE

It is important to remember that "recess" is a part of the educational curriculum. Having fun while you're in school or on the road is a goal that most of us should joyfully accept.

Yet, in many philosophies, having fun is viewed as hazardous in that it brings with it the *desire* for even *more* fun. It also brings *attachment* to having fun, and the *ego* of wanting the enjoyment for oneself. Soon, **D**esire, **E**go, and **A**ttachment (the "**DEA**") have developed into our dominant governing agency.

On the other hand, excessive efforts to avoid pleasure can result in austere practices in which enjoyment is shunned in favor of harsh and even masochistic self-control practices. Such extreme "purification" efforts can overwhelm playfulness and expressive forms of love.

The concept of "dispassion" is central in yoga philosophy. In this neutrality practice, one *observes and recognizes* the beauty that fills the world, but avoids dwelling on attachment to it. Genuine absence of ego, attachment, and desire is described as the very definition of "liberation" from suffering. It is one of the most difficult lessons we face.

An attachment to the desire to be *free* of desire, ego, and attachment is the acceptable exception to this philosophy!

Other philosophies allow the passionate aspects of humanity to surface. Sufism, mystical Judaism, and other philosophies concede the reality of enjoyment as part of the blissful nature of divine manifestations. In the "middle path" philosophy of Buddhism, neither extreme austerities nor frivolities are thought to be the way to peace and happiness. Whatever the tradition, a philosophy must deal with the role of pleasure and passion as a part of the journey.

PIMP MY RIDE
"SELF"-LOVE

No matter which highway or vehicle is chosen, the passenger must feel worthy of the trip.

If a person's upbringing is such that this sense-of-worth is lacking, it... be seen as a positive learning experience. The concept of "self-esteem" begs the definition of "self." This term is used with a great deal of confusion and equivocation in yogic/ayurvedic philosophy. It's important to feel the difference between the individual, "small-self" and the universal "Greater-Self" (see Part Four).

It is even more important to see the small and Greater selves as one entity.

Ultimately, it falls to the individual spiritual passenger to define the "self" in its many physical, philosophical, and heart-centered terms. For the trip to be successful, the mind-driver of the human taxicab *must* follow the spirit-passenger's directions.

TABLE 23-1: **PRINCIPLES OF MIND FUNCTION**

1. Mind Directs the Physical Body
2. Mind Problems cause Physical Problems
3. Mind has AIR, FIRE, and EARTH Qualities
4. Mind Quality Imbalances cause Illness
5. Adding Opposite Qualities helps lead to Mental Re-balancing
6. Mind Quality usually Matches Body Quality

7. Mental Food Determines Mind Quality
8. Mental Pollution (Toxins) can cause Mental and Physical Illness
9. Mental "Digestion" is Important for Health

10. Fear & Safety, Pain & Pleasure are the Primary Mental Motivators
11. Pain & Pleasure Associated Neurotransmitter Levels Determine Behavior & Mood
12. Pain Concepts & Responses Determine Behavior
13. Pain Defense Mechanisms are either Anesthetic, Diversionary, or Constructive

14. Mind seeks Activity & avoids Quiet
15. Mind & Breath are Closely Connected
16. Meditation Gives the Mind a Rest.
17. Mind Should Follow Spiritual Direction

18. Desire, Ego, & Attachment (DEA) are the Primary Mental Pitfalls
19. Behavior Changes can be Very Difficult.
20. Daily Routine Supports Self-Discipline and Health..

21. Mental Re-balancing involves Non-judgment & Acceptance
22. Love what You Do for a Living.

PART 4:

THE SPIRIT PASSENGER

IT'S ALL ABOUT ME

"Reggie, it's Margo, dude."

…Oh, crap…

"Reggie, can you get a party of four down at the Crow's Nest by the Yacht Harbor?"

"Got it, Margo. No problem."

"Thanks, Regg."

"No problem. 10-4."

… So, anyway, I'm drivin' down Highway One near the coast. Traffic is jammed-up pretty good as usual, and I see this gorgeous chick coming up slowly behind me in a brand new, metallic blue BMW convertible. Clean and shiny, top down (the car, not the woman), so, naturally, I turn and look.

She's absolute magazine material! Right out of Vogue or Cosmo. I know about these mags *only* because the women I used to live with read 'em all the damn time, OK? Alright, so *maybe* I looked at a few pages here and there…

So anyway, she's blonde with her hair pulled back into a tight, perfect ponytail with a blue metallic scarf-thing tied onto the ponytail that exactly matches the color of her car. Medium build, sexy, wrap-around shades, and full makeup - on a Saturday morning at the beach! Nice white, neatly ironed sleeveless blouse with nice tan shoulders, great fake tits, and a nice cute little nose. All in all, very well put together!

So I'm thinkin' "Damn, it must be great to have that much money!" I know what those gals spend on clothes, cosmetics, shoes and stuff cause I've driven 'em around on shopping trips. High-maintenance. Must be nice. You can tell she's not headed for any Habitat For Humanity house-building event! No sir. Pasatiempo Country Club. No doubt about it.

So she slows to a stop right in front of me and keeps looking straight ahead. No smile, no radio, not talking on her cell phone, or singing or anything. Just looking straight ahead. Motionless. Totally Stepford.

I'm thinkin' 'It doesn't look like she's having much fun out there in that shiny new car … Her old man's probably already escaped to the golf course, right?' So, then …

"Reggie, what's your ETA to the Nest?"

"Chillax, Margo. I got traffic on One. I'm guessing fifteen or twenty."

"Ten-four that."

… So I'm deep into fantasy and speculation about this chick when I notice the crowning touch – her bumper – or should I say – her *car's* bumper. Plastered right on her brand new car's ass is a neatly printed black and white bumper sticker. It says:

"IT'S ALL ABOUT ME"

…Yeah, that about sums it up…

Then she cuts me off and takes off toward Pasatiempo. Yep. That's what it's all about…"me … me … ME!"

IT'S ALL ABOUT WE

GREATER-SELF INTEREST

One of life's major lessons is understanding, feeling, and truly believing that humanity is one Soul-Spirit. We may be many in body and mind, but spiritually, we are ultimately One.

Accepting our unity and equality is difficult because it goes against the natural tendencies of the mind. The ego needs to divide and separate us from the rest of the world, and our bodies provide sufficient evidence that we are *physically* different.

Because the mind concerns itself primarily with the senses, it points to the other body-vehicles and says,

> "The tasteful leather in my quiet Mercedes is *different* than the cloth K-Mart seat covers in your noisy old Pinto! It *smells* and *looks* different, and it feels different to the *touch*. You can *hear* the purring of *my* engine and the clattering of yours."

The mind is all about creating partitions that separate. Without these sensory distinctions, the mind cannot identify itself. The mind would be committing virtual suicide to remove separateness from our existence.

As a result, the mind-driver gets only glimpses of the spiritual love-making that is going on in the back seat. It has difficulty seeing through the taxi's sensory partition that separates the spiritual back seat from the mundane front. The mind likes that partition. It makes the mind feel safe and in control.

When we turn off the mind in meditation, we turn off the need to experience differences. At that point, we move into the realm of the Spirit. In that place, we find peace, contentment, compassion, harmony, and health.

SMACK-DOWN OF THE CENTURY !

MOTHER THERESA vs. HULK HOGAN
of Calcutta   of St. Petersburg

SANTA CRUZ
CIVIC AUDITORIUM

FEBRUARY 30, 2009

HULK HOGAN vs. MOTHER THERESA

It wasn't exactly the bout of the century.

On paper, it was no contest. The betting line was a joke with the underdog pulling odds of 50:1. But the media loved it. The match-up was full of interest even if the outcome of the contest was not. The promoters were happy. Tickets were selling, and the network contracts had been inked.

The circus was in town!

The "weigh-in" was a good example. The Hulk was the first to enter, wearing a black skull-and-crossed-bones jacket and sporting reflective, wrap-around shades under his black bandana and over his white-blonde mustache. The camera flashes lit up the room as he strode to the stage, all smiles. The purse for this bout was to be the biggest of his career. It was a cinch. All he had to do was show up.

The reporters did their best to create something from nothing.

"Hulk!" someone shouted. "How do you feel about taking on a Nobel Peace Prize winner with only two days training?"

"I'm ready for ANYTHING she can throw at me!" he growled back, banging his fist on the table and sending water spilling out of the glasses that were parked in front of the dignitaries seated around him. The sound of his fist on the cheap folding table was thunderous, and many in the room jumped at the sound.

Everyone laughed nervously. They were frightened by this awesome man and by his incredible physical power. The laughter helped them dissipate their intimidation.

"When they first proposed this match-up," The Hulk continued, "I just laughed."

The reporters chuckled their understanding.

"But when they told me about the *purse* that The Donald was offering, I just couldn't refuse, no matter how embarrassing it might be."

His growling voice became softer as he finished his confession.

"I just wanna say… that this kind of event… just goes to show…"

He paused there, in front of the now silent crowd, and spent a poignant ten seconds wagging an admonishing finger at the hushed gaggle of pundits and panderers.

"...It just goes to show... what people can do ... when an event like this goes down for charity!"

The room hummed in consent. Cameras flashed their approval.

"Now, I called Mother Theresa last week over in Calcutta where she was wrestling with something a lot tougher than me," the confession continued,

"And I said, "M.T.! What's goin' down, girl?!"

Laughter again filled the room.

"She said,... '*YOU* are, dude!'"

The room erupted.

"I said, 'Oh yeah? How many rounds do you think you can last?'"

The audience was quiet in anticipation ...

"So she whispers... she says...'That's the beauty of it, my son! You'll just have to wait... and pray ... that you last long enough to hear... the *divine* bell... at the end of the *final* round!'"

No one spoke. A silent fifteen seconds passed while The Hulk stared off into space. The reporters sat silently in their folding chairs watching the entranced superhero.

"So, I'm here today" he continued, "to weigh-in for something we *both* stand for... something we can *all* stand for ... something that ..."

But his words were interrupted by a squeaking hinge on an opening door to the right of the stage where the Hulk stood suspended in mid-sentence ...

There she stood ... all alone ... in the doorway.

She was tiny. So tiny that the doorway appeared like a black cavern behind her. Her blue-striped nun's wimple reflected the bright spot lights from the stage on her left. She stood there quietly, glowing in the doorway.

In silence, the reporters rose to their feet.

The contest was over.

Everybody won.

SPIRITUALITY vs. SENSUALITY

The Hulk gets your attention. He's big and powerful, loud and active. He's controversial, stylish, modern, violent and masculine. He's genuinely awesome. He stimulates the senses.

Mother Theresa is also a powerful force, but in quite the opposite way. Her power comes from something that is strangely quiet and retiring, centered and balanced. Sensuality is not a part of her power.

It's human nature to be drawn to the active, the flashy, the powerful and the sensual. The senses grab a hold of us like a powerful wrestler. They are nearly impossible to resist. Why would anyone trade the glamour and excitement of hulking celebrity for the modesty, and demure dedication of a saint? One is a stimulating, entertaining sensation! The other *appears* to be a common drone.

This is the nature of the wrestling match between the mind and the heart that we fight everyday. Our senses pull us to enjoy things until we burst, and our stimulus-seeking mind convinces us to let the senses have their way. It rarely says "No" to pleasure in the immediate moment. It wants to party!

As little kids, we naturally go for the sensory Hulk. But as we get older, we realize the long-term limitations of constant sensory gratification, and the long-term fulfillment that comes from saying "No" to empty pleasure in the immediate moment.

What is it that allows for this maturity? Why do some people have it early in life and others never get over Wrestlemania?

Part of the answer is that we don't often *practice* saying "No" to our senses. From the time we were babies, we've been given what our senses ask for, and the media and Madison Avenue make sure that we know everything that's available for indulgence.

Saying "No" to indulgence is one of the first growing up lessons we learn. Saying "No" to some of the *basics* is a more advanced training lesson. We learn this self-control by practicing fasting, breath control, daily routine, and meditation.

Something more powerful than the Hulk-senses must step through the doorway and show us the way to greater things.

It is our self-respect and our concern for others that steps forward at those times. Our *hearts* tell us that some short-term pain is better than long-term suffering. A sense of self-worth tells us that we are something more than physical creatures seeking sensory gratification.

If we have already been given a sense of self-worth, then we can work to maintain it, and to deny ourselves sensory foolishness. If we have no basic sense of self-worth, then we will be tempted to seek pleasure outside of ourselves. Finding that sense of self-worth then becomes our primary goal.

OWNER'S CLUB
I-SELF VS. G-SELF

There is a confusing term that is frequently used in many philosophies. The concept of "S-E-L-F" is often applied to descriptions of an individual's personal nature, and to their relationship with the whole of creation.

The small "self" (with a small "s") describes the *individual* consciousness. The Greater "Self" (with a large "S") describes *the greater sum of all consciousness*.

Each individual is viewed as having an individual consciousness, an internal awareness of certain aspects of his or her surroundings—the "*individual small-self*." But each individual is also a part of the whole of creation. The combination of all individual consciousnesses is the sum-consciousness. That summary entity is called the "*Greater-Self*."

The Greater-Self (G-Self) is observed in the group behavior and emotions of the crowd at a football or soccer game, where as many as 100,000 individual selves (i-selves) are gathered. When a goal is suddenly scored, the entire crowd-combination of i-selves responds instantly as *one unison voice* in cheering that moment! That unison voice is a manifestation of the unified G-Self!

There is no other sound like it!

The G-Self erupts with *One* voice! "GOAL !!!"

If you are late to the game, and are walking outside the stadium just before it happens, all seems fairly quiet. You hear very little until the goal is scored. Then, in an instant, the G-Self erupts inside the stadium! As ONE huge voice!

"GOAL !!!"

It's startling! Unique! Energy-packed! It sends chills up the energy channels around your spine!

You can hear the same G-Voice at a music concert when an inspirational performance comes to its climactic finish! The audience jumps to its feet!

"BRAVO!!!" The G-Self erupts, and thunderous applause punctuates the performance! Energy tingles up and down the spine in response!

You may hear it again after a speech in Congress when the President dramatically stands before the people and climactically rattles his verbal saber!

"WAR!!!" the Congress' G-Self proclaims, and thunderous applause again follows.

The group responds as ONE. It is inspirational. Awesome.

If you were a visitor from another planet and heard that sudden, explosive community voice, you might well mistake it for the roar of some gigantic creature.

It would not be immediately clear that the creature had 100,000 individual parts. It roars as ONE!

At each of those climactic incidents, something different is created, or rather, revealed; Consciousness' can combine.

In fact, they have always been combined. According to yoga philosophy, each individual consciousness is continuously a small part of that *whole* of consciousness. Each individual football fan is always a part of the Greater Crowd. But once we leave the stadium or the concert hall, we *forget* that we are one great Fan Club. Consciousness can also be divided and separated.

We forget that we are one consciousness because the senses, and the mind's ego create interesting distractions and divisions for each individual. The mind tells us that, because my Yankee's hat is different from your Dodger's cap, we are different—that we *don't* have the same Baseball Consciousness. The mind does this because that's what the mind is—the creator of differences.

But when the mind is quieted, we can see another truth. In some ways, we are *not* different. We are ALL sports fans.

Once we have heard the Greater-Self's thunderous cheer, we are hooked. We *must* find it again. Why? Because, deep down inside, we know what that cheer means; it reflects all the power and safety that consensus, energy, inspiration, imagination and unity can create. It's huge!

That *G-voice* is one reason that we love crowd events. It's why we want to be celebrity performers - to hear that roar again and again! To have that fantastic *G-power* directed toward our small, individual selves is supremely intoxicating! If we hear that roar for our small i-self, then we know we are accepted. In those moments, we remember that we are one, huge, powerful, infinite consciousness being! In that instant, we are free of fear. We can spend a lifetime trying to be a part of that roar.

Individually, we don't get that many accolades in life. Civilization does not allow that many rock stars. It values the unusual. This addictive need for acclaim is one reason that celebrities sometimes destroy themselves with sex and drugs despite having everything sensual; they can't stand living without their personal, continuous G-Self roar once they have felt it. They seek something that mimics that vibration!

But that feeling is not only in the roar of the crowd.

It has a more powerful quiet side.

The "quiet roar" is what is found when we turn deeply inward.

When we are able to quiet our distracting and dividing minds, we can feel the quiet roar. We cannot hear it, nor can we see, touch, smell or taste it. It is an infinite sensation of unity. When we quiet the mind in some form of meditation, we find ourselves singing the silent alma mater with everyone else at the football game. We can feel the other voices. We know we are a part of it. We are safe.

We are One spirit, One consciousness. One.

CHAPTER 24:
COSMIC TRAVELERS
The Spiritual Aspect

COSMIC TRAVELERS
THE SPIRITUAL ASPECT

The third aspect of the trinity of life is "Spirit." As with the body and mind, the search for health requires that we deal with this controversial subject, but it is also important to clarify terms in this nebulous area. There is considerable overlap of the terms "spirit," "soul," and "consciousness." For the purposes of this discussion, the three will be considered similar enough to be used interchangeably.

It's difficult to define something that's naturally vague in terms that are concrete. This is especially true when describing something with characteristics that include being absolute, ultimate, supreme and impossible to characterize. It is equally difficult to define something with the finite mind that has been described as indefinable, self-revealing, and infinite.

Approaching the spiritual with *non-thought* techniques and practices (e.g. feeling, intuition, meditation, etc.) is one method of "understanding," but intellectual explanations can also help us get a bit closer.

Spirit is a vital force that enlivens and allows the body and mind to function. It is the supreme energy. It is connected to the Life Force Energy, and exists independently of the physical body. It may manifest into a new physical existence, or it may dwell outside of physical confines. It is separate from the mind, and can be described as a set of cognizant attitudes and approaches that generally direct the mind's activity. It has qualities that can range from positive to negative.

As mentioned, spirit can be an individual entity, or a composite of individual spirits. That cosmic composite spirit is unlimited and unchanging. The individual spirit is more limited, is more connected to the mind, and undergoes more changes.

Whether or not the Spirit is purposeful, or controlling of events is an open question, and its answer depends on personal philosophy. In any event, Spirit possesses a unifying sense of wholeness that gives one the sense that life has purpose.

GOOD DIRECTIONS – GOOD RIDE
SPIRITUALITY AND HEALTH

In the same way that a passenger in a taxi gives the driver the destination, the spirit tells the mind where to take the body-vehicle. Like the owner of a cab, the spirit also directs the mind-caretaker on how to maintain the vehicle. If the

693

spirit permits the mind to abuse the cab, the cab will eventually break down. The whole of psychogenic illness theory is based on this connection.

The mind needs the spirit's energized direction just as a driver often needs directions to find the way. Without some moral spiritual guidelines, the mind has difficulty with managing all the behavior laws and road health hazards. Failure to properly deal with these common obstacles can cause serious health accidents.

In order to avoid a feeling of confusion, the mind needs a sense of purpose and a sense of the non-futility of its work. It needs a sense of belonging, and it needs love. All of these things are provided by the spirit/soul/consciousness aspect of existence. It all begins with these conditions. Therefore:

Consciousness is Primary.

If the underlying spiritual questions of existence are not resolved or being actively developed, then an underlying sense of uncertainty and agitation can create tension in the mind and body that seriously undermines health. In addressing many health issues, it is important to examine the spiritual blueprints from which the mind and body are created.

Spiritual issues such as forgiveness, acceptance, discipline, compassion, and surrender, etc., must be addressed if health is to be achieved. Cruising the street in a cab without a passenger yields no profit.

THE PASSENGER'S DESTINATION
SPIRIT/SOUL/CONSCIOUSNESS JOURNEY

The School of Life is located at the intersection of Everywhere and Always. When we arrive at birth, we are all enrolled at the beginning level, and we take the same basic sociology classes. We may bring advantages or disadvantages from our physical, cultural, moral, and emotional present and past lives, but we must all face the rigors of the Life Curriculum.

Much of how we do in school depends on attitude. If we look at life as an opportunity to make ourselves into worthwhile people, then school will feel better than if we view it as an impossible, random, or worthless chore. If we visualize ourselves as ultimately successful, then the hours we spend in study will have a different character than if we view them as a waste.

The point of this educational life experience is to develop an awareness of what is worthwhile and what is trivial. We are then required to adjust our behavior accordingly. Actually living in ways that consistently reflect what we have learned about right living are the final exams that allow us to move on to the next grade level.

This learning is done by both the mind and the spirit. The mind acts, and the spirit observes and guides.

Just getting to school is a challenge. Sadly, many "students" have no genuine desire to learn, so they mark time in class, drop out, and eventually follow Pinocchio to the sensory circus. They earn donkey ears instead of awareness diplomas.

The true student organizes him/herself and develops the individual discipline and habits necessary to complete the behavior and morality courses, without parents pushing and organizing.

Toward the end of the life adventure, the older student has the option of continuing to work at the graduate level where serious philosophical issues are considered. At this point, very few continue to pursue their education. Most are satisfied to avoid difficult spiritual questions through anesthesia and diversion. They are content if their physical and sensual needs are met, but they continue to feel the uncomfortable emptiness of not being in a spiritually peaceful place.

But for those who continue to seek greater awareness at a deeper level, the new semester cannot come early enough! They are ready to sign up once again to work on their spiritual skills. They are ready to take on their own thoughts and beliefs, and are willing to try new approaches. They seek to gain abilities that will lead them to inspirational spiritual answers.

GRADUATE SCHOOL CURRICULUM
SPIRITUAL ISSUES

In the School of Life, we take many classes concurrently in different areas. First, we study our *physical* bodies, and the physical world they inhabit. Almost all of us pass *Survival 101*, and we also get passing marks in *Comfort and Entertainment*. We go on to take classes in healthy living from the point of view of at least one of the health sciences. The physical environment around us becomes understood as a result of completing experience-oriented laboratory experiments called "Day-to-Day Life."

After that, some of us go on to the next level and attempt an understanding of the mind. This level of study is mostly concerned with identifying our thoughts, beliefs, emotions, and our primary conflict areas. We then try for an understanding of our coping mechanisms, both helpful and difficult.

Once we've covered the basics, advancing to the study of spiritual concerns becomes automatic. Life situations naturally create spiritual questions such as:

Who are we?
How were we created?
Why are we here?
Why do bad things happen?

What is death?
Why do we have to die?

Why is there pain and difficulty in life?

Why are things not in my control?
Why aren't there enough resources?
What is really important in life?

How do we obtain true happiness?

What lasts forever?
What's the ultimate power in the universe?
Who controls the future?

Some students find these spiritual questions too perplexing. They give up and choose to remain Sophomores for life. They search only for ways to soothe their bodies, and divert or anesthetize their minds. They often remain discontent with being underclassmen, but they don't have the energy or intelligence to enroll in advanced classes. They fail to recognize that *one of life's primary purposes is getting some answers to the basic spiritual questions.*

Hard line scientific types may be content to live without a spiritual side, because it's difficult to detect or to prove spirit with limited sensitivity. Without an acceptance that love, faith, trust, surrender, peace, and harmony are real and pertinent, their minds and hearts will not be open enough to hear the spirit-professor's lecture.

The complexity and difficulty of life itself obscures the spiritual, yet it is the very weight of these worldly demands that underscores the importance of finding some sense of unity that brings peace, calm, and health to an otherwise onerous endeavor. If we can get through the prerequisite pain acceptance requirement, then a whole new field of spiritual endeavor opens to us.

Spiritual subjects deal with the nebulous and hard to explain. In addition to the above questions, spiritual courses often cover the subjects listed in Table 24-1 on Philosophical/Religious Issues.

It's comforting to have answers to these gnawing questions. Any answer is better than living in spiritual limbo. Having answers that are comforting to the mind can bring an extra measure of peace, contentment, and health.

It is important to recognize the multiplicity of paths to spiritual answers. To say that one path is best for all is to deny that we are all different and have diverse spiritual needs. We all arrive on the planet with different unresolved issues. We don't all enroll in school for the exact same purpose.

More detailed discussions of these and other issues can be found in religious and philosophical works including those listed in the bibliography. Most of the graduate level yoga courses revolve around how one develops the spiritual personality traits that lead to a conscious reunion with the divinity that we are.

TABLE 24-1: **SPIRITUAL CURRICULUM**
PHILOSOPHICAL / RELIGIOUS ISSUES

Acceptance
Action in the World
Aim of Life
Action with Devotion
Afflictions
Anger
Arrogance
Association
Attachment
Austerity
Autonomy, Individual

Being in the World
Bliss
Bondage
Body

Charity
Clarity
Cleanliness
Clergy
Compassion
Conceit
Concentration
Consciousness
Contentment
Conversion
Courage
Creation

Death
Demonic Character
Denial
Depression
Desire
Detachment
Devotion
Dispassion
Divine Character
Doer
Dreams
Duality
Duties

Ego
Emotions
Equanimity
Evil
Evolution
Expectations

Failure
Faith
Fate
Fear
Finite to Explain Infinite
Forgiveness
Freedom
Future/Present/Past

God
Grace
Greed
Guilt

Happiness
Hardship
Hatred
Heaven
Hell
Honesty
Hope
Humility

Icons & Images
Illusion
Individuality
Infinity
Involution
Ignorance
Intellect
Internal/External
Isolation

Joy

Knowledge

Liberation
Life as a Mirror
Life Force
Life's Sanctity
Love
Lust

Macrocosm
Materialism
Matter
Meditation
Mind
Ministry
Motivation

Nature
Obstacles
Omniscience
Omnipresence
Omnipotence

Pain
Passion
Past Lives Effect
Peace
Perception
Perfection
Pleasure
Practice
Praise
Prayer
Pride
Purity

Reality
Reincarnation
Renunciation
Responsibility
Rewards
Ritual

Sacrifice
Scriptures
Self-interest
Senses
Service
Silence
Sin
Social Groups
Spirit/Soul
Suffering
Surrender

Time
Transformation
Truth
Truthfulness

Union
Universe
Understanding

Violence

Will
Wisdom

697

MINISTER, BUSINESSMAN or BUM
PURITY, ACTIVITY, NEGATIVITY

We have an infinite number of choices about the way we live our lives. The choices we make are the *result* of our existing mental and spiritual character traits.

Ayurveda and yoga organize these character qualities into three groups; the Pure ("Sattvic"), the Active ("Rajasic"), and the Negative ("Tamasic'). These terms are often used to describe and summarize the nature of both the mind and the spirit (see Table 24-2).

Each of us is a mixture of these three mental/spiritual *character* types in the same way that we are mixtures of the *physical* AIR, FIRE, and EARTH qualities. A minister may have a personality that primarily reflects purity, but there is usually some of the businessman, and a tiny bit of the bum in him/her as well.

In the same way that we acquire physical qualities, we can also take on various mental and spiritual qualities as a result of our upbringing, and our environmental situations. According to yoga and ayurveda, many of our basic mental and spiritual tendencies are carried forward from previous life-classes we have taken and either passed or flunked.

An indolent, unhelpful, or evil set of personality characteristics can become a part of anyone's life, and these *"negative"* behaviors usually lead to significant pain and suffering. Some degree of "negative" heaviness and groundedness is balancing and necessary in life, but learning to let go of *destructive* negative behavior is an important goal for all of us.

Character traits that are summarized by *"activity"* (see Table 24-2) are necessary for productive functioning in a busy world. Social skills are needed for worldly success, and motivation and control are necessary for achievement. Movement toward activity is recommended for those who are mired in the inertia of negative character or heavy physical qualities. It is also suggested for those whose preoccupation with purity results in impractical isolation or immobility. A personality dominated by activity usually leads to a healthier body, but too much activity may lead to scattered and/or "run down" conditions.

Although the challenge of building character dominated by *"Purity"* is the goal of most religions, total and complete purity of behavior can be isolating as well as impractical. Those who only display characteristics of purity are often called "saints." They are the Nobel Laureates of behavior. The rest of us spend most of our class time moving slowly toward pure qualities, and many of the world's problems result from our inability to move far enough in that direction. Purity usually brings physical, mental and spiritual health.

In ayurvedic and yogic philosophy, the mind and spirit are separate. The function of the mind is practical, while the function of the spirit is that of observer, director, philosopher, and long-term student. The spirit has qualities that develop over many lifetimes as a result of the actions of its incarnated mind-driver and body-vehicle.

The physical AIR quality is frequently associated with Purity, the FIRE quality with Activity, and the EARTH quality with Negativity. This is by no means firm and fast, but it represents the general quality and character tendencies in nature.

TABLE 24-2: **CHARACTER ASPECTS OF SPIRIT & MIND**

PURITY	ACTIVITY	NEGATIVITY
Purity	Activity	Negativity
Uplifting	Worldly	Malevolent
Consciousness	Movement	Inertia
Light	Fire	Darkness
Right action	Change	Confusion
Spirituality	Excitability	Sadness
Space	Atmosphere	Earth
Perception	Attention	Experience
Knower	Knowing	Known
Observer	Observation	Observed
Cognitive	Creativity	Somnolence
Intelligence	Vitality	Unconsciousness
Clarity	Motivation	Elements
Alertness	Restlessness	Dullness
Attentiveness	Surveillance	Unconsciousness
Love	Selfishness	Gloominess
Compassion	Self-centeredness	Laziness
Cooperation	Control	Insensitivity
Happiness	Pleasure	Depression
Joy	Pain	Decay
Virtue	Possession	Veiling
Bliss	Passion	Suffering
Contentment	Conflict	Retarding
Devotion	Promotion	Resignation
Service	Motivation	Delusion
Goodness	Goal seeking	Materiality
Expansion	Disequilibrium	Limiting
Harmony	Fragmentation	Disintegration
Balance	Stimulation	Obstruction
Luminous	Radiance	Dullness
Still	Outward moving	Inward moving
Upward moving	Self-seeking	Gravity
Peace	Turbulence	Ignorance

BLIND CURVES AHEAD
FEAR OF THE UNKNOWN

The unknown often carries an element of fear. Because what follows the end of physical existence is a major unknown, great mental, emotional, and philosophical energy has been expended to create belief systems that propose the existence of something more.

Our next set of fears center around losing those things that help *keep* us from death. Fears of losing food and shelter are then supplanted by the fear of losing objects in general. This creates attachments that bind a person to physical objects, and inhibit recognition of the existing connection with spirit.

Once basic survival is assured, the desire for survival *beyond* death pushes us to produce offspring. Being sexual also proves our vitality and theoretical longevity. After survival and sexual power are established, power over others and accumulation of comforting wealth help assuage our fears of losing our security.

After these security measures have been obtained, a lingering fear of death and the unknown moves us to explore the spiritual world. We can avoid studying cosmic issues for a while, but as older people, we become uncomfortable living in fear without some cosmic answers.

Our inability to answer the questions of existence creates fear of the future and uncertainty about the present. Instead, we become preoccupied with non-spiritual things that pose simple questions that are easier to answer, or we give the answering responsibility to divinity.

GENERAL OPERATIONS DIRECTOR
DIVINITY

Since we can't live physically beyond death, we can't know what lies beyond. We ease the fears that come from that ignorance and impotence by creating a powerful entity that *can* know and do all of the things we cannot.

We create an entity that is infinite, omnipotent, omnipresent, and in complete control. We further define this entity as not needing its own creation or ending; it simply *is* the cause and the conclusion. Then, if we can't answer a cosmic question, we need not fear. Our creation has the answer, even though the answer may not be revealed to us.

We then set ourselves up to have access to that being, or trust that this creation knows what s/he's doing and will take care of us. We trust that the great director of life's drama will have all the answers. We give this **G**eneral **O**perations **D**irector a different three-letter name.

Who are we?	Creations of … God
Why are we here?	To serve … God
How were we created?	By … God
What is Death?	A return to … God
Why do we have to die?	So we can be judged by …..God
Why is there pain & difficulty in life?	We don't heed the will of ....God
Why do bad things happen?	As a punishment from …... God
Why are things not in my control?	God … is in control
Why aren't there enough resources?	God only knows
How do we obtain true happiness?	Follow … God
What is really important in life?	God
What lasts forever?	God
What's the ultimate power in the universe?	God
Who controls the future?	Big Bankers (Oh, God!)
What should I do?	Put it in God's hands

Questions answered. Problems solved.

Since we would prefer to have all the answers and be like God, we imagine God to be like we are. It feels better to know that, like us, God has two arms, two legs, a body and a head. A true superbeing is rarely visualized as a turtle or a duck.

Problems arise when different thoughts and beliefs about God conflict. Though no one has ever actually returned alive from God's domain, rumors continue to circulate about God's position on contraception, abortion, wearing veils, the priesthood, the identity of the "chosen" people, etc. Pretty soon, arguments escalate into full-on conflicts between different factions. Pretty soon, people are destroying each other because they are absolutely sure that *they* know exactly what the Super Being really wants.

This sort of conflict results from the imprecise use of that three letter word that means something different to everyone. When we talk about "God," we try to jam a thousand concepts and issues into those three letters. Even though we use the term all the time, we are almost never thinking about the same attributes as the person with whom we are having the discussion. The result is confusion, equivocation, misinterpretation, and difficult feelings.

One solution to this problem is to avoid using the term "God" whenever possible. Instead, clarity is introduced if the specific subject under discussion is named as a quality or concept. When we describe things that are divine or godlike, it works better to name those qualities that appear in the column under Purity in Table 24-2. The term "Divinity" works better than "God" for many people.

Divinity is given many forms as a means to focus on its many aspects. Giving divinity form makes the divine more approachable and available. Terms such as

"Heavenly Father," or "Divine Mother" suggest figures that are familiar to most all of us. Personification of the divine into saintly forms such as Christ, Buddha, Krishna, Moses and Mohammed can also help us feel closer to the infinite.

Giving over all of our unknown and unanswerable questions to the Ultimate Professor can be a positive thing if it relieves the tension of uncertainty. But if there is no *true acceptance* of a higher G-Self, and if those difficult questions linger, the uncertainties will continue to eat away at our minds and health.

Ultimately, yoga and ayurveda describe "God" as a quality of character or consciousness. When your own consciousness qualities start to look like the first column in Table 24-2, it's time to notify those pointy-hat dudes at the Vatican that you're ready to go marching in.

VEHICLE REPOSSESSION
BEYOND BODY DEATH

If you are traveling to school and your vehicle totally breaks down, you don't end the journey at the spot where the car dies. You find another vehicle and continue on. In the same way, the spiritual journey does not end at physical death when the body-vehicle gives out. According to yogic and Ayurvedic philosophies, the death of the body does not mean the death of the spirit.

Many philosophies and religions support the idea that part of a person's existence continues after death, but what actually occurs remains unanswered. This great mystery is possibly the central philosophical question. What is death? Movement ceases, responses to stimulation are absent, the body decays, there is no apparent awareness, and the active state does not return. But is this always the case?

Some of the great practitioners of yoga have reportedly delayed death for hundreds of years. One of the first yogis to bring the practice to the United States, Paramahansa Yogananda, is said to have left his body intentionally while in a state of good health. His body, unlike most, did not decay for weeks, and the official autopsy report described an absence of many of the usual postmortem findings of body stiffness and tissue decay. This suggests that there is more to bodily death than a simple cessation of biochemical function.

Neem Karoli Baba, the yogi teacher of popular author Ram Dass, was also said to have lived hundreds of years. Other yogis have also reportedly returned to their lifeless bodies to the amazement of their followers. Some historians claim that Jesus learned this advanced yoga technique while in India during his "lost years," and that his return to his body was a result of that knowledge.

Experiences with ghosts and the paranormal have also persisted over many centuries, and have given support to the belief that some kind of "spirit" exists after the body is gone. Beliefs in angels, devils, and returning saints have survived despite the inability to fully document their existence scientifically.

Some part of human existence remains after the body has decayed. The vast majority of otherwise logical people repeatedly validate this claim. They do so, not only because such an acceptance explains the otherwise unexplainable, but because the special nature of the unison roar of the stadium crowd cannot be ignored.

PINK SLIP OR RENTAL?
IDENTIFICATION AS SPIRIT

The possible existence of spirit is one thing. How closely we are connected to it in our everyday lives is quite another.

The vast majority of us are too busy or too distracted by physical and mental concerns to spend much time with spiritual issues. According to yogic/ayurvedic philosophy, that's the exact trap that has been set for us. We come to the planet as spirit, but are so distracted by shiny cars, reality TV shows, and the nightly news that we completely lose touch with this most important of concepts:

> *"We are not human beings having a spiritual experience,*
> *We are spiritual beings having a human experience."*

> - Pierre Teilhard de Chardin

This is the universal, State-mandated Graduate Exit Exam. If you fail to accept this principle, you'll find yourself in the cosmic Principal's Office signing up for another lifetime of study complete with all the confusion that life-situations and the senses can bring. But if we *do* accept this concept, and if spirit becomes the point-of-view of daily life, then we are well on our way to graduating to a Summa Cum Laude State of Bliss.

But let's be clear. Simple as it may sound, continuously feeling, and experiencing spirit is one of the toughest courses we can take. Numerous life-situation pop quizzes, relationship reports, lost love labs, parental projects, thought theses, and life-trauma term papers will continuously test our awareness of the spirit that we truly are.

As we progress in our studies, and quietly spend more and more of our time as a spirit masquerading as a person, we will often find doors opening for us. People will usually respond to people with Purity qualities with their own brand of positivity.

Eventually, everything is seen through spiritual eyes. Difficulty is seen as education. The transient, limited, and shallow aspects of life no longer hold our attention, and we live in the present moment in a waking state of observational meditation. The roar of the sporting event G-Self crowd constantly resonates within us.

We are Spirit.

THE CUSTOMER IS ALWAYS
REINCARNATION

Most of us don't achieve behavioral perfection during one lifetime just as a student doesn't learn everything in one year of school. The concept of reincarnation allows for successive chances to learn our life-lessons and to make greater spiritual progress in the same way that students return to school year after year to gain enough knowledge to graduate. We will automatically be enrolled in the specific classes we need.

If we make the assumption that one never returns to Earth after bodily death, then perfection in spiritual education is never achieved, since life is difficult and we make many mistakes. If, in spite of this underachievement, a perfect, heavenly, after-death existence were granted, then there would be no reason to attempt life's difficult spiritual work!

Each person has the opportunity to complete the curriculum in one lifetime, or in stages (successive lifetimes) depending on which belief system is chosen. The yogic/ayurvedic philosophy is that the spiritual curriculum is rarely completed in one incarnation. In some ways, this takes the pressure off since it allows us to take life less seriously, and to move toward *feeling* our way toward spiritual harmony.

Accepting the concept of reincarnation helps with letting go of the idea that death is an experience to be feared. All our natural survival circuitry and ego requirements must be overcome to believe this, so it's one of the most difficult life lessons we are here to learn. But if we can go beyond the fear of death, many of our everyday fears that evolve from death fears can be overcome as well.

Most of the great saints and martyrs are put to this death test. They become great by truly accepting that death is not the end. It allows them to do great things. The difficulty of this lesson is illustrated by the small number who have completed it to perfection. Jesus, Buddha, Moses, Mohammed, and the saints and sages of many other religions are the prime examples.

The time it takes to complete the whole curriculum is a function of the individual spirit's will to advance. Whatever the timeline, it is comforting to believe that almost everyone will eventually pass the exit exams and graduate. In the meantime, we must learn to enjoy the unremitting call of the spiritual school bell.

BLUEPRINTS
INHERITED BEHAVIOR PATTERNS

Somehow, birds know how to hatch their eggs, puppies know how to suckle, and whales know how to swim at birth without any instruction. These instinctual behaviors are ingrained in the brains and minds of all newborns as a result of thousands of years of previous life experiences.

In the same way that these gross survival skills are transmitted from one life experience to the next, yogic/ayurvedic philosophy states that more subtle life experiences and behaviors find their way from one incarnation to the next.

Repeated mental and physical choices create patterns in the mind and consciousness that transcend death. These traits are known in yogic/ayurvedic terms as "Samskaras." These inherited tendencies can include preferences for certain sensations, activities, behaviors, environments, associations, and even specific memories, languages and abilities from previous lives.

It is impossible to confirm that an impression or behavior is the result of previous life activity, so attributing current behavior to a previous life can be viewed as a rationalization or a realization. "It must be a result of something I brought from a previous lifetime." Such "previous life influences" can serve as catch-all explanations for events that are otherwise difficult to explain.

Most previous life experiences are not consciously recalled. Ostensibly, this is so that a widening of interests and options can occur without a dominant influence of the past. Free will allows a person to change these behavior patterns by responding differently after re-experiencing problem issues during the current lifetime. These behavioral issues act as recurring personality quizzes that must be taken until a passing behavior is developed.

CONSUMER REPORTS
COMPARISON & JUDGMENT

It is essential for the traveler on the spiritual path to pay attention when the mind moves toward comparison, discrimination, and judgment.

Because yoga views separation and duality as the false conclusions of comparison, discrimination and judgment, it is important to see *yourself* as the person you are about to judge. Perhaps, at a previous moment or in a previous lifetime, you have had similar problems yourself but grew out of them. Therefore, *observe* the problem behavior of others as a reflection of your own continued need to avoid the same difficult type of activity. Simply observe, and remain *non-judgmental* whenever possible.

On the other hand, many philosophies teach the development of "Right Association" which is spending time with the spiritually inclined ("Satsang") and away from those whose character is *judged* as negative. The resolution of this judgement conflict is often one's demonstration of exemplary behavior for people whose behavior is difficult. No effort is made to recruit them into a spiritual community. When they are ready to participate and learn, they should be admitted to the School of Life Lessons.

STAFF MEETINGS
RELATIONSHIPS

One way that we learn about our patterns of thinking and feeling is by observing our own behavior when we interact with other people. Whatever problem behaviors we have, they are usually brought out in our relationships.

If we can step back from the interactions that occur long enough to observe our reactions to different situations, then we can learn and grow. If we immediately blame the other person, then we lose the opportunity to examine our own reactive behavior. If we do see our own behavior, then we have the opportunity to make changes.

Some philosophers believe that the problems we encounter are the very issues we need to resolve. The problems we don't handle well will keep coming back to us, whether as a result of predictable circumstances, or by divine educational directive.

For this reason, ayurvedic psychology recommends that we see relationships as an educational opportunity and as a reflection of our educational needs. When we sign up for a relationship with a spouse, friend, or boss, then the "problems" they create become our lessons. Relationships can also lift us up and inspire us. Yoga and ayurveda often suggest that we view these positives as manifestations of the divinity in the world.

SMOOTH IDLE, ROUGH IDLE
SPIRITUAL PLEASURE & PAIN

Pain and pleasure are the basic motivators of our conduct. If we want liberation from slavery to pain and pleasure, then the mind must be trained by some restriction of physical pleasure, and by the acceptance of some physical pain. It must also be trained by the influence of spiritual pleasure, known by terms such as "grace" and "bliss," and by the spiritual pain of "heartbreak" and "despair."

Ultimately, spiritual practices are intended to move us away from despair and toward the uplifting. If they don't strengthen or lighten the heart, they should probably be abandoned. Negative spiritual practices that reprimand, impose guilt, and/or invoke the "not good enough" or the "didn't do it right" messages should be discarded.

Practices of "austerity," however, are an important part of the yogic path. Austerity is the practice of resisting the fulfillment of desires. Fulfilling desires does not satisfy them, according to ayurveda, but simply creates more cravings.

Pleasure is often accepted in yoga and other renunciative philosophies if it applies to pleasure derived from the divine. Rituals that induce this type of pleasure can include group singing, prayer, chanting, meditation, service, and simple association with other positive, spiritual people.

AVOIDING THE D.E.A.
BEYOND DESIRE, EGO, AND ATTACHMENT

Desire, Ego, and Attachment (DEA) are the mind functions that pose the greatest challenges to peace and contentment. All of us must contend with the DEA which is known on the streets of Yogatown as the "Three-headed Monster."

The DEA is all about our connections with the non-spiritual, transient, sensual world. We may bring DEA issues from previous lifetimes, and we use our

present incarnation to develop the understanding that physical objects, pleasures, and ego gratifications have only limited and transient utility. The yoga student learns to experience and accept many of these worldly things, but without developing an *attachment* to them.

This dispassionate renunciation of worldly desire, ego, and attachment, is a difficult and lifelong (or multiple-life-long) process. Many situations we encounter pull us in the direction of the DEA, but yoga students follow a program of meditation, restraints, and austerities that help them go beyond these attachments and toward a connection with "higher truths."

SKIDDING OFF THE ROAD
ERROR & SIN

We attend the school of life to learn from our mistakes as well as from our successes. If we didn't make mistakes, we wouldn't need to be here on the planet with all its difficulties.

The concept of "sin" is as curious as it is vague. The term is said to come from "missing the mark" in archery practice. This view of sin as a practical part of the learning process is in stark contrast to the common concept of sin as a manifestation of some inherently evil part of the human species. In yoga philosophy, we are not evil, but are simply prone to making mistakes as part of the learning process.

While it is important that we eventually learn from these mistakes, not everyone has developed the awareness to learn quickly. We need to be patient with ourselves and with others who are also unschooled at the beginning of the semester.

TIRE SLASHERS
EVIL FORCES

Pleasure and pain are intimately connected. If pleasure is experienced, pain will eventually follow. Pleasure in moderation usually leads to health, while pain usually leads to illness unless it awakens us to behavior that is healthier.

Pain and pleasure are mainly sensory *impressions*, while purity and negativity are inherited, or behavioral *choices*. Negativity is said to exist in order to provide a contrast so that we can recognize purity and the positive. Negativity is also viewed as a temptation that needs to be rejected.

When a person lives a life completely dominated by the Negative qualities described in Table 24-2, they often wind up causing great harm, pain, and ill health to both themselves and to others. They develop a mental and spiritual personality that is summarized as "evil."

The term "evil" is also confusing, because it means many different things to different people. Some believe that evil is connected to an actual "devil" or that evil behavior is deliberate or non-reversible. Others routinely describe their political opponents as "evil." This vague term should be discarded in favor of a description of a person's specific character problem.

If one spends a lifetime in the negative column, a negative personality remains after the body dies. It will return to a different body for another try at learning the pure or the active, or it may linger outside of the life-classroom in a nebulous astral alley as a ghostly collection of negative spiritual traits with an unfinished agenda. Negative personalities affect us in like schoolyard punks. If we hang out with delinquents, we'll soon be in trouble.

Can evil possess us without our actions or our choosing? Can we be "cursed" by an outside evil influence? Such invasive, negative spirits are said to be rare, and are said to be unable to withstand the influence of those who are strongly grounded in purity. Using that saintly strength, these bullies can be chased out of the school exorcise yard.

DESIGN ENGINEERS RULE
CONSCIOUSNESS IS PRIMARY FOR HEALTH

It is difficult for many of us to accept that a spiritual foundation is important for good physical health. People are usually born healthy without any prior spiritual practice, and they can stay healthy for a long time without one, as long as the mind does not lead them to unhealthy behavior.

The mind-driver of the vehicle will operate as it has been trained. The employees in a post office will follow the style of the postmaster, and the students in a class will respond to the directions and demeanor of the instructor. There needs to be a monitor for the mind, and spiritual practice is that overseer.

Like a teenager, the mind is prone to rebellion, but it is generally happier with the security of parental guidance. A teenager will only clean up his/her room if a higher (parental) power takes charge. If there is no one to train and monitor the mind, then it will wander into the circus of self-indulgence and error. Just ask

Pinocchio. He needed Jiminy Cricket. England needed Gandhi, and America needed Martin Luther King and Dr. Phil.

There needs to be a philosophical outlet for mind-stress that explains pain, and lessens it. Religious traditions provide such answers as well as spiritual routines that allow the mind to feel comfortable in predictability.

RULES OF THE ROAD
CONSCIENCE

Most of us have an internal concept of healthy and moral behavior that is often overcome by immediate sensual needs and desires. When that happens, "crimes against wisdom" ("Prajnaparadha") create behavior that eventually leads to ill health.

The ability to hear and to follow this internal wisdom and to accept its delayed benefits is one of the hallmarks of the mature and enlightened person. We are either children in need of immediate gratification, or adults who are able to delay it. Spiritual practices help us become adults.

It is important to feel comfortable with the spiritual rules that one is following. They should make sense, feel loving, and be supportive. If they aren't, if they send negative messages, or if they are imposed externally, they may induce rebellion rather than reassurance.

Developing the ability to follow one's internal guide is usually a long, trial and error process. External resources such as support groups and mentors are important initially, but ultimately, the strength to remain on course must come from within. Often, it comes from the pervasive awareness of both the i-self and the G-Self.

CHAPTER 25:
DRIVING STYLES
Philosophies
and Religions

THE DIFFICULT QUESTIONS

"Hey, Reggie. You there?"

"Yeah, Margo."

"Regg. Are you sober today, boy?"

"Stone-cold."

"Did you say "stoned-cool?!"

"I wish. But, no. I'm painfully clear-headed for the moment."

"Well, in that case, we need you to drive Babaji from Bonny Dune to Mt. Madonna. D'you remember how to get there?"

"I do."

"How long shall I say it'll take you?"

"Twenty. Twenty-five."

"Will do."

… Reggie's not too big on religion, but he likes old Babaji. So does everybody else here in Santa Cruz. Nothing like watching someone take up jogging when they turn eighty! Seriously! Every morning at 6 am, white robes and all, there he goes, running down the road, grinning … with disciples huffing and puffing behind him!

Myself, I was raised ultra-religious by my mom. I think the reason Mom loved the church so much was because she felt so guilty about trapping my Dad with my pregnancy. That plus the habit of being raised in a strict Lutheran family in Ladysmith, B.C., and going to church almost every day.

I do see where religion can be helpful in providing some sense of discipline and order. It gives us answers to the tough questions in life, and explains a lot of the crap that we all go through.

But there's a difference between going through the motions of a religious life, and actually living those principles every day from the heart. My mom went to church every weekend because, in between weekends, she was a bitch on wheels! The way she blamed and berated everyone around her, especially my Dad. The way she held a grudge. She was the least forgiving pseudo-Christian on the planet!

715

For her, the *only* way was Christianity. She was right, and every non-Lutheran was damned! She hated it when I took religion and philosophy classes in college, and started talking about other religions. The idea that there could be other ways to God was just impossible for her mind to handle.

And she was a thankless person; completely ungrateful for everything she had been given. She was a total phony. At church, she was very upright and "proper." But at home, she remembered none of the thoughts behind the sermons and the hymns we listened to and sang week after week.

When I got into yoga philosophy, she rolled her eyes and acted like I was the world's biggest fool, even though practicing the yoga poses and the meditation was clearly helping me turn my life around. She even tried to make me get rid of the little Buddha in my own apartment just because it made *her* feel uncomfortable.

Living in S. Cruz helped cure me of Mom's hypocrisy. Anything goes in the People's Republic of Santa Cruz. It's damn near impossible to feel self-conscious here.

Everyone is part of the big play.

CRUISE CONTROL
RELIGIOUS ANSWERS

If a religion or philosophy is fully and willingly accepted, it can provide comfort, order, and predictability, as well as answers to the classical life questions. It can provide a world view of existence, and appropriate behavioral guidelines.

Religion also deals with issues that are beyond scientific answers, and too difficult for many people to tackle. Religion can provide pre-packaged conclusions, dissolve doubts, abolish anguish, and remove the need for critical thinking.

However, if a religion is not willingly accepted, then it can become a serious obstacle to true spiritual growth. Religions often become bogged down in ritual, dogma, and social stratification. They become the essence of comparison, judgment, ego, attachment, and discrimination, all of which are antithetical to ayurvedic and yogic philosophy.

Religions often leave behind their underlying philosophies and become social clubs that can be both useful and harmful. They frequently compress many divergent issues into one doctrine, and require total adherence as the price of belonging.

Individuals should come to their *own* philosophical conclusions, rather than being told what to think or feel. Even if the end results of a personal search are the same as the religion's teachings, traveling the spiritual path can only be done with one's own feet.

THE ONLY WAY TO DRIVE
SPIRITUAL EXCLUSIVITY

One of the main drawbacks of narrowly following any religion or philosophy is that we begin to feel that the religious choices we've made *for ourselves* are best for everybody.

This is a fairly natural result of the fearful ego's need to separate and defend us from whatever is different. After all, what if we have made the *wrong* religious choice? What if another sect or religion is right, and we have the wrong beliefs? That would make us inferior and them superior!

The ego can't go there. By definition, *they* must be wrong and we must be right. This exclusivity is not accepted by yoga and ayurveda which teach that there are many paths to the realization of the same truths. Ayurveda is built on the foundation that all people are different, and, therefore, they all may have different (religious) needs. Ultimately, however, the human search for love is understood as the unifying experience.

Feeling separate from others (duality) has been described as a universal disease that most of us are on here the planet to grow beyond. If we do not recognize some level of unity with others, then we remain bound to the downward cycle of comparison, judgment, discrimination, and exclusion. This is the nature of human bondage, and the cause of much human misery.

WALKING THE TALK
LIVING YOUR BELIEFS

No matter what philosophy, spirituality, or religion we "practice," if we don't try to *live* our beliefs at every moment, then we are just playing with ourselves.

Praying at church on Sunday morning, then cursing & drinking at the football game on Sunday afternoon is an obvious example of spiritual hypocrisy. The problems with this type of hypocrisy include a nagging subconscious guilt that slowly eats away at us, and a loss of self-esteem. When self-esteem is lost, even more pain is created. That pain generates more "pain-killing" behavior that further damages self-esteem. This negative spiral continues to build on itself, and results in mental and physical illness, as well as further spiritual emptiness.

It is important to be able to look into the mirror in the morning and see a person who is honest with him/herself as well as with others.

Of course, it's virtually impossible to *completely* achieve the perfection toward which we strive. Even Christ, Buddha, Mohammad and Gandhi had their faults, but they kept on trying to live their beliefs. Yoga and ayurveda teach that we may eventually equal their achievements, but it may take us a few more lifetimes. Much of life is about discovering what makes a person feel worthy, confident, and happy about who they are. Find those things and live them as much as possible!

CHAPTER 26:
HIGHWAY MARKERS
Spiritual Milestones

THE BRIDGE

… Did you ever hear the one about the motorcycle biker who's riding alone down California Coast Highway One, when the sky darkens with clouds, and he hears the voice of God booming out from above:

> *"Lefty! I am granting you one wish! It can be anything at all. What is your desire?!"*

So Lefty pulls over, thinks about it for a minute and says "O.K., Lord. Build me a bridge to Hawaii so that I can ride over to Maui anytime I want."

> *"Your request is far too unrealistic and wasteful! Just think of the resources that would be squandered building a bridge of such length and depth! Make another wish, my son."*

Lefty thinks for a while. Finally he gives in and says, "OK, Lord, then help me understand my wife! I really want to know how she feels inside, what she's thinking when she gives me the silent treatment, why she cries so easily over nothing, what she really means when she says there's 'nothing wrong,' and how I can make this woman truly happy?!"

> …

> *"Do you want two lanes or four on that bridge?"*

Of course, I always wondered what I would ask for if God or a Genie were to appear and grant *me* a wish or two. I know that what I'd ask for *now* is different from when I was younger, and that it has nothing to do with women!

When I was in my teens and twenties, all I wanted to do was party and play football. I didn't give a hoot about my schoolwork. But my parents were old-country strict, and doing well in school was a duty, not an option. When I didn't live up to their expectations, they began to treat me like I was an adopted, retarded orphan. Sure, I knew that my job was to do well in school, and to do my chores around the house. But school was so frikin' boring and stupid. I figured it was enough that I did most of my damn chores.

Yeah, I hit my peak in high school. That's when I was king. Football was my life. I can even remember giving my required speech in English class … on football! I was the starting quarterback every year since my Sophomore year and everybody knew who I was. And, being the only white guy on the Ravensbrook team also brought me a lot of extra attention. Back then, I was known as "Supercoose"—the white guy that all the tough black guys respected. Totally boss.

After I finished school and got out into the world on my own, I began to need all the necessities, and crave all the toys. I had to have my own place to live, a righteous stereo, a boss theater system, a hot car, and season tickets to the Niners, Giants and Sharks.

But it wasn't 'til I got married the first time that the real purchasing projects started. Man! We had to have everything from a house in the right neighborhood, to the best frikin' brand of waffle iron! Then the kids came along, and almost every minute seemed like an effort at keeping up with *their* growing needs.

After my first divorce ruined me financially, I had to start all over again. I was too stupid to learn from that experience, and had to repeat the whole process after the Inferior Court of the State of California colluded with my second "wife" to pummel me into poverty again.

So here I am, working to stay afloat and trying to finally learn how to enjoy myself. It's not easy to do on a shoestring, but I still get laid from time to time. I even got one lady to take me to the Big Island for a week, and another to take me to Bermuda!

My apartment is no showplace, but I still have my big screen TV, my home brewery equipment, and my ganja garden out back in the little green house. I've got other more exciting things that I'm into, but that's personal. You understand.

But now that I'm getting older, and my frikin' health is starting to falter, I *do* think more about the end, and about the "God" questions that I ignored when I was in Sunday school. I give Margo a hard time, but she's been pretty cool about keeping her day-to-day issues connected to her "spiritual goals," as she puts it.

She always says …

"Reggie. Are you on the planet, dude?"

See what I mean? … "Uh, … What planet is that, Margo?"

"Planet Hollywood for you, babe! I got a real celeb for you to pick up if you want to come by the office and get the limo!"

"Who is it?"

"You won't believe this, Regg…"

"Yeah?…"

"Ok. Who's your full-on favorite Bay Area celeb?"

"Uh …Robin Williams?! Oh Shit! Tell me it's old Morky, Margo!"

"Female…"

"…Sharon Stone?!..."

"Politically correct…"

"Uh, …Nancy Pelosi?..."

"Black, dude…"

"… not … not … Whoopi?!..."

Try gay!

… ?? … uh, … who the … Degeneres? (no) … Who the hell is it?...

DESTINATIONS
GOALS OF LIFE

In yoga philosophy, there are spiritual stages through which most people pass during their lives. In the same way that the body grows, develops, and ages, the mind and the spirit should move from basic necessities to exploration, recognition, and union with the divine. Most of our culture gives only tangential attention to the spiritual, and we often remain unaware of the big picture. We see the temporal trees, but not the spiritual forest.

Our religious orientation may re-direct us toward the spiritual, and may provide milestones to follow in the effort to achieve spiritual goals. In yogic and Ayurvedic philosophies, many of those basic Goals of Life are described in Table 26-1.

TABLE 26-1: **GOALS OF LIFE**

1. Experience the World

2. Freedom from the DEA (Desire, Ego, Attachment)

3. Develop Spiritual Qualities

4. Remove Non-spiritual Qualities

5. Develop of self-control

6. Distinguish the Transient from the Eternal

7. Peace

8. Love

9. Joy

10. Contentment

11. Bliss

12. Service

13. Surrender

14. Merge with Divinity

15. Absence of Need for Reincarnation

TABLE 26-2: **SPIRITUAL AND NON-SPIRITUAL CHARACTERISTICS**

SPIRITUAL

1. Fearlessness
2. Purity of heart
3. Knowledge of God
4. Charity
5. Sensory Control

6. Sacrifice
7. Scriptural Study
8. Austerity
9. Straightforwardness
10. Harmlessness

11. Truthfulness
12. Non-Anger
13. Renunciation
14. Peacefulness
15. Honesty

16. Compassion
17. Non-covetousness
18. Gentleness
19. Modesty
20. Non-fickleness

21. Vigor
22. Forgiveness
23. Fortitude
24. Purity of mind
25. Non-hatred
26. Humility

27. Reflectivity
28. Sacrifice
29. Wisdom
30. Surrender
31. Faith

32. Keeping good company

33. Contentment
34. Grace
35. Equanimity
36. Generosity

NON-SPIRITUAL

1. Hypocrisy
2. Arrogance
3. Conceit
4. Anger
5. Harshness

6. Ignorance
7. Materialism
8. Deception
9. Covetousness
10. Fickleness

11. Hatred
12. Self-pride
13. Stubbornness
14. Ignorance
15. Wealth preoccupation

16. Sensory intoxication
17. Lust
18. Haughtiness
19. Passion
20. Hoarding
21. Gluttony

SLEEPING PASSENGER
SPIRITUAL UNEMPLOYMENT

If we are unable to deal with the difficult spiritual quizzes, we can always drop out of metaphysical school. Many people do, and they can be fairly happy enjoying the physical and mental pleasures of everything from grandchildren to TV wrestling shows. Modern culture makes it easy to keep our interests superficial.

As we age, however, most of us begin to realize the limitations of sensual indulgence. The body starts to weaken and painful body sensations become more common. The approach of death raises spiritual questions that we can no longer ignore. We can either find a spiritual path to follow, or we can continue to feel unfulfilled by living without any of these crucial answers.

According to yoga and ayurveda, there are certain stages in life through which most of us pass on the way to finding spiritual answers.

MECHANIC'S APPRENTICE
DUTY

One of the four pillars of spiritual life is to perform one's "duty" in the world ("Dharma"). Righteousness is the first duty – to earn one's livelihood by honest means.

In yoga philosophy, there are different duties for different parts of society. According to tradition, a member of the intellectual class focuses on the performance of mental and behavioral tasks. The duties of a member of the laboring class are more physical. Although duties are often grouped by social class in the older yogic tradition, all can benefit from cultivating the qualities of all types of people. No matter what the level of society in which one is born, it is important to avoid the traps that come with expected social and personal behavior.

Duty also means developing certain qualities and abilities. Developing *serenity* means spending time on spiritual activities, and diverting the mind from worldly objects and achievements. It involves developing self-control that creates a spiritual focus for the sense organs. The duty to observe *austerity* means channeling sensory desires toward Greater-Self interest, and away from the small self. *Purity* is supported by physical cleanliness as well a cleanliness of character. This includes taking food that is wholesome and pure.

Forbearance means being patient and understanding without hatred, even after injury by others. *Uprightness* means developing candor, honesty, openness, sincerity, and truthfulness in one's actions. *Knowledge* of the outer, non-intellectual world as well as the scriptures and philosophical, theoretical teachings is also suggested. *Wisdom* on subjects of direct practical nature should also be acquired. Developing *faith* in the power of the divine conscious principle is also a duty of the spiritual aspirant.

BRINGING HOME THE BACON
ACCUMULATION

In the next stage of life ("Artha"), accumulation of material resources is emphasized. Developing the ability to provide the necessities of life for one's family is an acknowledged requirement, and can be done while developing spiritually.

Going beyond providing the necessities can bring problems of excess accumulation, and may bind the collector to their maintenance and upgrading.

While devouring Wall Street, it is important to remember that making money and obtaining possessions is not the ultimate goal. If one can maintain this spiritual perspective on accumulation, then it is OK to achieve financial success. The principles of Right Action should not be compromised in the process of accumulation. Regrettably, modern society makes this combination extremely difficult since "wrong" behavior is often the way that material success is obtained. Selling misogynistic rap music or violent videos is not consistent with the ayurvedic/yogic definition of success.

ROAD TRIPS & HOLIDAY VACATIONS
APPRECIATION

Once the necessities of life have been secured, it is time to more deeply experience and appreciate life's positive pleasures such as freedom, and loving kindness.

It is natural for the mind and the physical body to desire pleasure. If pleasures and desires are completely suppressed in excessive austerity, then they build up inside the mind and weigh heavily on the consciousness. Suppression can create frustration and resentment that can obstruct progress toward letting go of attachments.

To manage this type of emotional constipation, it is important to experience the pleasures of life ("Kama"), but in a way that allows the spiritual seeker to maintain a perspective of separation from pleasure.

From the outset, it should be recognized that the experience of pleasure is a reflection of the experience of divinity and the Greater Self. In some way, pleasure should connect the individual with the Greater Consciousness. It must be learned and remembered that pleasure is not something that can be owned or retained. On the contrary, it is something that must be released, as everything must eventually be released when the spirit leaves the body.

Life's pleasures must, therefore, be experienced with some neutrality and moderation, and without excessive desire, attachment, or indulgence. They must ultimately be recognized as pleasant way stations on the road to something even more important.

PERMANENT VACATION
LIBERATION

The word "liberation" is another confusing term with as many meanings as the number of people who use the word.

On a macro level, minorities can be liberated from discrimination, women can be liberated from traditional social roles, or an entire population can be liberated from occupation by a foreign power. At a more personal level, couples can be liberated as a result of divorce, and individuals can be liberated from addictions.

For the purposes of this discussion, liberation is used in the spiritual sense and is taken to mean freedom from preoccupation with non-physical difficulties ("Moksha"). It is a mental/spiritual term. One can be mentally and spiritually liberated while alive with significant personal problems or physical pain. Complete liberation differs from specific issue liberation in the same way that two weeks vacation differs from permanent retirement in comfort, safety, security, contentment, and happiness.

In order to get such an extended vacation, most of the spiritual processes need to be mastered. Needless to say, achieving that type of broad and consistent awareness is an overwhelming task that few people can successfully complete. However, many philosophers feel that simply following the path *toward* this goal is liberation enough for any one lifetime.

Once again, reincarnation theory allows for multiple return efforts at reaching these goals. It's an individual choice. You can either move in the *direction* of sainthood, just mark time, or give up altogether and backslide to become a dung beetle or tobacco company executive.

The short list of requirements for the graduating class of the Liberal Arts College of Liberation consists of the courses of study and practice listed in Table 26-3 on the next page.

What could be simpler?!

Most of us are like the perpetual doctoral students who spend year after year working on (or taking a break from) their Ph.D. dissertations. Since it takes considerable time to finish our spiritual tasks, it's important that we do one thing with some consistency:

Enjoy and Learn from the *Journey!*

TABLE 26-3: **LIBERATION CURRICULUM SUMMARY**

1. Develop self-discipline.
2. Master the Eight Parts of Yoga (Table A-14).
3. Perform Selfless Service.

4. Develop a Positive Mental/Spiritual Nature (Tables 24-2,26-2).
5. Cultivate Purity (Tables 24-2,26-2).
6. Achieve the Goals of Life (Table 26-1).

7. Live with an Expanded Awareness in the Present Moment.
8. Follow the Principles of the Noble Eight-fold Path (Chapter 27).
9. Ditch the DEA (Desire, Ego, & Attachment).

10. Achieve a Meditative Union with the Divine.
11. See the Divine G-Self in Everything.

CHAPTER 27:
PASSENGER MAKEOVERS
Spiritual Therapies

MORE THAN DUMB LUCK

… Yes, I used to be a real screw-up. Believe it or not, I was into partying big time in high school. I'd sneak out at night and meet my friends, even on weeknights. We'd basically get drunk and just drive around. Radio, jokes, smokes, coke. Checkin' out the guys, maybe burn some weed. One time, Jen had to pull me out of a ditch by the side of the road, when I got out of the car to puke, and lost my balance. Another time, on a trip to Austria with the marching band, I got caught drinking with Jen, Tracy, Peterman, and Sloan, and got suspended from school for a week. Mom was right there to ground my butt for a month. I deserved it.

When I left home and went off to "college," I was no student. Dude, I was FREE! It was great to be on my own and have someone else pay all the bills! It was one huge social safari that only ended when I flunked out in my sophomore year. I deserved that too.

I worked a lot of crumby jobs after that. Mostly in the "food service industry." I got really lonely just working, and got into smoking weed pretty much 24/7. After a while, I started seeing a shrink and doing anti-depressants too, but it all seemed to drag on without any purpose. The drugs helped for a while. But I started getting sick with the flu all the time. It never seemed to go away. My apartment was way too cold.

It's one thing to be messed up mentally, or to be sick and overwhelmed with physical stuff. But it's another thing to be a lost soul. I knew that sooner or later, I had to deal with the "God" thing, but I was too cool back then to have anything to do with religion, especially after seeing my Mom's religious hypocrisy.

It took me forever to make the time for real divinity to find its way into my everyday life and into my heart-self. Life kept me so distracted, I never had time for long-term philosophical stuff. At least I *thought* I didn't have time. Somehow, I had enough time for TV, but not for meditation, or church, or bible study, or any thinking about the fact that we are really spiritual beings.

When I was young, I din't think I needed God. I thought I could figure it all out on my own. I didn't want anybody telling me what to believe. It was only when I really hit bottom that I finally accepted that I needed help. Lots of help! It was only when I began to believe that I was not alone that I found the energy to pull myself up again.

I used to think it was just dumb luck that I met my teachers. Later on, I decided to believe that those meetings were *meant* to happen. I couldn't prove the destiny thing, but I decided that it just *felt* better to believe in destiny. I decided to *feel* a little more often than I *thought*. I decided to view my life as something that would result in my growing emotionally, and becoming a better person. I decided to *believe* that all the crap that happened to me took place to teach me some worthwhile lesson.

It took me a long time to recognize the questions that my problems were asking me. I began to open myself up to different ways of thinking about things, and not seeing myself as being alone and separate anymore. I began to get into routines that reminded me of spiritual things.

I turned off my TV cold turkey. I've been TV sober for seven years, now.

It felt so much better to be thinking about the positives instead of worrying, and moaning all the time. I changed my "self-talk."

What felt really good was to get into community service. At first, it felt weird because I thought I was just using more unfortunate people to make myself feel better. Then I decided that it was a total "win-win" situation! After a while, the whole thing began to feel more natural. People are supposed to spend their extra energy helping others instead of getting more for themselves.

I know I've still got a long way to go. I still make mistakes and get sidetracked. I still need to be better with people. I need to learn to forgive my Mom for being such a phony bitch, and my Dad for his drunken cowardice.

But I just can't seem to do it. Even though I understand how they grew up with …

"Hey, Margo. … … You … you there?" …

"What is it, Regg?"

"Margo, … I … I need … an ambulance…"

"A what?!"

"An … ambulance … ambulance …"

"WHAT FOR?! WHERE?!"
…

"REGGIE? … … REGGIE?! … WHERE ARE YOU?!"
…

"REGGIE?!…"

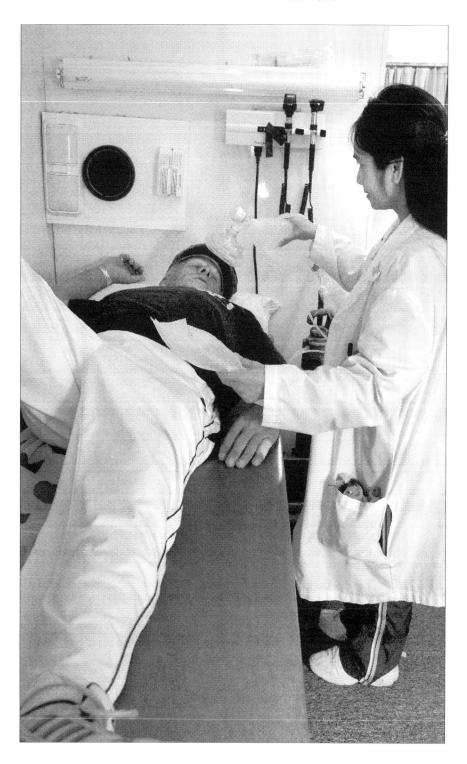

PASSENGER MAKEOVERS
SPIRITUAL THERAPIES

According to ayurveda, the body is a physical precipitation of the mind, and the mind is a condensation of the spirit. So developing spiritually is an extremely important process for long-term mental and physical health.

The ultimate goal of the life-process is the development of spiritual health. It may take the onset of old age and the approach of death to force us to actually face this issue, but for those whose concerns go beyond soap operas, this set of inescapable spiritual issues cannot be ignored.

TRASH IN THE BACK SEAT
MENTAL & SPIRITUAL POLLUTION

If we can recognize pointless mind-activity, then we are well on our way to quieting the mind. Mind-quieting is a necessary step for clearing mental and spiritual pollution (Chapter 23).

Most of the time, we experience difficulties because the true spiritual nature of the world is covered up with mind-cluttering objects and activity. The mind is repeatedly lured away from the divine by the senses, and sensory-seeking activities take over. Activity is the key ingredient in this process. The mind seeks activity, no matter how pointless or destructive.

Recognizing spiritual trash is an important part of building spiritual strength. The symptoms of absent or wrong spiritual practice include those characteristics described as "Negativity" in Chapter 24.

If you sense that your life is dominated by some of the spiritual pollutants noted in Table 27-1 below, you need spiritual healing!

TABLE 27-1: **SYMPTOMS OF SPIRITUAL POLLUTION**

Anxiety	Vengeance
Guilt	Inequality
Sin	Exclusivity
Judgment	Individuality
Comparison	Buying and Selling
Fear	Noise
Negativity	Living in the Past
Desire	Sensuality
Ego	Violence
Attachment	Anger
Loneliness	Stress
Separation (Duality)	Preoccupation w/ the Transient

Initially, most of us behave like spiritual two-year-olds, and make a mess of things. We are then meant to discover the effects of those mistakes, and to make repeated efforts toward peace and contentment. It's a long process with no quick fixes. That's why it's called spiritual "practice."

Don't feel too bad about messing up the back seat of the cab with your spiritual trash. Even famous movie stars do it. It's difficult to avoid this problem in a world that functions as a result of the production, distribution, sale, and resale of certifiable spiritual garbage. No television network executive, or violent video game distributor will ever find spiritual repose as long as their carnage and negativity permeate our mental airwaves.

BODY SHOP
PHYSICAL THERAPIES

It's hard to be spiritual when you have a backache. The primary goal of the physical aspect of yoga is to prepare the body to be comfortable for spiritual work. If your back is throbbing, your mind will go the spine, and will not be quieted in meditation. Mind-quieting is necessary for spiritual development.

For that reason, we take care of the body, and use awareness practices to avoid distractions. Some physical techniques that are used are reviewed in Table 27-2.

TABLE 27-2: PHYSICAL-SPIRITUAL SUPPORT METHODS

1. Fresh, Clean Food
2. Body-type Appropriate Food
3. Robust Digestion
4. Quality Rebalancing
5. Yoga Postures
6. Exercise
7. Breathing Exercises
8. Daily Routine
9. Herbal Remedies
10. Cleansing Techniques
11. Rejuvenation
12. Advanced Techniques (Part Five)

Clearly, this is a heavy load to carry. It should be remembered that the learning process is intended to be lifelong. Hopefully, we can maintain enough physical health to sustain a routine that promotes spiritual development into old age and beyond.

PSYCHED
MENTAL THERAPIES

For spiritual progress to be made, the chattering mind must be quieted. The breathing techniques described in Chapter 8 are especially important in this process, as are the techniques described in the Chapter 22 on Constructive Defense Mechanisms, and Chapter 23 on Behavior Pattern Changes.

We must also become aware of the anesthetics and diversions we use (see Chapters 20 and 21), and the stories we are playing in our heads.

Some of the essential aspects of mind therapy are given below in Table 27-3.

TABLE 27-3: **MENTAL-SPIRITUAL SUPPORT METHODS**

1. Physical Therapies
2. Restraints & Observances
3. Breathing Techniques
4. Meditation Preparation & Practice
5. Daily Routine

6. Healthy Mind Food
7. Mental Quality Re-balancing
8. Mental Exercise
9. Workplace Adjustments
10. Relationship Adjustments

11. Cleansing Techniques
12. Anesthetic & Diversion Awareness
13. Negative Story Awareness
14. Constructive Defenses
15. Behavior Patten Changes

16. Letting Go
17. Energy Practices
18. Visual Techniques
19. Sound
20. Phrase Repetition
21. Music
22. Color
23. Gemstones
24. Astrology

If one is deeply stuck in mental doldrums, it is difficult to jump from stagnation to spiritual work. The intermediate step of moving from inertia to activity is often necessary. Once into activity, awareness of the spiritual can move that activity in spiritual directions. When spirit is recognized, one can let go of activity and move into unambitious calm and the bliss that can accompany a more spiritual existence.

In ayurvedic medicine, psychology and mental health are closely connected to spirituality, so spiritual effort is necessary. Most modern psychology is non-spiritual by design, but most ayurvedic psychologists hold that spirituality is essential for mental health since the mind is a condensation of spirit.

BACK SEAT CLEANUP
SPIRITUAL THERAPIES

Once the body and mind are in good shape, then spiritual progress becomes easier. It is not necessary to have a perfectly healthy body and mind for spiritual advances to be made, but not being distracted by mind and body helps a great deal.

Mind quieting allows for introspection, meditation, and natural spiritual evolution. For that reason, many of the *mind* healing techniques (Table 27-3) are also spiritual healing techniques. Beyond those and the physical methods described in Table 27-2, some additional approaches are outlined below in Table 27-4.

TABLE 27-4: **SPIRITUAL SUPPORT METHODS**

1. Physical Therapies
2. Mental Therapies
3. Witnessing Awareness
4. Meditation
5. Phrase Repetition

6. Rituals
7. Noble Eight-fold Path
8. Avoiding the DEA
9. Living in the Present Moment
10. Living from the Heart

11. Surrender
12. Selfless Service
13. s-self Awareness
14. G-Self Awareness
15. Seeing Divinity in Everything

One part of yoga is changing the nature of a person's consciousness. This area, known as "Tantra," makes use of many subtle techniques including color, sound, gemstones, phrase repetition, deity visualization, deity identification, and worship to help raise the awareness to a higher level. Taking vows concerning morality can also be involved. Channeling sexual energy toward creating a connection with the divine is a well-known aspect of Tantra that is often misused for the sole purpose of achieving sensual pleasure.

In addition, certain ayurvedic herbs are used to assist with spiritual efforts. Brahmi, jatamamsi, shankapushpi, and jyotishmati are among those recommended for use in specific circumstances.

Other spiritual goals include allowing yourself to just "be" instead of constantly being a "doer." Finding harmony with nature and the seasonal changes is very helpful. Developing an understanding of one's place in the universe, and putting life goals into perspective are processes that help heal the troubled spirit.

Witnessing awareness, living from the heart, and surrender to the divine remain crucial to spiritual advancement. Recognizing what is transient and what lasts allows us to live in the present moment without clinging to the past or dwelling on the future. After many years of practice, divinity becomes ingrained in our nature, and we can no longer separate it from whatever else we are.

WHAT WE CHOOSE TO SEE
PERCEPTUAL/ATTENTION CHOICES

Either consciously or subconsciously, we choose to give our attention to certain things. Those are the things we truly love.[87]

When we *choose* to give our attention to the non-spiritual, the superficial, the mundane, and the limiting, then our lives take on those characteristics. If we decide to give our attention to the special, unlimited, and extraordinary concepts, our lives become special in those ways.

The way we *choose* to perceive something can completely alter its character. The liquid in the half-full glass will be more satisfying then the same liquid found in the half empty one. One choice leads to a heavenly existence, while the other creates its own hell.

Why would anyone knowingly choose limitation over liberation? Part of the reason is that the limited is more easily grasped than the limitless, and is, therefore, more immediately secure. *Accepting* that life is an unpredictable "mystery" removes much of the tension and limitation that keeps heavenly existence far off in the clouds.

We can also choose to give more of our attention to our *feelings* instead of our thoughts, plans, and stories about our lives. If we do that, then spiritual growth happens much more readily.

FAVORITE RIDE
RULING LOVE

If you can choose to drive any car, then the car you choose is the one you love. Your personality is reflected in the characteristics of those vehicles. If you choose a Rolls, you love luxury. If you choose a hybrid, you love economy.

In the behavioral and spiritual sense, you are that to which you choose to give your attention. If you give your time and attention to fear, then you love suffering. If, on the other hand, you spend your time connecting with others, then you love sharing.

It's important to know what receives your attention, because that is what you will become. Once your ruling love has been made more obvious, you can change it by giving your attention to something else. That's not an easy task, but stepping back from your own situation and seeing what it is that occupies your time and thoughts is a good beginning.

NO COMPETITION
NON-DUALITY

One of the greatest barriers to spiritual progress is the separation from others that comes naturally from ego development. When we think of ourselves as spiritually separate, comparison and judgment invariably follow and lead to conflict. This negative separation is known as "duality."

When you see someone else who is different, visualize yourself as that person. Put yourself in his or her place. Perhaps, in a previous situation or lifetime, you were in that same physical, mental, or spiritual position, but you became different by following a different mental/spiritual path. You appear different, but you are both on similar spiritual journeys.

Examine any fearful beliefs that you may have that lead you to separation from others. Thinking that you are better than another person only protects that part of your mind that is afraid. Thinking that you are worse than another only protects you from taking responsibility for your situations and your actions. Grow up. Be strong enough to accept equality. You don't need more.

The spiritual school of life is an equal-opportunity institution. The poorest minority group saint is the sister of the richest wrestling star.

FELLOW TRAVELERS
EQUITABILITY

When the idea of spiritual separation is dropped, the natural result is to treat others equally. Without accepting equitability, spiritual advancement is difficult.

Much of the unequal treatment that people practice is the result of the fear that there isn't enough to go around. If we feel that there isn't enough, then competing for what there is becomes important. Obtaining an unequal advantage in that struggle becomes part of that effort. On the other hand, if we believe that there *is* enough for everyone, there is no need for discrimination or double standard advantages.

Spiritually, there is enough for everyone. Love is free. The more of it you give away, the more love is generated. Pretty soon, the place is awash in love. It's easy to experience this at weddings, graduations, and holiday events. The challenging part is to carry those loving and giving feelings into situations that are less joyous.

Physically and mentally, it sometimes feels like there *isn't* enough to go around. When people focus on money and pride, then competition and discrimination naturally arise. It is only when people accept that physical and mental needs are less important than spiritual ones that they can let go of their efforts at hoarding, and begin greater sharing with others.

Of course, such sharing requires that minimal survival and comfort amenities be obtained. For many in the world, this is not the case. Because it's difficult to be spiritual when one is hungry or worried about keeping what one has, physical and mental concerns often obliterate consideration of spiritual needs. The result can be anything from tyranny to terrorism.

It is the rich who are most often challenged to rise above a sense of superiority and "greater than" thinking. Because they have more to lose from physical (fiscal) equitability, they are more prone to protecting themselves by creating separation. This disconnection from others can leave them so spiritually isolated that they are pushed into anesthetic and diversionary behaviors.

It is important to pay attention to the part of driver's ed. class that allows us to pull our mental Mercedes over to pick up Mother Theresa. If we don't, the next time around, the cosmic car dealer may send us a used Pinto.

DRIVING TWO CARS AT ONCE
ANXIETY OR FAITH

It's often difficult to do several things at the same time. Acting both positively and negatively simultaneously is one such contradiction. A thousand times a day, we have the opportunity to be positive or negative. Do we buy a glutanous gas guzzler, or do we drive a holy hybrid?

In spiritual terms, it boils down to a choice between participation in those activities that are limiting or those that are unlimiting (see Table 27-5). We can choose the transient or the eternal. A prime example is the choice between love and fear. Loving behavior is limitless and expansive and brings happiness and health. Fearful activity causes contraction and brings sadness and sickness. Fear generates separation while love creates unity.

Love also means living in worldly uncertainty with faith, and surrendering our anxiety to the unknown. If, as we fear, trusting turns out to be a mistake, and we wind up "getting screwed," then the resulting adversity should force us to look even harder at the issues that were involved in our choices.

The list of positive and negative choices is long, and the positives are often more difficult *in the short term*. Once again, we are given Delay of Gratification (DoG) training. If we're as intelligent as DoGs, we will learn that doing it the hard way in the short term means doing it the easy way overall. A DoG will wait patiently for results.

TABLE 27-5: **SOME SPIRITUAL CHOICES**

LIMITING	UNLIMITING
Transient	Eternal
Negative	Positive
Fear	Love
Physical	Spiritual
Anxiety	Faith
Thoughts/Beliefs	Loving
Manipulating	Trusting
Vengeance	Forgiveness
Past and Future	Present
Event	Witness
Scarcity	Abundance

DRIVING GRANNY TO THE DOCTOR
COMPASSION & SERVICE

One of the most important ways one can improve his or her mental or spiritual state is to divert attention from one's own problems to the needs of others. This is not to say that personal problems are not significant, but sharing difficulties may lessen the burden considerably.

Compassion involves cultivating sensitivity for the less fortunate without pity. This awareness of other's needs brings a sense of belonging that distributes pain over a larger area. Ayurveda teaches that the pain and problems that exist for an individual are common to the whole world.

True compassion means feeling for *all* who struggle in the world, not just for some. It involves a personal prayer for the whole world, and seeing the suffering of others as our own. It is difficult to be at peace individually knowing that the rest of the world suffers. Therefore, the healing of humanity as a whole is important in our individual spiritual therapy.

Of course, it's easier to give of oneself if there's already some personal strength from which to draw, but this is not necessary. No matter how difficult a situation may be, one can usually give something to someone else.

When compassion grows into a manifest form of action it becomes service. Service is a demonstration of those pure character qualities that define divinity. It can take almost any form including work in education, the healing arts, or ecology to name just a few.

Giving to others usually results in a sense of psycho-spiritual well-being. Attitude is critical when participating in any giving activity. Although any giving has merit, *giving without expectation* brings the most spiritual healing. Giving *with expectation for reward* is a sterile business transaction. The heart is not involved, and the healing is superficial.

ALONE IN THE REPAIR SHOP
ISOLATION

When spiritual progress has become difficult, removing the distractions via isolation can be helpful. Just as meditation is made easier by sensory reduction, life itself can be made simpler by withdrawal into relative isolation.

We are basically social creatures with worldly desires and attachments, so we become addicted to all things mental, social, and sensual. The difficult "cold turkey" isolation approach can be helpful in severe social addictions, and it can be used as a preventive measure when life begins to become problematic. If the DEA (Desire, Ego, Attachment) is breathing down your neck, then hiding can be helpful.

Even though considerable mind quieting can occur in isolation, hiding from one's conflicts and difficult thoughts is not the ultimate goal. Once isolation has settled the mind, an improved perspective on the world can be obtained.

Oftentimes, isolation is practiced in places that are primitive. When basic amenities that are taken for granted become areas of concern, self-sufficiency is often strengthened in both mental and physical areas.

Isolation can also be an opportunity for strengthening personal routine and ritual. Because self-control and self-esteem are crucial parts of mental stability, their development in isolation can be quite helpful for the development of spiritual clarity and purpose.

SUSPENDED LICENSE
RENUNCIATION & DISPASSION

One of the central principles of yoga and ayurveda is the development of the ability to live in the world without being attached to it.

The worldly and the sensual are here to be experienced, but once experienced, a realization that they are not essential is expected. As a result, attachments to, or desires for the worldly and sensual are to be renounced internally.

Renunciation is not intended to mean experiencing a minimalist life without sensations, experiences and pleasures. Being a hermit in the woods has its place, but true renunciation need not require severe austerities. It requires a change in attitude.

If one's attitude change also includes a lowered sense of small-self importance, and a spiritual world view, then the development of a healthy spirit progresses. "I, Me, and My" are traded in for "Us, We, and Our." Small-self interests are made secondary to the interests of others in greater need. When this happens, one is no longer a threat to others, and harmony is the result.

Ideally, the process of renunciation should not be an emergency escape from stress, but rather, a part of a planned process of personal development. Negativity and activity are abandoned in favor of purity and quiet.

True renunciation must occur in thought as well as in action. Of course, this is extremely difficult, and usually follows prior changes in behavior. But a decrease in recurrent difficult thoughts is a good measure of spiritual progress.

The result of practicing this type of renunciation is "dispassion." It does not mean that one leads a life without "passion," but it means that the passion is tempered by attitude changes. Leaving the DEA doesn't mean giving up all partying. It just means not *needing* to party, and not being upset when you can't.

PASSENGER BEHAVIOR
RIGHT LIFESTYLE

Once the temptations of activity and negativity have been controlled, positive qualities can be built into one's life. The 26 classic yogic qualities for realization of the Greater Self are listed in Table 27-6 below. Each can take a lifetime to master, but there is no hurry. Sooner or later we are all destined to learn them.

TABLE 27-6:
26 ROYAL QUALITIES FOR SELF-REALIZATION

1. Fearlessness
2. Purity of heart
3. Knowledge of God
4. Charity
5. Sensory Control
6. Sacrifice
7. Scriptural Study
8. Austerity
9. Straightforwardness
10. Harmlessness

11. Truthfulness
12. Non-anger
13. Non-expectation
14. Peacefulness
15. Non-crookedness
16. Compassion
17. Non-covetousness
18. Gentleness
19. Modesty
20. Non-fickleness

21. Vigor
22. Forgiveness
23. Fortitude
24. Purity
25. Non-hating
26. Non-pridefulness

RIGHT TURNS

*Right View, Intentions, Speech, Action, Livelihood,
Effort, Mindfulness, Concentration, & Association*

Yoga and ayurveda are considered by many to be the parent philosophies of Buddhism, so it is not surprising that the Buddhist take on spiritual thought and behavior is compatible with much of yoga philosophy.

In the Buddhist philosophy, eight issues are among those considered key to spiritual living. They are ways of living, and require considerable practice to achieve.

A *Right View* of the world is without delusions or distortions about what is real, lasting, and important. This includes an internal understanding of what is, how it all works, and an understanding of oneself and others. We all develop fantasies and stories about our lives that help get us through the day, but they may not serve our spiritual development well in the long run. Positive perceptions of suffering, death, impermanence, and cause and effect are important.

Developing *Right Intentions* means using the mind to become free from selfishness, negativity, delusion, and ignorance. This involves thinking about the well-being of others as well as oneself. Having the proper (selfless) motivation for an action is just as important as the act itself. For example, charity given with the expectation of praise does not have the selfless motive that it should-the welfare of those for whom the charity is given.

Right Speech is also important to cultivate. Since words are effective transmitters of emotions, they can either be gifts or weapons depending on which ones are chosen and how they are used. Truthful, kind, helpful, gossip-free, ego-free, heart-felt words are recommended for spiritual advancement. Using special "sacred sounds," repeated phrases, and chants can be helpful as well.

Right speech also works on a subtle energy level to open the energy center in the throat area. It also includes the absence of speech—silence—as a tool for spiritual advancement and mind quieting.

Right Action means actually living your life according to your beliefs. Philosophy and religion are fine in and of themselves, but they mean much more when they actually affect a person's behavior. Specific behaviors include non-violence, giving, gentleness, generosity and so on. Rechanelling sexual energy toward spiritual awareness, avoiding intoxication, and not giving in to cravings are other practices that are taught.

Loving the world through the work that we do is the essence of *Right Livelihood*. Work that helps others, brings spirituality, avoids negativity, creates equality, promotes happiness, and reduces ego and attachments is necessary. It is impossible to bring these qualities into the world as an arms merchant, thief, or health insurance company executive.

Following a spiritual path is the essence of *Right Effort*. Inquiry into the cosmic questions of life through introspection, contemplation, and prayer are important. Meditation, yoga, service, and the above listed qualities of purity are positive paths to follow. Avoiding the negative options, overcoming our difficult habits, and giving up our attachments is another part of this approach.

Right Mindfulness means mastery of the mind; making it a servant instead of a master. It also means cultivating awareness of one's environment and actions. It is the ability to see one's part in life in a real-time mode, and to understand the motivations, emotions, and behavior of others as well as oneself. It includes the effort to live in the present moment.

Right Concentration means focus with spiritual intention using most the above-mentioned disciplines. The focus should be on obtaining insight and wisdom from life's lessons. Taming and training the restless mind, and testing ourselves with distractions from the path toward spirituality are part of the concentration process. Once this is done, the mind is transformed into a tool for spiritual exploration, and we can transcend from the worldly toward unity with the divine.

Beyond these classic aspects of the Buddhist Noble Eight-fold Path, there is the important concept of *Right Association*. Spending time with like-minded people ("Satsang") who share a partnership that includes a sense of community, selfless service, and common virtuous ideals makes the journey infinitely easier than trying to travel with a spiritually malodorous hitchhiker.

LUCKY DRIVING GLOVES
RITUAL

Ritual is created when spiritual issues are addressed in a regular, ordered, sequential, and ceremonial manner. This organization of spiritual practice is good for making spiritual progress, and for healing the mind. It helps put us in the proper frame of mind for movement to deeper levels of consciousness.

Although there are many rituals, a common thread in yogic rituals is to offer oneself and one's actions to the divine. Light and fire are used frequently to represent the light of awareness and the flame of desire for the divine. Another custom is to let go of negativity by writing down problems, and burning the paper in a fire ritual.

Ritual also helps us understand the concepts that rituals symbolize. Once truth blossoms in devotional behavior, a personal connection with divinity is obtained. At that point, the rituals, forms, and deities have served their purpose. They are not the goal. Once they have shown us a divine way to live and love, they can be reverently remembered as useful guides.

DASHBOARD MADONNA
PRAYER

Prayers are efforts to communicate with the divine. They are frequently requests for help, love, guidance, or other assistance. According to Ayurvedic tradition, sincere prayer involves a heartfelt *spiritual* request, and not just a request for the fulfillment of a physical or emotional desire.

Because we are all part of one consciousness, prayer should include wishes for the good of all beings, and all positive prayers should be respected. Since the divine is often thought to be a form of consciousness, prayer is largely an internal communication rather than a connection with something external.

Nonetheless, external icons are often used in prayer to help focus the mind. The mind relates primarily to the physical, so a physical object representing divinity is often used to settle the mind. Concentration on the form, essence, and symbolism of a devotional object can be helpful in cultivating its qualities.

Objects of prayer can be selected for their specific psychological/spiritual effects. Some represent the ability to overcome negative emotions or anger, while others involve the practitioner in thoughts that bring contentment, spiritual awakening, overcoming obstacles, or other effects.

Other prayer practitioners choose not to focus the mind on an external object. Formless devotion and prayer may focus on mantras, holy names, or divine qualities such as love, truth, and peace.

As a prayer practice is developed, the devotee begins to see the divine in everything! At that point, prayer, the object of prayer, and the devotee merge, and become unified with the Greater Self.

COMMITTED TO THE DRIVE
DEVOTION

Devotion is a form of deep love, commitment, and attunement with an object, spiritual process, or symbol. Although one may be devoted to worldly things, devotion in this context is meant to be applied to a love of the divine. Devotion to those individuals who embody divine qualities is often observed, but carries with it the potential trap of infatuation with the messenger instead of the message.

Devotion is one of the few acceptable forms of attachment in yoga philosophy because it is attachment to the divine instead of the transient. Once established, devotion becomes an attitude of the spirit in which a spontaneous, intense pursuit of knowledge of the divine becomes a consuming passion.

The practice of devotion usually involves contemplation and study of divine power, wisdom, and goodness. The practices of prayer, chanting, story-telling, and ritual often become part of devotional development.

Eventually, frequent thoughts of the divine, and dedicating all acts of service to the divine become a part of the devotee's lifestyle. Life becomes an offering of oneself to the divine through an external symbol. A devotee who lives his or her life as a conscious manifestation of divinity, eventually imparts that spirituality. The divinity that is already within that person is revealed, and s/he moves closer to union with purity.

Devotion is an effective process to help organize, focus, and establish a rhythm to the spiritual search. The practice is said to cure many ills, both mental and physical, and a lack of devotion has been described as the root of all psychological suffering.

DRIVING INSTRUCTORS
SPIRITUAL TEACHERS

One important tool for spiritual maintenance and repair is the guidance of a teacher or guru. This usually takes the form of an inspirational person, living or not, with knowledge that is deeper than that of the student. The teacher is usually distinguished by his or her ability to effectively transmit that knowledge by word, action, example, or by their inspirational presence.

The function of a spiritual teacher is to point the way for an individual to follow. Their spiritual guidance should convey the truth as it applies to everyday living.

The true spiritual leader is a consistent reminder of the fruits of following a positive spiritual path. The guru can also function as a temporary focal point for students. Focusing on the guru can be helpful in the practices of ritual, devotion, meditation, and moral conduct. In the process, the guru's positive qualities are internalized.

The spiritual teacher should be thought of as a *means* to obtain spiritual knowledge. The guru may be a conduit for divine truth and knowledge, but he or she is not the cause or ultimate source of that wisdom. Although any teacher is to be respected and honored for his or her abilities, no teacher should be worshiped. If one is awakened by a divine light shining through a window, one should not make the mistake of worshiping the window.

Just as there are both good and bad school teachers, there are genuine and less genuine spiritual leaders. The false guru can be identified as a person who does not embody the traits of a liberated person (see Table 26-3). A genuine teacher should set an example by *living* his or her beliefs without vanity, claims of extraordinary ability, judgments, or profit-generating sales of spiritual paraphernalia.

True gurus exemplify the liberating criteria of Table 26-3, and should outwardly radiate the divine consciousness of purity that resides in all of us.

96

MUFFLERS
SILENCE

According to yoga philosophy, silence is beyond time, space, and causation. Complete silence disappeared during creation when the first sound, "OM." was generated by the merging of primordial consciousness ("Purusha") and creative will ("Prakruti"). Sounds then became more and more differentiated, vibrating at slower and slower frequencies as energy condensed from the ethereal into the physical.

Moving back toward primordial spirituality, therefore, involves moving back toward silence. Controlling one's speech is one of the first steps in this effort. Less total speaking combined with well-chosen words helps with quieting the mind.

Observing periods of silence is a yoga technique that conserves energy, quiets the mind, and decreases arguments. Practitioners of yogic silence may carry note pads or small writing boards to communicate with others when necessary. This practice slows down communications which allows for a more careful choice of words. This, in turn, leads to greater introspection, and to a greater awareness of one's own thoughts.

Inner silence is often the product of outer silence. When inner silence is created, purification of spirit and reunion with the Greater-Self consciousness is possible.

TORN-UP TRAFFIC TICKETS
FORGIVENESS

True forgiveness is not an intellectual exercise. It's a difficult response to real-life offenses, and an important milestone in the spiritual curriculum.

Superficial forgiveness means dismissing past transgressions. Sweeping an issue under the rug with a shallow pronouncement that the problem is "forgiven" may not be reflected in the depths of the heart where festering anger, resentment or pain can do long-term emotional, spiritual, and physical damage. Superficial forgiveness is tempting because heart-felt forgiveness is so difficult.

Deep forgiveness is difficult because holding a grudge is a survival tool that is used to protect us from those who treat us badly. The mind and the ego thrives on the negative, and holding a grudge keeps all the negative feelings of anger, injustice, and pain active. With these emotions in play, the ego's protective role is strengthened, fear is awakened, and "security" is increased. While these negatives may strengthen the ego, they weaken the spirit which is built on unity.

Practices that build forgiveness include prayer, and visualizing offenders realizing the nature of their errors and being surrounded by healing light.

Forgiveness always concerns something that has happened in the past, so not forgiving means holding onto the past. Forgiving means letting the past go in favor of the present or the future. Yoga and ayurveda recommend living in the present whenever possible.

Changing one's attitude about life events is also key in the forgiveness process. If one views the "negative" things that happen in life as positive learning experiences, then there is really nothing to forgive. Those whom we regard as our tormentors can be our teachers, if we choose to see them that way.

If one maintains the point of view that life experiences are manifest projections of our own mind (we are shown what we need see), then non-forgiveness means holding a grudge against the needs of our own mind!

Forgiving *oneself* is often the most difficult, because we expect more of ourselves than is reasonable. Accepting our failures requires us to accept that we are mortal, fallible, and not the gods we are pressured to be. If we never made mistakes, we wouldn't need to be here.

DRIVING INTO THE UNKNOWN
SURRENDER

To achieve peace and higher awareness, it is necessary to "surrender" to some greater power. One definition of surrender is to "relinquish control," but control is one of the primary means by which the ego deals with fear. If one is in control, the odds of being overwhelmed by adversity go down.

757

Yet one of the primary aims of yoga philosophy is to actually *accept* losing control, especially of "unimportant" things. Attachment to objects and outcomes must be overcome, and objects that are known to be of low spiritual value are surrendered first.

In most cultures, surrender indicates weakness. The idea of purposely allowing oneself to become vulnerable through surrender is an anathema to the basic survival instincts inside each of us. Certainly the masculine image men are given does not allow for vulnerability or surrender.

Nonetheless, we all know that we *are* ultimately vulnerable, and will all die. It is when we change our focus to the goal of becoming *spiritually* invulnerable that the idea of surrender becomes more thinkable. Risky spiritual behavior means *not* surrendering attachment to those things that we are certain to lose. In much of yoga philosophy, the only things that we take with us after death are the bits of awareness or ignorance that we have gained.

Being human, however, we don't often think that far ahead. We are living more immediately, so we hold on to the fear of the consequences of surrendering our present security. We continue to respond defensively to issues and problems. It is only when we begin to understand ourselves as being primarily made of spirit, that we can let go of our non-spiritual attachments.

To become spiritual, we must take a significant "leap of faith." In this process, physical and immediate security are traded for the possibility of spiritual advancement. There is no guarantee. The spiritual is simply given a try.

The outcome of this decision is placed in the hands of the mysterious divine. The assumption is made that this divine consciousness is benign, and that the overall result will be positive in spiritual terms, if not in physical ones. Oftentimes, positive results are seen in both.

In another aspect of surrender, there is an admission that we can't solve our own problems through our own personal power. There is a sense that excessive control efforts only bring further stress and agitation. There is also a realization that the frustrating details of life are not so important after all.

Yet another aspect of surrender is letting go of the identity of being the "doer" of deeds. In this liberated mind-set, many of our actions, thoughts, and emotions are considered to be the result of divine direction and intrinsic spiritual growth needs. By surrendering everything to the divine, and by focusing on the divine, we become more closely united with that divinity.

Another type of surrender involves surrendering the past. One can consider the difficult past to be the consequence of happenstance, previous life errors, or a directed learning experience. In positive surrender, there's an "attitude of gratitude" for a useful life lesson. The difficulties of life are not taken personally.

Another aspect of surrender involves spending more time reflecting on the power of being a part of the Greater-Self, and living from the heart in the present moment. It means not surrendering your attention to the negatives.

Surrender takes time and practice. Every time the DEA knocks on your door, you must let them confiscate a little more Desire, Ego, and Attachment. Surrender also involves releasing physical stress with many of the techniques described in Part Two of this work. Breathing, yoga postures, and exercise are very helpful. It takes years of practice.

Surrender also involves "letting go" of the infinite number of negative stories we tell ourselves every day. Some of the common tapes we play in our heads are listed in Table 27-7.

TABLE 27-7: **MENTAL/SPIRITUAL LETTING GO**

LETTING GO OF:	ACCEPTING THAT:
"I can't stand the pain."	"Pain is part of life." "Fear of pain is a mind/ego creation." "I can make something positive from pain."
"I will die"	"Most of what I am never dies."
"Life is too difficult."	"My excess desires are not needed."
"I won't be able to go on."	"I can go on after it resolves."
"I can't get what I want."	"I have what I really need."
"I have to do it my way."	"It can be done many ways."
"I don't understand."	"I'll understand later." "We can't know everything."
"I'm afraid of it."	"My essence is not fear." "It will turn out for the best." "I will trust in a good future outcome." "I'll get over it."
"I'm angry, anxious, distrustful."	"My essence is not that emotion." "I can wait for the outcome." "I am love."
"It shouldn't be like that."	"This experience is not what I'm about." "I am here to learn from this." "It will pass." "It's just one experience."
"This always happens."	"ALWAYS thinking can be a mind trap." "I have the choice to let go & change."

SPECTATOR SPORT
WITNESSING AWARENESS

Spiritual growth means the growth of awareness; becoming conscious of things that were not observed before.

In order for something to be perceived with awareness, there are at least three parts to the process are required. There is the object or concept that is being perceived, the perceiver, and the process that connects the two.

In ayurvedic thinking, the perception/awareness process involves the initial movement of awareness energy *from* the perceiver to the object, and then back to the perceiver. There is active movement of awareness energy *from the perceiver.* This differs from the physical scientific concept in which energy comes only from the object to the perceiver, and is simply registered as some type of sensory input.

From the scientific point of view, the perceiver is passive; whatever comes by is taken in. In the ayurvedic scenario, the perceiver is more active, and directing his/her attention. In this three-part interaction, there is a greater sense of the whole process.

A movie projector operator beams a light onto a theater screen. The light is reflected back to his eye and is perceived. The audience below him laughs. In the wings, the theater manager smiles his approval. The manager has witnessed the whole three-part interaction. He perceives the *process* of what has transpired. Although involved himself, the operator may also be aware of the process.

In everyday situations, we can interact either with or without an observing awareness. While we are interacting, it is easy to have a perspective on what the *other* person is doing. This is because we are removed from that person to a degree. But if we add another degree of separation, and simultaneously observe the interaction as a whole, like the theatre manager, then an entirely different perspective is obtained.

When we *observe ourselves* interacting, additional learning takes place. We see our own behavior as well as the other person's more objectively. We can observe how our behavior patterns develop, what effects they have, and how we can alter them for everyone's benefit.

If we can learn to observe ourselves sneaking into McDharma's for a triple cheeseburger, then we have a chance of changing course before the fat, sugar, and salt ruin our health. If we observe ourselves when we stop listening to someone who is trying to communicate, then we have an opportunity to slow down, keep our mouths shut, and our ears and minds open.

If we can develop this manager/observer/operator point of view, then we are much less likely to be swept away by the surge of events that often dominate our active lives. We are less likely to make mistakes and repeat them. Instead of diving into the river head first and being swept down stream, we become the fisherman/observer on the bank of the river of life, watching the current carry our life-events down stream. We observe and learn.

Practicing observation, like the manager at a play, or the fisherman by the river, is an important part of meditation. The intent is to learn to observe our own thoughts and beliefs. After some practicing, we become able to do this self-observation without needing to sit quietly or close our eyes. We can do it while we are fully active. This "walking meditation" helps bring the positive peaceful aspects of sitting meditation to the rest of our daily activities. Eventually, our entire life can be conducted with this type of awareness. The ability to do this continuously is one of the qualities that define the great leaders, saints, and sages.

When this witnessing awareness is present, we develop additional skills and improved behavior. We can learn not to take things personally or too seriously. In the same way that the manager in the theatre knows that it's just a play, we can become aware that life is just going to school. We can begin to see the lessons and avoid the pitfalls. This is especially true when life gives us situational reruns. We can become more aware of our place in the universe and our relationships with its various parts.

Witnessing awareness is a key part of the yogic/ayurvedic development of spirit. Most of us enjoy watching a movie or sporting event. Witnessing allows us to be on the stage and in the audience at the same time. When this happens, the activity expands, and the limits of the experience dissolve into the Greater Self.

DRIVE-IN MOVIE
LIFE AS A MIND PROJECTION

Another life philosophy holds that everything that appears in the physical world is actually a projection of the mind. Two people can view the same event and have completely different experiences because what appears on each one's visual/mental screen is influenced by their own mind concerns.

Each individual mind has its own issues. It makes sense that everything the mind sees is colored by those concerns. In delusional/illusional states, the mind creates a "false" reality. In less delusional states, the mind is also creating much of what is perceived.

The mind does this because it is preoccupied with itself. At home, the videos we pop into the TV are the ones that we want/need to see. The challenge is to recognize that the way we perceive reality is the result of those needs. With that perspective, we can take more responsibility for whatever happens.

IT ALL HAPPENED TOMORROW
BEING IN THE PRESENT MOMENT

When events actually occur, they do so in their own present moment. They become part of our past, present, or future as a result of the timing of our interaction with them.

If we are in school, and we are preparing for a mid-term exam, then that exam is in our future. If we are in the process of taking the exam, then the exam is happening in the present. Once we are finished with it, it moves into our past. The only time that we actually interact with that exam is while we are taking it - in the present. We may influence the outcome by preparing for its occurrence, and we may learn from it once we find out what the correct answers were, but the only real *influence* we have over it occurs in the present.

If we spend all of our time preparing for the future, or analyzing what happened in the past, then we miss out on the only opportunity we have to really interact. We must use witnessing awareness to catch ourselves when we focus on the past or the future. If we remain distracted from the present, then we will miss out on what's happening while we are preparing or remembering.

On the other hand, much of the process of delayed gratification is predicated on focusing on the future. The ability to practice delayed gratification, however, relies on our ability to see our choices clearly in the present when the choices are actually being made.

One technique to help us keep our attention more focused on the present is breath awareness and control. For some reason, it is difficult to think about all the breaths we will be taking in the future, or the ones we have taken in the past. When we focus on alternate nostril breathing, for example, we focus on each individual breath as it is occurring in the present moment.

Phrase repetition, and focusing on a single object can also hold us closer to the present instead of reviewing the thought and belief stories the mind loves to replay. Preoccupation with the past and the future chain us to our difficult mind games. In contrast, the present is the playground of the spirit.

Time is largely defined by the past and the future. They give temporal dimension to existence in the same way that two points create a line, and several points create depth. Without the past and the future, there is only a single point on the page of time—the present.

The past and the future are creations of the mind that no longer exist (past), or may never exist (future). The mind needs to create time so that it will have enough to do. Just imagine how bored the mind would be if there was nothing to anticipate or regret. The past gives us identity, and the future provides hope. Being in the past or the future is sometimes a manifestation of the mind's not accepting the reality of the present moment. When the present is too painful, the mind moves to the future or the past.

If we can narrow the dimensions of time to the present, then we can narrow the influence of the mind. When this happens, our natural, internal spiritual nature is uncovered. We can do this by paying attention to what is happening right now!

HIGHWAY COURTESY
LIVING FROM THE HEART

When answers to spiritual questions are needed, thoughts and beliefs are less useful than responses from the heart. In many philosophies, the heart is the seat of emotions, but the idea of actually *living* from the emotions in an unforgiving world is difficult to accept.

Going through life with an "open heart" is a perilous endeavor. It involves accepting increased emotional vulnerability, and the real possibility of getting hurt. But by opening ourselves to our own feelings, and by dealing with others on a feeling level, we allow for deeper spiritual exchanges to occur. If we stay on the more superficial levels, we are likely to get caught up in the mundane and the transient.

Living with an open heart means giving attention to the positive qualities that have been described in previous chapters, and by acting in ways that put selfless qualities first. Many of the essential teachings of Jesus were about living in a loving and giving way, and accepting vulnerability (turn the other cheek, love thy enemy, crucifixion, etc.). He practiced this behavior because he was devoted to achieving something enduring, and letting go of the transient. He understood that love, trust, and being in the present moment are the currency of *spiritual* salvation, and the doorway to a higher level of consciousness.

Yet few of us have the Christ-like courage to accept this type of vulnerability. We are still consumed by the fear that such an exposure will lead to injury or destruction. If we open our hearts so fully, aren't they likely to be broken?

Jesus knew that his *emotional* heart would be broken, but he also knew that his *spiritual* heart would be liberated. He knew that the very purpose of the heart is to open, and that hearts are routinely broken for the sake of affirming and trusting in the positive. He also knew that the heart has great strength, and that it can become even stronger as it heals.

Opting for an approach to life that involves such openness, loving, and trusting requires an attitude of acceptance without defiantly questioning or resisting the difficult. We are here to experience and get over certain problems, so problems are exactly what we need. Without problems, heart-math class would be empty and pointless.

We begin to know that we are passing the graduate courses in openess when we check in with our feelings. If we are feeling confident, nurtured, self-assured, carefree, expansive, powerful, grounded, capable, supported, etc., then we have learned openness and acceptance. If, on the other hand, we find that we are still feeling resentful, contracted, unsupported, worried, etc., then we can bet that our report cards will indicate that this open book life-lesson will need to be repeated.

JUST WHAT THE DOCTOR ORDERED
ACCEPTING LIFE AS PERFECTION

It is perfectly obvious that life is imperfect. A perfect life would have none of the difficulties we encounter every day. It would be like a "perfect" school—no exams, no homework, no difficult teachers, no labs, no term papers, and (while we're at it) no classes to sit through either!

We can adopt one of several attitudes toward school. We can be upset by its difficulties, or we can focus on the challenges that difficulties present. If we always received good grades without working for them, we would be learning very little. Getting a *difficult* education gives us the experience that is necessary if we are to make difficult emotional and spiritual progress. No one can become a spiritual rocket scientist without wading through emotional algebra. We need the difficult classes if we are to advance toward graduate level abilities.

We can even go a step further and decide that we are being made *very* strong by the very difficult. But the giant step of concluding that the high hurdles we face are the *perfect* tests for us presupposes a faith that is strong given the difficulty of our experiences.

Why should we believe that we get the exact challenges we need? Because making that assumption leads us to remove counterproductive negative responses to difficulty. It turns despair into challenge. It keeps us in the classroom, and off the road to the circus.

If we presuppose that it's all necessary for our enlightenment, then we will dig deeper for a better understanding. It's more heartening to believe that the curriculum is not random or pointless; that it's designed to get us somewhere specific and special. Why not be uplifted by believing that the lessons life provides are precisely the ones we need?

EVERY CAR A ROLLS ROYCE
SEEING DIVINITY IN EVERYTHING

In the same way that we can choose to adopt the point of view that life is a series of lessons to be learned, we can also choose to recognize an omnipresent awareness in every situation. There are three basic types of awareness. We can be aware of the details, the greater overall picture, or both. When we are trying to drive to work through heavy traffic without getting totaled, we are using our *temporal* awareness to manage details. We are thinking about our small-selves and our need to be secure.

When we have a moment to reflect on our overall struggle to survive, and when we can *feel* that we belong to mass-transit humanity, then we become conscious of the greater picture. We become aware of something greater than ourselves. In that awareness, we move into the Greater Consciousness.

If we look hard enough, and if we allow ourselves some sensitivity, we can begin to feel the "Greater" in most of our everyday experiences. Eventually we do not need the explosive cheers of the football crowd to remind us of our spiritual unity. After a while, we can continuously choose to see ourselves at every moment as one of many on a spiritual journey.

Yoga and ayurvedic philosophy teach that a positive, divine consciousness is pervasive. It has always been there, but it has been obscured by the flashy trappings of the sensual world and by our ego-based sense of separation from others. There is no need of proof that the Greater Consciousness exists and is ubiquitous. In the end, it is a matter of *choosing* to believe that it does, because it FEELS right, comfortable, enduring, and whole.

To the "successful" Wall Street banker, some cars just don't have the necessary "bling." But to the starving or the dying third-worlder, every rickety relief vehicle is miraculous beyond measure. It's all in our point of view. One thing life does give us is - choice. We can choose, or we can lose the opportunity to see the positive and the unity in everything we encounter!

Running
Through the streets
Screaming,

Throwing rocks through windows,
Using my own head to ring
Great bells,

Pulling out my hair,
Tearing off my clothes,

Tying everything I own
To a stick,
And setting it on
Fire.

What else can I do tonight
To celebrate the madness,
The joy,

Of seeing God
Everywhere! [50]

- Hafiz

ONLY ONE OWNER
UNIFYING CONSCIOUSNESS

When we have made our bodies healthy enough that they no longer make undue demands for extra satisfactions, we can more easily silence the distracting chattering of the mind and its ego accomplice. When we have trained our minds to let go of its stories, attachments and desires, and we find ourselves desirous only of unity with the Greater Self, we become One with that Greater Spiritual Consciousness. At that point, we run the risk of being labeled as either "saintly" or "insane."

It is more than a coincidence that most of the world's religions embrace some form of unifying monotheism. The Hebrew concept of God (Yaweh) "is one." There is only one Allah, with Mohammed as the principal prophet. The Christian trinity is a manifestation of the one God. The Chinese Tao is the one ruling force. The Buddhist middle path leads to unity in Nirvana.

This tendency of the universe to gravitate toward the concept of unifying consciousness is mirrored by physical gravity itself. There is a natural tendency for all objects in the universe to be attracted to each other. It is the most basic of tendencies, and it is the basis for the formation of the stars, planets, and all other objects in creation.

People and their spirits also gravitate toward each other. For the most part, we like the comfort of the presence of others around us. We like to get together to celebrate. We don't go off in solitude to rejoice.

We can easily feel some measure of unity with the animals who become our pets and friends. We can even feel affection and connection with the flowers and plants. We learn to love the mountains and rivers because they are made of the same stuff we are.

We are all stardust and energy. We are all condensations of consciousness. When we are able to continuously feel the divinity/awareness/consciousness in all aspects of life, we will be living in the divine.

MERGING TRAFFIC
REJOINING THE INFINITE

Once we recognize our unity with spirit, we can begin to merge back into it. Yoga and ayurveda both teach that we are never truly separate from our spirit-consciousness, but we forget that we are spiritual beings having a human experience. Like fish in a lake, we are attracted to the flashy lures that Hollywood and Madison Avenue put in front of us. All too soon, we are hooked.

Because we have been distracted in this way, we no longer "have the time" to focus on what is ultimately important. Nonsense! We have as much time as we need for whatever it is that's vital to us. If we honestly felt that leading a spiritual life was important, we would use any technique necessary to pursue that goal, like an athlete trying to win Olympic gold!

The problem is that we really *don't* believe that spirituality is that important. After all, how can sitting quietly, or being of service to others be more important than who wins the World Cup, World Series, World Wrestling Championship, or Miss World? Why would anyone care more about Mother Theresa than they would about the Hulk or Richard Petty? After all, in this world, we take whatever we can get—right now!—because we only go around once!

Or do we?

It's an either/or situation. We can conclude that we are *not* primarily spirit, that there is *only* this one lifetime, and that we must live it to the fullest without sacrificing anything significant for whatever happens after we die. Or, we can decide that within us there is a vibrant spirit-consciousness that endures beyond life's little super bowls.

Even if we believe in only one lifetime, living with the soul-nurturing behavior of a spiritualist will allow less flashy life experiences to be more deeply lived. We will feel better in this lifetime by practicing awareness, kindness, service, and understanding.

If we choose to believe that our actions carry forward beyond the end of our physical existence, we can move on to the question of whether the goal itself is actually reachable. Can we actually lead spiritual lives in a difficult, modern world? Can we really achieve spiritual liberation/enlightenment?

Like everything worthwhile, spiritual living takes practice and patience. Even Mother Theresa, Nelson Mandela, and Oprah had to pay the spiritual electric bill. People like these, and the saints that have come before them demonstrate that spirituality and liberation are quite possible. It's the ultimate in DoG training. We can train ourselves to delay gratification for as long as it takes.

Ultimately, working toward spirituality requires removing expectations of reward in this lifetime. It also requires training ourselves to believe that we are the very essence of loving Spirit.

Life also provides us with glimpses of what it's like to reunite with our divinity. The bliss feelings of drug rushes, sexual orgasm, and the roar of the stadium crowds have similar ecstatic qualities. That is why we pursue them even though they are transient. When we work for an *enduring* rush using the long-term techniques for developing purity, we can find bliss that is gentle and enduring.

TABLE 27-8: **SPIRITUAL PRINCIPLES**

1. Consciousness is Primary for Health.

2. Spiritual Direction Brings Mental Health & Purpose to Life.

3. There is One Enduring Interconnecting Greater Spirit ("G-Self").

4. There are many Separate Individual Sub-Spirits ("i-self").

5. The i-self and the G-self are Connected.

6. Spiritual Separation from Others is Illusion. Unity is Reality.

7. The Spiritual Character qualities are Purity, Activity, & Negativity.

8. All Spiritual Qualities are Potential in Everyone.

9. We Incarnate on Earth to:

    Remember what is important
    Let go of what is unimportant
    Improve your character
    Realize the G-Self within & around us

10. Death is a Transition from Physical to Spiritual State.

11. Spiritual Qualities Carry Forward from Previous Lives.

12. See Divinity in Everything.

13. Serve Others without Expectation

14. Live from the Heart.

15. Be Aware of the Present Moment.

16. Surrender to the Purpose of Life's Lessons.

PART FIVE:
ADVANCED TUNING
TECHNIQUES
Advanced Ayurvedic Studies

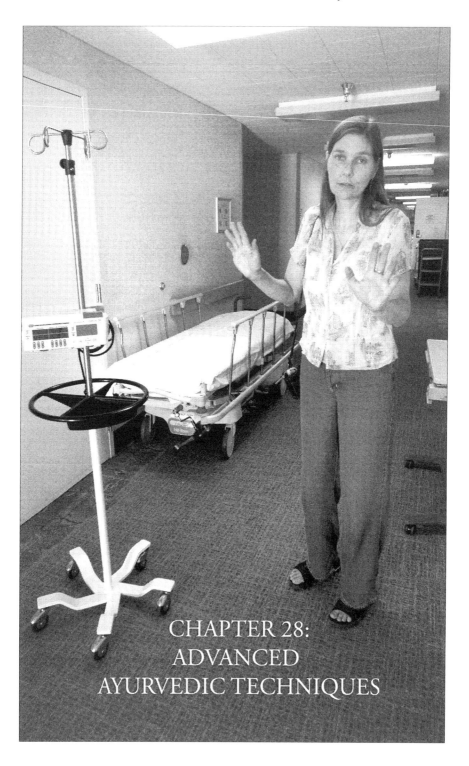

CHAPTER 28:
ADVANCED
AYURVEDIC TECHNIQUES

IF NOT NOW...?

…Reggie can't talk right now. The nurse said he's sedated after the procedure…

It's kind of odd to think of Reggie unable to talk, or resting for any length of time. But he's probably very at home and comfortable being asleep under the influence of drugs.

Maybe now, he'll stop listening politely and start trying some real lifestyle changes. The tough thing is that he's going to need a lot more than lifestyle changes to deal with the mess he's in right now. The doctor's say there's the possibility that surgery will help, but they're turning up their hands at what to do if that doesn't work.

If he's going to beat this, he's going to need to try everything he can; things that he's going to think are really off-the-wall!

The main thing is whether or not our old driver will have the drive-to-survive? Some people just give up when they hit bottom. For others, it's the wake-up-call that they need. Some people even get several wakeup calls. Some get several a day!

I guess we'll just have to hope that when Reggie wakes up, he wakes up!

…

Well, I'd better go. I've got to get Alan to drive the limo up to the city to pick up some of Regg's old celebrity clients to come cheer him up. When they heard what happened to Regg, they all said they'd make the time to come pay him a visit. Some celebs actually care about other people beside themselves.

DIFFERENT GARAGES FOR DIFFERENT VEHICLES
QUALITY BODY LOCATIONS

Different vehicles are often housed in locations that fit their characteristics. Motorcycles are kept in small spaces, sports cars in average size garages, and large trucks are parked outside. Curiously, there are different locations in the body where the AIR, FIRE, and EARTH qualities are dominant. When an excess of the quality is present, these are the places that are primarily affected.

The gaseous AIR quality is found primarily in the gassy colon. There is also a considerable amount of AIR quality in the lungs, and in the spaces inside of the long bones as well, but the dominant area of AIR quality, in ayurvedic thinking, is the colon. When excessive AIR quality builds up, it can go anywhere in the body, but very often, it will manifest in the colon as extra gas, cramping, diverticulosis, or constipation.

When the AIR quality moves out of the colon into other tissues and systems, AIR-type problems develop. When the AIR quality is returned from the tissues to the colon by the *Five Cleansings* technique, the AIR quality can be reduced by using different types of enemas.

The hot, liquid FIRE quality has its home location in the small intestine. There is also considerable FIRE quality in the liver, gallbladder, spleen, and blood, but its primary location is in the small intestine. When extra FIRE quality accumulates, problems often manifest in the small intestine as diarrhea or Crohn's disease. Manifestations of FIRE migration outside the small intestine include skin inflammations, eye disorders, blood and liver diseases. The FIRE is removed from the intestine with various purgatives.

The EARTH quality resides primarily in the stomach and the lungs. It is also found in the joints, brain, mouth and other places as well. Extra EARTH accumulation results in mucous congestion of the stomach and lungs with cough, asthma, and sluggish digestion.

One of the natural reasons that vomiting occurs is to remove excess EARTH quality from these sites. In ayurveda, vomiting is used therapeutically to treat disorders of excessive EARTH quality. The *Five Cleansings* technique can move excess EARTH from the tissues to the stomach, and from there it is eliminated by vomiting.

THE GLUE
COMPOSITE VITAL STRENGTH

That great new car smell is an experience that many people love. It's the glue. But there's something about that particular glue smell that feels a little different from the other glue-sniffing highs that we get in life. Maybe it has something to do with the whole idea of having a brand new car! Perhaps it's the combination of the glue with the new plastic and the fresh fabric and leather that energize a new owner!

Glue not only stimulates the olfactory sense, it holds things together and gives the combination of materials function and strength as a group that they don't have as individual pieces. If there were nothing holding them together, the parts of a motor vehicle could not function collectively, and that flimsy Ferrari would fall apart.

In the same way, the body combines various protein and hormonal components to make its own protective, energizing, and non-toxic "glue." This cohesive combination not only holds parts of the body together, it gives them strength, power, and the ability to resist assaults by the elements and biological invaders.

This *Composite Vital Strength* (CVS), known in ayurvedic terms as "Ojas," is crucial to survival. In ayurvedic thinking, this substance is responsible for protecting and maintaining the body's tissues. The nerves that control the heartbeat, for example, are nourished by this strengthening amalgam. The ability of the red blood cells to endure their difficult transportation duties is also considered to be a function of this protective biological blend. It also helps by combating oxidizing and aging influences.

Composite Vital Strength has a definite effect on the consciousness. It affects neurotransmitters such as serotonin, melatonin, and dopamine. As such, the effect of CVS on the mind and on relaxation is significant. It has a component (called "Soma") that is closely connected to a blissful state of consciousness.

Plasma proteins are associated with CVS. Albumin and globulin permeate many tissues throughout the body and are important for infection-fighting when they work together with other products of cellular metabolism.

Some claim that hormones are also associated with CVS since they contribute to the body's ability to fight infection, and are well known for their ability to help strengthen and energize muscles and other tissues.

As with many other body systems, proper digestion is necessary for the production of building blocks for tissues. Without proper digestion, the components of CVS can't be created, and without proper chemical Transformational Intelligence (see the following section), these components cannot be properly combined. If the body's Composite Vital Strength is not made properly, its functions become disturbed and its protective effects are weakened.

Composite Vital Strength can also be affected by the AIR, FIRE, and EARTH qualities. If excess EARTH quality affects the CVS, then the circulating CVS will be too heavy, and sticky. A feeling of lethargy and dullness of mind can result. If extra AIR quality affects CVS, then weakness and fatigue are often present. Too much FIRE quality can burn up the CVS leaving the body without protection and susceptible to autoimmune disorders. Burned CVS can also result in multiple sclerosis, liver disease, gout, lupus, psoriasis and eczema.

Like vehicular oil, CVS can leak out of the system. When this happens, and levels of this protectant fall, various types of coma can result. Composite Vital Strength is important in maintaining consciousness. In addition, breathlessness, chest pain, palpitations, dehydration, osteoporosis and muscle loss have been ascribed to CVS depletion. Loss of Composite Vital Strength can activate dormant negative processes. Relapses in hepatitis, chronic fatigue, and even AIDS can be triggered as a result of depleted CVS.

An overload of Composite Vital Strength may stimulate symptoms that suggest excess EARTH quality such as diabetes, obesity, high cholesterol, glaucoma, hypertension, heart attack, edema, lipomas and lymphoma.

Psychological issues are a common cause of disorders affecting Composite Vital Strength. Grief, worry, and other emotions can disturb the protective effects of CVS and lower immunity. Physical trauma, excessive sex, and too much exercise can also cause depletion of CVS. Chronic diseases and toxins can also cause enough stress to affect the Composite Vital Strength and weaken the body's ability to defend itself.

The body's Composite Vital Strength can also be thought of as the protective sealant on the paint of a car. That sealant not only protects the car, it also gives it a shiny luster, an "aura" that makes it look strong and capable. When our bodies are strong and protected by this natural defense mechanism, our own aura of health and vitality can shine more brightly than any Bentley or Benz.

THE SPARK
TRANSFORMATIVE INTELLIGENT ENERGY

In a motor vehicle, gas and air are mixed in the carburetor and transported to the engine cylinder. When mixed together, they have the ability to burn and release energy. But they need something extra to actually make it happen. The mixture needs a spark. Once the spark hits the gas/air mixture, a mini-explosion occurs and the engine is energized. Without the spark, nothing happens.

In the human vehicle, a spark is also necessary for the transformation of many chemical, mechanical, and behavioral reactions to take place. The transformational spark that catalyzes these changes must be specific for the particular body reaction that is occurring. In the specificity sense, the catalyst must be correct; it must be intelligent.

In the intelligent design of a motor vehicle, there are specific issues that must be considered in creating a working machine that uses many different parts. For each part, the dimensions, sensitivity, durability, importance, speed of operation and proximity to other parts must all be appropriate. In the body too, all of the interrelationships must be correct for each cell, organ, and system to function properly. The intelligence, accuracy, and propriety of these relationships is what allows them to function together.

Energies that transform with purpose, specificity and intelligence are known in ayurveda as "Tejas." This *Transformative Intelligent Energy* (TIE) is akin to the modern transformative energy of enzymes, hormones, nucleotides, neurotransmitters and other controlling chemicals. It is not only the physical chemicals themselves that govern the transformations. It's also their characteristics, their *intelligence* that directs metabolic changes.

Mechanical activities that are transformative are also included in this concept. Chewing, cooking, fermenting, and sprouting are all examples of the way biological systems mechanically transform. Heat and light also have transformational capacity as exemplified by the transformation of melanin and vitamin D in the skin.

This transformational power/potential also controls the *degree* to which processes happen in the body. The amount of coloring in the skin, eyes, muscles and other body parts is partly a function of how much transformation occurs in the body's chemistry.

Psychological and spiritual transformations are also influenced by TIE intelligence. Changing from a fear-based psychology to a more trusting, love-based way of seeing the world is an example of a psychological transformation for which intelligence is needed.

Everything about us is the result of a complex intelligent construction from essential building blocks. The spectrum of influence of that intelligence necessarily includes such vital areas as general health, longevity, vitality, nutrition, and energy. Nourishing our Transformational Intelligent Energy is, therefore, vital for health.

THE FORCE
LIFE-FORCE ENERGY

In the *Star Wars* stories, some of the characters make use of a powerful energy source to accomplish certain tasks. Through various techniques, they connect to this mysterious "Force" that pervades the universe. On the planet Earth, the energy that changes atoms and molecules into living creatures is known as the "Life-Force."

It's not a new concept. In the Chinese tradition, this force that enlivens is called "Chi," and in the ayurvedic/yogic traditions, it is known as "Prana."

Life Force Energy (LiFE) is one of the *subtle* energies. Like Composite Vital Strength (CVS) and Transformative Intelligent Energy (TIE), it is difficult to isolate and to define. One illustration of the manifestations of LiFE is the difference between food that has been canned and the same food that has been freshly harvested. They both contain similar atoms and molecules, but the fresh food has an "enlivened" quality and energy. Old food lacks this vitality.

Another example is death. When the physical body "dies," this Life Force Energy (LiFE) dissipates. At one moment, a person is "alive." A second later, the very same collection of tissues, systems, and chemicals is there, but the collective, coordinating, sustaining, enlivening energy is gone. Giving the body an electrical shock can sometimes bring that LiFE back. According to some, returning the LiFE energy may also be done by extraordinary supernatural means (e.g. Lazarus).

LiFE is more than chemicals, electricity, adrenalin, or oxygen. These substances can be put into an isolated container, but they will not create a living being.

One reason we don't fully understand all of the chemistry of "life" is because it involves more than chemistry. LiFE is the mysterious, intelligent force/energy that properly combines these ingredients in a way that results in biological life. It does not come from the physical or the mental worlds, but is derived from the spiritual. It is difficult to describe with pictures and words.

There are several aspects of LiFE that are important. Movement, interaction, and coordination are essential components of living organisms. Simple breathing is an interaction and coordination of many processes that result in the movement of air, water, carbon dioxide that permits us to stay alive. The energy and intelligence of these processes is LiFE.

In the same way, the movement of thoughts, emotions, memory, and intelligence in the mind requires LiFE. The movement of oxygen into the tissues is a result of the LiFE. The coordination of the senses, the balance of the blood circulation, the transportation of oxygen to the tissues, and the stimulation of physical and mental digestion are the results of the action of LiFE. It coordinates the heart and higher cerebral functions, as well as the actions of the CVS and TIE.

From its primary locations in the heart, hypothalamus and cranial space, LiFE *governs* expression, enthusiasm, bliss, and the development of higher consciousness. It is a part of the life-creating capacity in reproductive fluids.

LiFE is affected by many factors including food, environment, taste, aroma, breathing, and spiritual behaviors. An awareness of the benefits of cultivating Life Force Energy can lead to improved health, self-control, and power.

In the final analysis, both Jesus and Yoda were probably using yoga techniques to control Life Force Energy. So can we.

CORVETTE VIBES
SUBTLE ENERGY

In modern medicine and in physics, energy assumes many forms. In the human body, there is *electrical* energy that is measurable with electrodes, and there is chemical energy that is measurable by heat production and other means. There is also the *kinetic* energy that one measures by recording the speed, mass of the body as it moves.

But there are more subtle types of energy in the body. *Mental energy*, for example, is more difficult to define and measure. Brain waves can be recorded and measured, and mental stamina can be quantified by aptitude tests.

Some people radiate an *enthusiastic energy*. They are alert, connected, focused and ready to go! Being around them makes us feel alive and energized! Other people generate only somnolence, passivity and inertia that feels like an energy black hole. Still others have an energy that seems other-worldly. Famous people on public display generate a sense of awe that has its own special energy.

If we allow ourselves to accept the possibility that these subtle forms of energy exist, then understanding how they work opens up healing options that escape us if we demand energy systems that must be grossly measurable. The Eastern healing arts and philosophies recognize these and other subtle energy systems. It is understood that dealing with the subtle is not easy. It takes an open mind and a higher degree of sensitivity.

There is something extra exciting about a highly polished, perfectly tuned, powerful, shiny new Corvette Stingray that is impossible to measure. But, dude! … those "vibes" are REAL! - if you can FEEL!

CHANNELING THE FORCE
LIFE FORCE SYSTEMS

Ice is a solid condensation of liquid water, which is itself a condensation of gaseous steam. It's all water, but in different density forms.

In a similar way, according to quantum theory, the physical body is a form of condensed matter, energy, and consciousness. It's all consciousness, but in different density forms.

Ultimately, everything derives from a *condensation of consciousness*. In the yogic/ayurvedic system "consciousness" is condensed into "intelligence" which is, in turn, condensed and arranged in patterns known as "mind." There is still another distillation into the "life-force" and other subtle energies, and from there, yet another condensation produces the physical body.

These condensations (known as "Koshas") are depicted in Figure 28-1.

FIGURE 28-1: **ENERGY CONDENSATIONS**

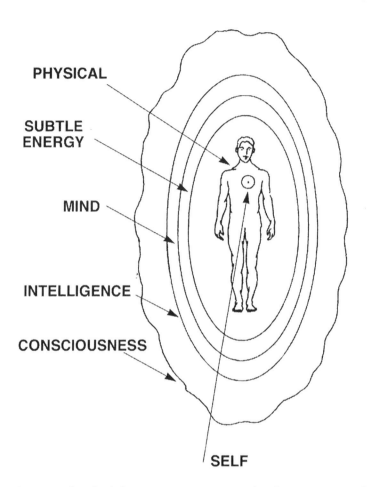

PHYSICAL

SUBTLE ENERGY

MIND

INTELLIGENCE

CONSCIOUSNESS

SELF

An example of subtle energy movement is the electromagnetic field that is created around a wire through which electricity is conducted. The gross electrical energy that is transmitted through physical nerves also generates a subtle electromagnetic field.

Both subtle and gross energies are real, and both have effects on the body. Subtle energy also moves in patterns that are fairly consistent. One study of these patterns of subtle energy movement and their effects is called "*Polarity*" theory.

Human evolution began in the saltwater environment of the ocean. In its simplest form, the body can be viewed as a large bag of evolved salt water. Salt water conducts electricity, and there are subtle electrical currents that move

782

within the human saltwater body. Outside of the physical nervous system, these currents move in definite patterns, like the water currents in a the ocean. These patterns of subtle energy movement also form the basis of the science of acupuncture. Lines of energy movement in the body are defined by acupuncture "meridians" often seen in illustrations depicting acupuncture (Figures 28-2).

FIGURE 28-2: **SUBTLE ENERGY MERIDIANS** [68]

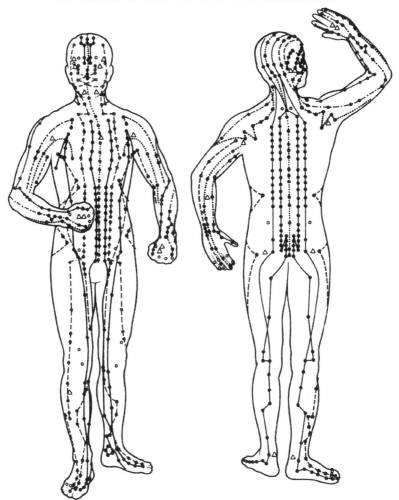

Each individual line of subtle energy flow functions like an individual nerve fiber. These subtle energy nerves, known as "*Nadis*," permeate the entire body and connect organs and tissues for functional purposes (figure 28-3). 72,000 of them converge in the area of the umbilicus. They branch throughout the body terminating at many different points of sensation and action. Their termination in the hands and feet form the basis for the science of Reflexology.

FIGURE 28-3: **SUBTLE ENERGY NERVES** [68]

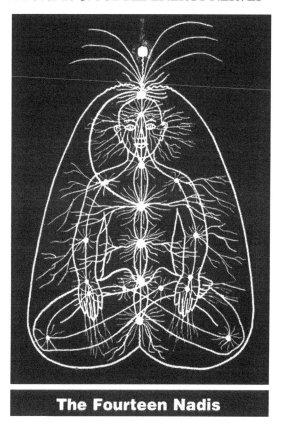

The body is also divided into subtle energy compartments or Oval Fields. At the junction points of these fields are energy centers that also function as capacitor storage points for subtle energy. These *chakras* are also important transfer points for subtle energy. Their approximate locations are shown in Figure 28-4. Chakras also serve as connections between the body, mind and spirit, and are discussed in the next section.

The flow of energy can be impeded at any point in this energy system. This can lead to inadequate energy in some parts of the body and too much in others. Such energy imbalances can be the cause of innumerable illnesses such as headaches, high blood pressure, fatigue, abdominal pain, anxiety, appetite loss, gastrointestinal disorders, and breathing difficulties.

The techniques that are used to release subtle energy blockages and to restore the proper flow of subtle electrical currents are an important part of many Eastern medical sciences. The subtle energy system can be influenced by physical manipulations of the pathways and centers by techniques such as exercise, yoga postures, and deep massage work. It can also be affected through the subtle system's connections to the skin where acupuncture, acupressure, massage, yoga poses, polarity, and other modalities are used.

Acupuncture is the best known of these forms of treatment. It has been accepted as an effective tool for many types of maladies, especially for pain and chronic musculoskeletal conditions.

MAJOR HIGHWAY JUNCTIONS
PRIMARY ENERGY CENTERS

There are many energy centers in the subtle energy system that serve as energy storage and connection points. Seven of these centers are major areas for this energy transfer.

These centers, known as chakras, are described as spinning wheels of energy that govern the five primal elements of earth, water, fire, air, and space. They also exert control over the five senses and the organs of action. They function as connection points between the mind, body, and spirit, and represent a person's spiritual progression from preoccupation with the mundane to blissful union with spirit.

They are connected to the body systems, and especially to the autonomic nervous and endocrine systems. They function as valves for controlling the energy flow to various parts of the body. If there are problems with energy flow through these centers, then problems will manifest in the areas they influence. The presence of Life Force Energy helps to open these interchanges, and the buildup of Composite Vital Strength helps these interchanges to develop.

Because they are also connected to the mind, psychological symptoms can manifest in the areas the energy centers govern. Virtuous activity will result in smooth function and interaction of these energy centers, while difficult behavior will cause blockages of energy flow.

These invisible centers are usually described by their location and sometimes by their function. The major centers are located near the front of the spine along the center of the body, and are arranged from the base of the spine up to the top of the head (Figure 28-4). Each center is also associated with different qualities, colors, sounds, deities, gems, and spiritual issues.

The first center is located near the base of the spinal column and is known as the *Root Chakra* or "Muladhara Chakra." It is associated with the earth element, but with the AIR quality. It is concerned with food and survival experiences, and is connected to the physical body manifestation of energy condensation. It is connected most intimately with the spleen, stomach and gonads. Its proper function yields groundedness.

FIGURE 28-4: **PRIMARY ENERGY CENTERS (Chakras)** [12]

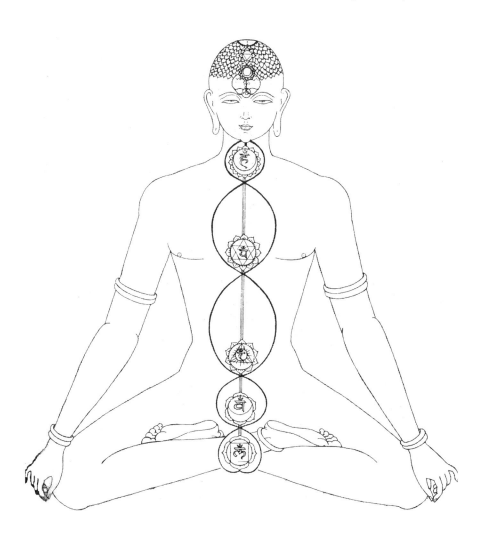

There is also said to be a reservoir of subtle energy located in the root energy center. This *kundalini* energy can be released by special practices and rise dramatically up the chain of energy centers ending in euphoric bliss at the top energy center. Such a release can be an awakening experience, but, if poorly controlled, can create problems as well.

Energy center number two is located in the pelvic area and is related to the water element and the EARTH quality. This energy hub ("Swadisthana Chakra") is concerned with procreation, self-identity, self-esteem, and prestige. It is connected to the kidneys, adrenals, sexual organs and to the Life Force Energy.

The third chakra center is located behind the umbilicus and is known as "Manipura Chakra." It is associated with the FIRE quality and element, and relates to the small intestine, heart, pancreas, gallbladder, and liver. It is closely connected to the mind, and is important in issues of power, control, achievement and ambition. Many inflammatory disorders may have their origin in a disturbance at this point.

The heart area is the location of the fourth energy center known as "Anahata Chakra." It is also functionally connected to the lungs and large intestine, and influences the thymus and immunity as well. Psycho-spiritually, the heart center is connected to forgiveness, knowledge and love.

Next is the throat energy center. It relates to the AIR quality and its disorders. The organs most directly affected by this "Vishudha Chakra" are the vocal cords, larynx, thyroid and parathyroid. When energy is concentrated into intellect, it connects with the throat center and influences communication, expression and will.

Between the eyebrows just behind the forehead is the sixth energy center known as "Ajna Chakra." It is closely connected to the mind and to spiritual desires. It is also concerned with intuition and connects to the pituitary gland. It connects to the ethereal bliss layer of consciousness.

At the top of the head, the Crown ("Sahasrara") chakra is the bridge between the upper levels of the mind and actual spirit. Some traditions describe a silver transitional energy/consciousness thread rising from this location to areas of higher consciousness. Psycho-spiritually, development of an awareness of the greater G-Self happens here. On the physical level, this energy center is connected to the pineal gland.

Running vertically through the center and connecting these energy centers is a major Central Subtle Energy Pathway ("Shushumna Nadi."). A pair of pathways ("Ida" & "Pingala") spiraling up and around this column of energy centers from the first to the sixth, trace the movement of subtle energy from root to top.

An awareness of these subtle energy centers and pathways can be helpful in diagnosing and treating many disorders of chronic and insidious origin. Some basic disorders associated with dysfunction of the primary energy centers are given in Table 28-1.

TABLE 28-1 **PRIMARY ENERGY CENTERS, ORGANS, ISSUES, DYSFUNCTIONS** [62, 63]

ENERGY CENTER	ORGANS	MENTAL/EMOTIONAL	PHYSICAL
Root	Spine base Legs Feet Rectum Immune system	Family & group safety Providing life necessities Self-assertion Feeling at home Law and order	Low back pain Varicose veins Sciatica Rectal tumors Immune disorders
Pubic	Sexual Large intestine Vertebrae, lower Pelvis Appendix Bladder Hips	Guilt, blame Sex, money Power, control Creativity Ethics Honor	Low back pain Sciatica Gynecologic problems Pelvic pain Sexual potency Urinary problems
Umbilicus	Abdomen Stomach Intestine, upper Liver Gallbladder Kidneys Pancreas Adrenals Spleen Spine, middle	Trust Fear, intimidation Self-esteem, confidence Self-care, care for others Decision making Criticism sensitivity Honor	Arthritis Ulcers, gastric & duodenal Colon, intestinal problems Liver dysfunction Anorexia, bulimia Indigestion Hepatitis Adrenal dysfunction
Heart	Heart Lungs Shoulders, arms Ribs, breasts	Love, hatred Resentment, bitterness Grief, anger Self-centeredness	Heart failure Heat attack Respiratory allergy Mitral valve prolapse

Location	Organs / Systems	Psychological	Disorders
Heart (cont.)	Diaphragm Thymus	Loneliness, commitment Forgiveness, compassion Hope, trust	Cardiomegaly Asthma Lung cancer, breast cancer Pneumonia Back pain, upper Shoulder pain
Throat	Throat Thyroid Trachea Spine, neck Mouth Teeth & gums Esophagus Parathyroid Hypothalamus	Choice Will Personal expression Dream pursuit Creativity Addiction Judgment, criticism Decision-making	Hoarseness Sore throat Mouth ulcers Gum disorders Temporomandibular dysf. Scoliosis Laryngitis Lymphadenitis, neck Thyroid disorders
Forehead	Brain Nervous system Eyes Ears Nose Pineal gland Pituitary	Self-evaluation Truth Intellect Inadequacy Openness Learning Emotional intelligence	Brain tumor, stroke Neurological disorders Sight Hearing Spinal (full) problems Learning disabilities Seizures
Crown	Muscular system Skeletal system Skin	Trust Ethics, courage Humanitarianism Selflessness Macro Perspective Spirituality, devotion Knowing	Energy disorders Depression Exhaustion, non-physical Light sensitivity Sound sensitivity Environmental sensitivity

TRAFFIC LIGHTS
ENERGY JUNCTION POINTS

The primary energy centers described above function as the main controllers of subtle energy flow in the body. Just as there are small highway intersections that control the flow of lesser amounts of traffic, there are many minor subtle energy interchanges scattered throughout the body.

These smaller energy junction points ("Marmas"), can become obstructed by injury, toxins, emotions and other factors. This can lead to wrong distribution of energy and subsequent illness. Working on these energy points with pressure (Acupressure, Turiya), needles (Acupuncture), heat (Moxibustion), or medications can relieve these obstructions restoring Life Force Energy flow and health.

These Energy Junction Points (EJP's) not only connect the major subtle energy pathways with the minor energy junctions, they are also the interface points where subtle energy "condenses" into physical energy.

There are 107 primary EJP's. Their location on the body is not precise because subtle energy itself is not as precisely condensed as is physical energy. They are identified during therapy by their approximate location, their sensitivity, and the effect of their being touched or manipulated. They can be small or large in size.

Some examples of these EJP's are shown in Figure 28-5.

FIGURE 28-5: **SOME ENERGY JUNCTION POINTS** [47]

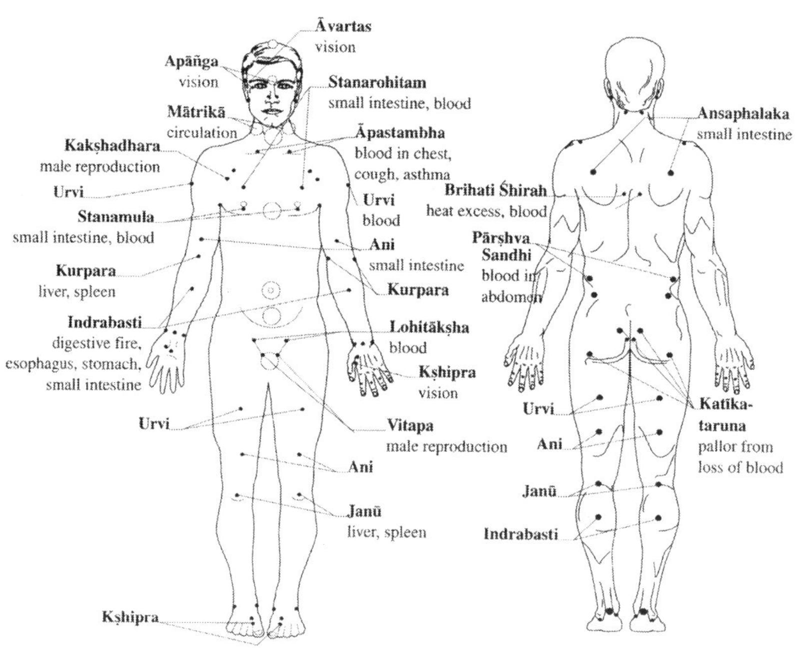

790

The EJP's are organized into groups depending on their association with a muscle, blood vessel, ligament, bone, or joint. EJP's are also classified by the intensity of response to touch. Martial arts make use of the importance and extreme sensitivities of some EJP's.

Knowledge of the location of the EJP's is useful in bodywork and massage because toxins, stress, and emotions can become stuck at these points. Yoga postures help stimulate and balance conditions at the EJP's. Breathing practices can also be helpful since the breath is closely connected to the movement and production of subtle energy itself.

Illness and disease can manifest as pain, blockage or swelling at the marma points, and relieving the blockage can help relieve the symptoms and improve the disease's outcome. Detoxification, rejuvenation, tonification, and making use of hidden energy reserves can also be aided by fixing the stoplights at these intersections.

BALANCED CIRCUITS
POLARITY ENERGY SYSTEM

When energy moves, an electrical field is often created in which one area is positively charged, another is negative, and a third area remains neutral. When gross nerve energy or subtle LiFE energy moves in the body, similar areas of positive, negative, or neutral charge are created. Both positive and negative energy need to complete a circuit back to their original source, or a charge buildup is created.

In the Ayurvedic subscience of Polarity Therapy, the movement of these energies and the buildup of their charges in different areas of the body is studied. Since energy is always moving from the physical to the subtle and back, the areas of concern in polarity therapy are wide-ranging. They include everything from the buildup of physical and emotional energy to one's connection with cosmic forces, as well as the effect on physical organs.

In polarity theory, there are several Energy Zones that are defined by the physical body and by the subtle energy body and its Primary Energy Centers (Figure 28-6). The five elements of ether, air, fire, water, and earth are also considered in the definition of Oval Fields of energy in the head, neck, abdomen, chest, and pelvis. The elements and fields are connected to the Primary Energy Centers.

Within each of the zones there are energy relationships that are either normal and functional, or abnormal and dysfunctional. There are also relationships between the zones such that a disturbance in one zone may resonate with a disturbance in another distant zone. In this way, distant energy issues can be the cause of local problems.

The transitional areas between zones are important energy transfer points. A good flow of energy inside and between zones gives health, while blockages in energy movement create excess energy buildup and illness.

There are other patterns of subtle energy movement that are identified in polarity. There are Long Lines of subtle current that run up and down the body from head to toe (Figure 28-6). There are also currents that run in a Spiral pattern starting at the belly button in the side-to-side plane of the body and another spiral pattern that starts at the top of the head and spirals down around the body like a hula hoop. These current patterns create an "invisible anatomy" that is described by several energy systems.

Connective tissue bridges many of the zones, and is a means of energy transfer. In this way, body functions are integrated. Energy disturbances can lead to connective tissue disorders and vice versa. Emotional energy is especially likely to lodge in the connective tissue. In the ayurvedic tradition, many connective tissue diseases are associated with specific emotional issues. In polarity therapy, special attention is paid to the role of connective tissue in health and illness.

Trapped energy can even crystallize and condense from the mental/emotional level into the physical. These crystals act as foreign bodies that irritate and are rejected by the body's immune system. This rejection forms the basis of some autoimmune disease. Areas of excess fat, or abnormal skin texture, elasticity, temperature, and color may appear as manifestations of trapped energy.

When these energy imbalances occur, they can manifest outwardly in the subtle and physical bodies. The posture may become imbalanced and body language may reflect the state of internal energy balance. The expression of thought and emotion are also reflections of internal energy status. One of the functions of the polarity therapist is to help the patient become aware of how their energy is being used or misused, and guide them in developing goals for healthier energy use and balance.

In the bodywork that is done in polarity therapy, the hands of the therapist are used to reflect energy imbalance patterns back to the patient. Patients can then learn to soften the blocked boundaries by letting go of whatever fear creates these blockages. There are specific physical exercises for helping the energy move from zone to zone.

DIGITAL ELECTRONICS
ENERGY POSES

Normally, subtle LiFE energy escapes from the body and dissipates, so techniques that help to retain subtle energy are important. One such set of techniques is known as "Mudra."

Mudras are most often recognized as positioning the fingers in certain patterns

FIGURE 28-6: **POLARITY CURRENTS & ZONES** [76]

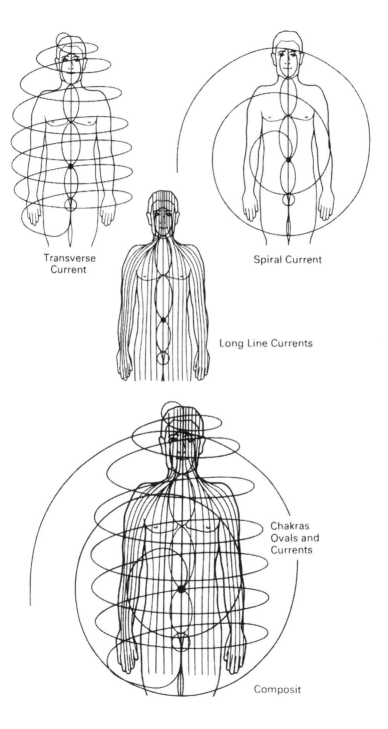

Transverse
Current

Spiral Current

Long Line Currents

Chakras
Ovals and
Currents

Composit

(Figure 28-7), but they can also be hand, eye, or arm poses. They may also be combined with yoga poses, breathing exercises, muscle locks, colors, or visualizations. Energy poses are subtle physical positions that may deepen the awareness, concentration, and effects of other activities. They are said to awaken LiFE energy, stimulate primary energy centers, and open the LiFE reservoir at the base of the spine. They direct energy to the upper primary energy centers, promote an awareness of the flow of LiFE, and help move energy toward higher states of consciousness.

These poses also help establish a link between body, mind, and LiFE. They link individual LiFE force with universal forces. They help to develop expression of the state of mind, mood, attitude, and perception. The mind also becomes introverted, aiding in processes such as concentration, and sensory withdrawal. In this way, they are said to help with deepening meditation, coming to terms with the past, solving everyday problems, improving relationships, and building character.

Because subtle energy travels in definite patterns in the hands and fingers, connecting different parts of the hand to each other can be useful in dealing with energy issues in these distant areas. As with foot reflexology, areas of the hand form reflex zones that are connected to different areas of the body. The fingers can reflex to specific internal organs, Primary Energy Centers, minor energy transfer points, psychological characteristics, the basic natural elements, and even the different planets.

FIGURE 28-7: **ENERGY POSES (Mudras)** [36]

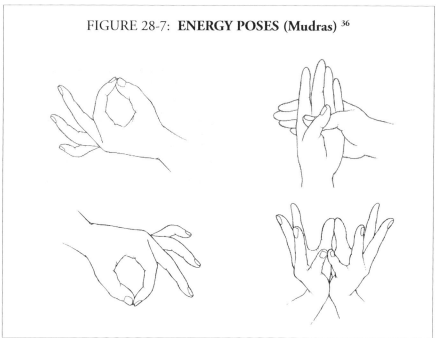

LOCKS & KEYS
ENERGY LOCKS

Body locks are another technique for managing the subtle energy in the body. In this practice, muscles in a particular area of the body are held in contraction to redirect the flow of LiFE to the central energy pathway for purposes of health improvement and spiritual awakening.

During this practice, the breath is usually held in exhalation and the awareness centered to one or more points in the body. This process acts to open three of the psychic control centers (known as "Granthis"). The Locks can be done alone, or with breathing or hand pose exercises.

There are three basic locks and one combination of the three. They all have physical and psychospiritual benefits, and are performed on an empty stomach.

The Anal Lock ("Moola Bandha") is similar to the Kegel exercise done by women to strengthen their perineal muscles. It involves a pulling up of the muscles of the perineal floor between the anus and the testes in the male, and behind the cervix in the female. This practice stimulates the pelvic nerves, and tones the urogenital and excretory systems. It stimulates intestinal movement, and helps to relive constipation and hemorrhoids. It is also therapeutic for anal fissures, ulcers, prostatits, prostatic hypertrophy, asthma, bronchitis and arthritis. It is also good for depression, as well as for psychosomatic and degenerative illnesses.

It is also used for the relief of many sexual disorders. It improves ejaculation control, and aids in the redirection of sexual energy toward spiritual development. It also helps with the alignment of the physical, mental, and spiritual bodies, and energizes the perineal energy center. It is not a good practice if there are problems with hyperactivity.

The Abdominal Lock ("Udiyana Bandha") involves exhaling, sucking the stomach inward and upward, and holding the breath. This practice is good for abdominal ailments such as indigestion, constipation, and diabetes. It helps stimulate digestive energy, balance the adrenals and relieves anxiety and tension as well as improving the blood circulation. This practice is not to be done if there are problems with colitis, stomach or intestinal ulcers, high blood pressure, heart disease, or glaucoma.

The Throat Lock ("Jalandhara Bandha") is done by exhaling and bringing the chin to the chest creating an energy stimulating lock in the neck. This lock helps regulate the circulatory, respiratory, and metabolic systems. It helps with mental relaxation, stress reduction, and the development of meditative introversion and one-pointed concentration. It energizes the primary throat energy center and helps to regulate the circulation, relieve stress, and reduce anxiety and anger. If neck disorders, vertigo, high blood pressure or heart disease are present, it is a good idea to avoid this practice.

Once these three energy locks have been mastered, they can be combined together in the Triple Lock. Those with contraindications for doing the previous three locks should not do the Triple Lock either, and pregnant women should also refrain from using this technique.

Those who are able to do the Triple Lock get the benefits of the individual locks and a balancing of the entire endocrine system. Aging and degeneration are said to be markedly slowed by this practice, and rejuvenation of the body is aided. It helps to open the flow of subtle energy in the Primary Energy Centers, and helps quiet the mind for meditation.

FIGURE 27-8: **BODY LOCKS** [33]

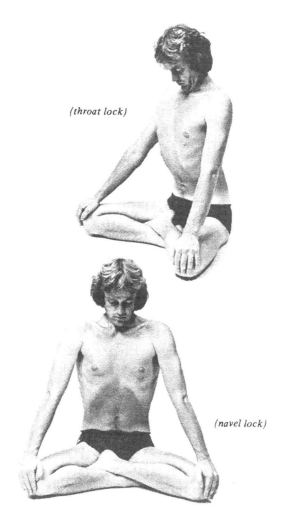

(throat lock)

(navel lock)

HOOD ORNAMENTS
VISUAL PATTERN THERAPIES

When trying to center a car on a highway, a hood ornament can be helpful in a subtle way. In a similar manner, aids for centering of the mind and spirit on life's highway can be helped by the use of visual patterns.

Some concepts are better understood or expressed with images than with words. When trying to quiet the mind, the use of words can be counter-productive because the mind is often activated by words and thoughts. An appropriately sized visual pattern is held at reading distance, and a steady gaze at the pattern restricts the field of vision and limits stimuli to the mind. Visual patterns are used for promoting peaceful tasks, developing attention, and stopping excess mind chatter.

These patterns ("Yantras") are usually square shaped, and contain a point in the center that signifies the origin, unity, manifestation, and emanation of creation. There are also circles, triangles, and squares that have different effects on the field of vision, and different effects on the stability of the mind (see Figure 28-9). The patterns also are symbolic of different aspects of nature, behavior, and divinity. In the Ayurvedic tradition, they may also be connected to deities, astrological elements, numbers, and they may form the basis for sacred architectural plans.

Circular visual patterns known as "Mandalas" can also be therapeutic. They consist of a center, radiations from the center, and the periphery of the circle. The center represents the spiritual force, the radiations from the center the connection of the inner with the outer periphery. This radiating circular pattern is common in nature and extends from patterns of crystals to patterns of stars radiating out from the center of galaxies.

Mandalas are designed to draw thoughts toward the center—toward the origin of divine consciousness that is everywhere. The eye is easily attracted to this pattern, and the iris of the eye is itself a mandala that points the way to internal eternal consciousness. The journey toward that inner consciousness through meditation can be aided by concentration on these visual patterns.

The combination of a visual pattern with a spoken or thought-referenced phrase engages both the verbal and visual parts of the brain. This renders both techniques more effective.

Qualities are created in visual patterns by the use of colors and shapes that enforce the different qualities.. Most of these patterns give EARTH quality stability while those that are more activating promote the FIRE and AIR qualities. The AIR quality is balanced by shapes that are square, thick, and symmetrical, and by textures that are soft instead of rough and harsh. A FIRE quality excess is helped by shapes that are round and soft. EARTH types do best with pyramidal shapes with sharp angles rather than with round or square images.

Creating such a geometrical pattern is a good practice because it requires accuracy, discipline, concentration, and patience. Focusing on these patterns helps to develop these qualities in the mind, reduces distractions, and stimulates the right hemisphere of the brain. Looking at these visual patterns can be calming and centering for the mind.

FIGURE 28-9: **VISUAL PATTERN (Sri Yantra)**

SHRI YANTRA

ROCKIN' TUNES ON THE RADIO
SOUND THERAPY

In some philosophies, sound is the primary manifestation of divine consciousness. According to ayurvedic tradition, sound controls and conditions the waking consciousness, the subconscious, and the super conscious as well as the sensory mind and intelligence. Since health ultimately derives from mind and consciousness, sound is an important health consideration.

Sound moves the heart as well as the mind. Sound connects us with the outside world. The sound of words and speech are crucial for our mental conditioning, mind structuring, communication and expression. The sounds of words have a subtle energy component, and their vibrations connect us to the sensory and psychological fields of others. Words are the powerful vehicles by which the mind can express itself. Thoughts have sound components that are colored by desires, aspirations, and conditioning.

Sounds are closely connected to emotions and are vehicles for expressing emotion. Singing sounds usually reflect joy, shouting sounds reveal anger, crying sounds show sorrow, groaning may mean pain, and screaming sounds often convey fear. Soothing repetitive sounds can help to release emotions.

Sounds are most closely associated with the AIR quality, so the use of sound therapies can be especially helpful in AIR quality imbalance disorders. Sounds that harmonize help in mental and emotional digestion, while discordant sounds that don't fit create stimulation and stress.

An excess of the EARTH quality can be balanced with sound that is light, and high-pitched. FIRE excess is balanced with sweet, soft music, and AIR with low-pitched sounds.

UNFORGETTABLE RADIO JINGLES
MANTRA PHRASE REPETITION THERAPY

One such sound-oriented healing technique involves the repetition of a sound or phrase with special therapeutic energy. These phrases (known as "Mantras") are repeated in a regular manner and in so doing, they change the subtle energetic structure of the mind.

The mind and consciousness have a vibratory background pattern like the rhythm of a song. Repetitive phrases work on this vibratory pattern and change dysynchronous and unhealthy rhythms into more pleasant and effective ones. Part of mental "digestion" involves creating this harmony of internal sound. Mantra phrases do this well because they carry sounds that are soothing and healing, and sacred phrases with "special power." Of course a phrase with a negative energy effects can be repeated as is the case in the curses of voodoo practice.

Positive phrases bring an infusion of Life Force Energy and balance the AIR, FIRE, and EARTH qualities. They purify the environment, change the patterns of the mind and elevate subconscious thought patterns.

As tools for healing the mind, mantra phrases work differently from other psychological transformation techniques. The physical sound characteristics of mantra phrases work by energetically "dissolving" problem thought patterns instead of reinforcing the difficulties by focusing on them.

Psychological disorders are viewed as imbalances of energy in the mental field. Mantras with balancing energy are used to rebalance the mind. Some phrases with active, rough energy are needed for overcoming mental inertia, while others have energies that help with ego dissolution, self-awareness, love, wisdom seeking, and the pursuit of higher truth. Mantra phrases are used to overcome deep-seated latent psychological tendencies known as "Samskaras." They are also used in preparing the mental field for meditation by simplifying and quieting the mind. Like white noise, they help remove thought distractions.

Coordinating mantra with many other healing techniques can help improve the outcome. Using repetitive mantra patterns with breath control, visual patterns, or physical therapies such as acupressure or yoga postures enhances their effect. Doing most anything with mantra support can raise its effectiveness.

Mantras can be used as exercises for the mind in the same way that physical exercises are used for the body. They help with mind control, mind strength, and the ability to resist negative external influences. Extended periods of repetition may be used for mental or consciousness clearing.

Repetitive phrases can be used anytime, but they can be especially helpful when used at night for restful sleep. The specific health benefits of some simple one-word Mantras are given in Table 28-2.

TABLE 28-2:

MIND / SPIRIT EFFECTS of PHRASE REPETITION

Energizing, Empowering, Emptying Primary Mantra	"OM"
Negative Energy Dissolution, Nerve function, Expression Negative Influences	"Hum"
Life-Force, Divinity, Protection Strength, Peace, AIR excess Mental Disorders, Immunity Digestive Energy	"Raam"
Concentration, Thinking, Speech Intelligence, Creativity, Mental & Nervous Disorders Learning, Communication	"Ayeem"
Health, Beauty, Creativity, Prosperity, Plasma, Reproduction, Refinement, Sensitivity	"Shreem"
Cleansing, Transformation, Energy, Joy, Realignment, Atonement, Detoxification Cardiac strengthening	"Hreem"
Work, Action, Power, Efficacy	"Kream"
Strength, Sexual Vitality, Emotional Control, Grounding, AIR excess, Food Preparation Medicinal Preparation	"Kleem"
Pain, Agitation, Peace, Calm, Tremors, Palpitations Detachment, Nerve Degeneration	"Shaam"
Energy, Vitality, Sexual Vigor, Fertility, Artistry	"Shooom"
Cerebrospinal Fluid Nourishment, Energy, Mind, Heart, Nerves, Rejuvenation	"Sohm"
Knowledge, Intelligence, Math & Science Ability Logic, Patience, Endurance	"Gum"
Wisdom, Power, Transcendence, Transformation EARTH excess	"Haum"

In addition to having effects on the mind and the spirit, mantra sounds also relate directly to each of the different types of body tissues. According to Ayurvedic tradition, mantras can be used to strengthen and stabilize these tissues.

TABLE 28-3: **PHRASES for STRENGTHENING BODY TISSUES**	
Plasma	"Yam"
Blood	"Ram"
Muscle	"Lam"
Fat	"Vam"
Bone	"Shaam"
Nerve	"Shum"
Reproductive	"Sam"

AIR quality excess individuals should not chant out loud for more than a few minutes and should not use too much "OM" as it increases space. They can use "Ram," "Lum" "Vum" and "Hreem,"

FIRE quality excess can use "OM," "Ayeem", "Shreem," and "Shaam." EARTH excess problems should be helped through the plentiful use of active mantras such as "Hum," "OM," and "Ayeem."

More complex mantra sounds for specific situations can be found by consulting a yogi skilled in matching people, situations, and problems wth therapeutic sounds.

SOOTHING IN-DASH STEREO
MUSIC THERAPY

Subtle energy is reinforced by music. Putting repetitive phrases to music in the form of chanting is an important part of yogic/ayurvedic practice. The calming, organizing effects of the repeated phrases with special vibrations help to calm and quiet the mind. When the mind is quieted, union with spirit is more easily achieved.

Music has many different qualities. As such, different types of music can be either soothing or unbalancing for those with quality disturbances. For those with excess AIR quality who are troubled by excess motion, music that is slow, warm, soft, and sweet is best. Tones that are lower in the scale may be more soothing to the AIR types who should avoid listening to fast, high-pitched, agitating, or loud music.

FIRE types can also listen to slower music to calm their normally active natures. Higher pitched, sweet tones such as flute and harp are good for them. EARTH quality people, on the other hand, need the stimulation of faster, loud music. Marches and dance music are good in this case.

Different types of music are appropriate for different times of day. When energy is needed in the morning, lively music is used. When evening comes, calming is in order. Different seasons also require music that balances their qualities. Hot summers are improved by light, cool music, while heavy winters need more stimulating sounds.

The vibrations of the body's subtle energy system resonate with musical notes as well. Specific notes on the scale are associated with each of the Primary Energy Centers. Their use helps move subtle energy through the body's subtle energy channels, and the use of tuning forks can be helpful practice.

IMITATING THE PROBLEM
HOMEOPATHY

Subtle energy disturbances can be treated with the subtle energy science of homeopathy. The principles that govern this approach are also derived from the ancient Ayurvedic texts.

Each illness produces symptoms that are the result of the body's efforts to fight the cause of the disease. A primary homeopathic principle is that illnesses may be decreased by encouraging the body to more easily recognize and fight the *symptoms* the illness produces. The body's ability to recognize and fight these symptoms can be stimulated by introducing molecular imprints from tiny amounts of substances that produce the same symptoms as the primary illness. These *similar* symptom-producing substances are not toxic like the primary cause of the original disease. The body learns to fight back.

This principle of "like cures like" symptoms is known as the Law of Similars. In modern medicine, immunizations can work in a similar way. The body is trained to attack particles produced by weakened vaccine germs that are similar to the offending bug, but unable to produce actual disease.

The modern medical practice of allergy "hypo-immunization" may be another way of looking at what is happening in homeopathy. A very small amount of the substance that created the problem is given. This causes the body to build a familiarity with the irritant and avoid reacting to it.

The fact that the amount of stimulating substance used in a homeopathy prepa-ration is so small often leads the Western mind to conclude that no effect can be possible. The issues of concern in homeopathy are largely those of *subtle* energy responses, so *subtle* amounts of material are thought to be effective. In fact, the more subtle the amount, the more effect it may have because *subtle* qualities are being cultivated. The result is that less substance gives more results. This gives rise to the homeopathic Law of Infinitesimals in which very dilute amounts are used. A further reduction in the interactive particle size is achieved by a shaking of the solution.

Homeopathy is used to strengthen the body's defense systems and to stimulate emotional and mental healing. It appears to work best in chronic illness, although many people use it for acute problems as well.

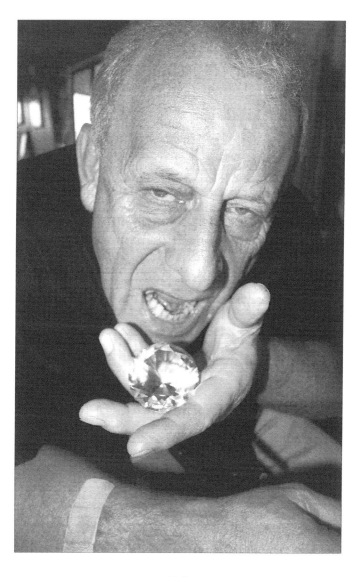

REAR-VIEW MIRROR ORNAMENTS
GEM THERAPY

Another subtle energy therapy involves the use of gems. They are said to vitalize, energize, and protect the body and mind. They strengthen the aura, the astral body, and their connections with the mind. As natural substances, they help to align a person with the healing forces of nature. Because most come from deep inside the earth, they are said to act on deep-seated emotions.

For the gems to exert their subtle influence, they need to be of sufficient size, and they need to touch the skin when being worn. In the ayurvedic tradition, gems are also correlated with specific planets, and work to balance the influences of the planets on the mind, body, and spirit.

When gems are ground into a powder and the power burned to an ash by a special procedure, gems can act as medicines for certain conditions (see Table 28-6). They can also be soaked in alcohol to make a medicinal tincture that works on the Life Force Energy of a patient.

The more expensive gems are said to be more powerful, but substitutes of lesser quality but larger size can be used if necessary. Traditionally gems are associated with an ability to provide psychological and emotional qualities to the long-term wearer as outlined in Table 28-4.

TABLE 28-4: **GEMS & PSYCHO-SPIRITUAL QUALITIES**

ATTRIBUTE	GEM
Self-esteem, Energy, Leadership	Ruby, Spinel, Garnet
Love, Peace, Calm	Pearl, Moonstone
Vitality, Will, Acceptance	Red coral
Balance of Mind, Perception & Judgment	Emerald, Peridot, Green Tourmaline Green Zircon, Jade
Wisdom, Strength, Creativity	Yellow Sapphire & Topaz, Citrine
Love, Sensitivity, Imagination	Diamond, White Sapphire & Coral, Clear Zircon & Quartz
Detachment, Patience, Independence	Blue Sapphire, Amethyst, Lapis
Perception, Judgment, Thinking	Garnet
Insight, Focus, Concentration	Cat's Eye

PAINT JOB
COLOR THERAPY

Colors have qualities. They can be bright and stimulating, dull and calming, or fairly neutral. As such, colors affect the different body quality types and therefore, the health of the individual.

A person with an excess of the AIR quality can be helped by being around colors that are warming such as gold, orange, and yellow. Calming colors like white, whitish-blue, and white-green can also be helpful for the hyper mobile AIR types. Colors should not be too bright or iridescent, and flashy colors like red, purple, and bright yellow may be too much for imbalanced AIR types. Black, brown, and grey may serve to devitalize the AIR quality, so they should avoid them as well.

FIRE quality excess is balanced by pastel colors that are cool, calming and mild such as white, blue, gray and green. The FIRE quality is aggravated by hot, stimulating colors like red, orange and yellow. Neon-like colors that are very bright and intense can make a FIRE imbalance worse. Color is helpful for balancing the FIRE quality because visual input is especially important for FIRE-types.

Those with excess EARTH quality do best with warm, stimulating colors. Strong contrasts and bright colors work best for them. Orange, yellow, gold, and red are best for EARTH quality people. Their colors should be light and luminous and not soft like pink or baby blue. Avoid black color, which darkens the outlook.

Clothing coloring that is consistent with the need for quality balancing is important, and an environment with these colors can be quite helpful.

Colors can also profoundly affect the mind, and, therefore, healing. Stimulation can result from contrasting colors such as red and green, or blue and yellow. Sedative colors include green, gray, and white. Colors are important in shaping and communicating moods and emotions. They act as nutrition for the mind, life force, and for the blood.

Bright colors are associated both with motivation and anger, and they can increase clarity, focus, action, perception, passion, anger, irritability, and criticism. They can also stimulate the digestive fire, but an excess can burn up the Composite Vital Strength. Color helps with orientation, perception, and attracts attention.

Color helps with external and internal visualization practices. Focusing attention on the golden color of a ghee-fueled flame is a common meditative practice. Color is an important part of visual pattern therapy and gem therapy and can create a harmony among the natural elements.

Color often reflects the state of a person's health. Jaundice, pallor, and plethora are examples of the way that color can be observed in the diagnostic process.

Blue light and green light can be used to help heal wounds, and visual color therapy is often used for psychological healing effects (Table 28-5).

TABLE 28-5: **COLOR EFFECTS**

Red	Stimulates circulation, alertness, aggression, warming
Orange	Lightness, balancing sexuality, superficiality, mood lightening
Yellow	Digestion, alertness, obtrusiveness
Green	Calming, regenerative, initiative
Blue	Stability, security, protection, yearning
Violet	Transformation, spirituality, higher consciousness
Brown	Stability, earth, stagnation
White	Contains all beneficial effects, purity, inclusivity
Black	Protection, emptiness, regrouping, sadness, pessimism, avoidance

WHAT'S YOUR (ROAD) SIGN?
ASTROLOGY

Another influence on the consciousness and body in traditional Ayurvedic thinking is the position of the Earth and the heavenly bodies.

It is clear to anyone who deals with the tides that the moon's influence on the ocean is significant. Because we are also made mostly of salt water, the influence of the moon on our physiology is significant.

The other planets and stars are said to influence our lives by their vibrational radiation, according to astrological thinking. The moon is close enough to give an obvious gravitational effect on our world. The other heavenly bodies exert a much smaller gravitational effect. Planets orbiting distant stars exert enough pull on those stars to cause detectable changes in the star's shapes and vibrations. Presumably, the planets do the same subtle things to us.

The positions of the stars and planets relative to each other are different at every moment in time. Unlike a clock that repeats itself at twice daily intervals, the celestial clock is never the same from moment to moment. This uniqueness is an attractive way to highlight the uniqueness of each individual being.

An awareness of the predictable planetary movements is helpful since any predictability lessens life's uncertainty. Elaborate and differing astrological systems have been developed to associate planetary positions with life events. Like any other religion, this belief system has its basis in tradition. Tradition provides a helpful rhythm and security to life.

Traditional ayurvedic medicine takes these influences into account in explaining the presence of problems, and predicting optimal times for medical interventions. It is difficult for the analytic scientific mind to accept that such subtle and vague influences have significance.

Astrology also highlights the nature of physical existence as a manifestation of the qualities that the planets represent. Venus represents the love influence, Mars the violence aspect and so on. It highlights the influence of cosmic consciousness. An awareness of one's place in the cosmos is emphasized by thinking about celestial objects and events. Knowing one's place in a larger scheme of the solar system and universe may thereby bring a sense of understanding, security, and predictability.

PENETRATING OILS
MEDICINAL CARRIERS

In order for a medication to be effective, it must be able to get to the area of concern. In ayurveda, the choice of such a vehicle ("Anupan") is very important.

Different vehicles have different abilities to access the various tissues, organs, and systems. They have varying abilities to function quickly, penetrate deeply, and affect energy levels. They can help or hinder the balancing of the AIR, FIRE, and EARTH qualities, and they are more effective in certain disease conditions than in others. If toxins are present, their effects can also vary.

For the delivery of medication in a condition of AIR quality excess, warm water is often the preferred vehicle. If excess FIRE is the problem, then milk, cool water, or maple syrup can be used. EARTH quality excesses are improved with hot water, honey, or ginger tea as carrier substances.

If extra penetration into the tissue, organ, or system is required, then a deeply penetrating vehicle (a "Yoga Vahi") may be required. In the AIR disorder situation, deep penetration is achieved using ghee, or gold water. For FIRE disturbances, ghee or milk are preferred, and for EARTH quality excess, bitter ghee, gold water or copper water are used.

The various food carriers, their quality effects, and some of their specific actions and uses are listed in Tables A-12 & A-13 in the appendix of Volume One.

Delivery of a medication also depends on the way it is prepared. Freshly harvested herb, herb pulps, concoctions, infusions, and teas are among the many choices for medication delivery.

HEALING ASHTRAYS
MEDICINAL ASH PREPARATIONS

Minerals are important in health maintenance for everything from the calcium in bones to the trace minerals needed for complex enzymatic reactions.

In modern medicine, minerals such as calcium, magnesium, zinc, iron, and chromium are commonly taken internally for health maintenance, and sulfur is also used externally. Minerals are also used in ayurveda, but they are often given in a purified ash form that makes them stronger, more easily absorbed, more rapid acting, and more effective.

These ash preparations ("Bhasmas") are made by repeatedly heating the material and then dipping it seven times into each of several purifying liquids. These preparations are said to be good for longevity, and support of the mind and nervous system. They increase Composite Vital Strength, Transformational Intelligent Energy, and Life Force Energy as well.

In addition to the minerals mentioned, ash preparations are also made from metals and gems. Gold has been used in modern medicine for the treatment of arthritis, and iron for the treatment of anemia, and these metals are also used more effectively in ash form in ayurvedic medicine.

Mercury is considered to be highly toxic *in its elemental form*, but the ayurvedic preparations that use mercury ("Ras" preparations) for its highly potent and penetrating qualities use only the *highly purified and non-toxic forms* of this metal. Just as poisons are carefully used in modern chemotherapy, purified ash preparations of mercury are used just as carefully in ayurveda. They have been utilized effectively this way for thousands of years without toxic results. An open mind on this subject allows for the inclusion of these powerful treatments for serious problems that have no effective modern medical cures.

The medicinal effects of some of the ash preparations are described in Table 28-6.

TABLE 28-6: **MEDICINAL EFFECTS of ASH PREPARATIONS**

GEM	ASH NAME	USED FOR
Agate	Akika	Bleeding, thrombocytopenia
Amber	Trunakant	Peptic ulcer, ulcerative colitis, diabetic ulcer
Conch	Shanka	Colitis, gastritis, gastric ulcer, vomiting
Copper	Tamra	Cirrhosis, hepatitis, fatty degeneration, lipoma, aphrodisiac
Coral	Praval	Osteoporosis, hyperacidity, pyrexia, osteoporosis
Cowry	Karpardic	Malabsorption, sprue, enteritis, diarrhea
Diamond	Hira	Bronchogenic carcinoma, diabetes, TB
Dearhorn	Shringa	Coronary artery disease, degenerative arthritis osteoporosis, asthma, hypertension
Egg Shell	Kukkutanda	Bone, nail, hair disorders, teething, ulcerative colitis, rickets, aphrodisiac
Emerald	Panna	Multiple sclerosis, ADD, depression, hepatitis, schizophrenia, heart disease, nervousness
Gold	Suvarna	Heart failure, arthritis, memory
Iron	Lauha	Anemia, bleeding
Mica	Abrak	Immune support, TB
Pearl	Moti	FIRE disorders, gastritis, ulcerative colitis, osteoporosis, tooth degeneration
Ruby	Manikkya	Energy, CVS, TIE, fatigue, heart failure, heart attack
Sapphire (blue)	Nilam	Rheumatoid arthritis, insomnia
Silver	Raupya	Sperm inadequate, osteoporosis
Tourmaline	Vaikrant	Asthma, TB, malignancy, diabetes

CHROME FINISH
METAL THERAPY

Metals have their own unique qualities. They may be heating or cooling, so they affect the AIR, FIRE, and EARTH qualities in different ways (see Table 28-14). Their effects are used in jewelry and in the ash preparations described above. Metals are also boiled in water, or combined with purified sulfur and/or mercury to make highly potent medicines.

When used as jewelry, both their subtle energies and their gross medicinal qualities are transmitted by touching the skin, or by slow absorption through the skin according to ayurvedic tradition

Gold and copper are heating and are therefore good for balancing excesses of the AIR and EARTH qualities. Silver, on the other hand, is cooling so it is avoided by those dominated by AIR and EARTH, and used by those with abundant FIRE quality.

When processed into an ash preparation, metals become much more biologically available and non-toxic. For example, getting adequate iron absorption from the gastrointestinal tract is a common problem when using the unrefined iron salts commonly used in modern medicine. According to ayurveda, increased iron levels can be more rapidly achieved using the ash preparations. Metals go to all tissues.

Gold is good for balancing excesses of the AIR and EARTH qualities. Its major effects are on the heart, arteries, blood, nervous, and reproductive tissues. It is used for hypotonia, Parkinsonism, coronary constriction, palpitations, heart failure and flutter. ADD, arthritis, tinnitus, sciatica, arrythmias, hypotension and memory problems can also be helped by the use of this metal.

Silver is cooling and is used for decreasing the FIRE quality, and it works especially well on the blood, nervous, and reproductive tissues. It is used for nervous system inflammations including encephalitis, neuritis, meningitis, and demyelinating conditions. It is also used in epilepsy, cerebral hemorrhage, syncope, vertigo, labarynthitis, and dizziness. When combined with other metals and minerals it is also used for juvenile diabetes, and low sperm count.

Copper is heating, has an affinity for the blood and fatty tissues, and is used to balance the AIR and EARTH qualities. It is used as a liver cleanser, and to decrease fat. It is also good for hepatitis, lipomas, osteoporosis, obesity, high cholesterol, acne, eczema, psoriasis, and gallstones.

Iron is also heating and decreases the AIR and EARTH qualities. It works best on the blood, muscle and bone tissues. It is used in anemia, leukemia, osteo-degeneration, receding gums, lymphadenitis, ascites, edema, and enlarged liver and spleen.

"*Purified*" lead is heating and is only rarely used if there is an excess of AIR and EARTH qualities. It has an affinity for the fat, nervous tissue, and bones. In Ayurvedic medicine it has been used successfully to treat irritable bladder, dysuria, leukorrhea, diabetes, diabetic nephropathy, and obesity.

Tin is cooling, so it is used for conditions where the FIRE quality is increased. It is most effective in the reproductive tissues and is used for eczema, psoriasis, low sperm count, bladder and prostate problems. It is used for syphilis, gonorrhea, and the safe awakening of the subtle energy reservoir at the base of the spine.

Zinc is heating and has affinity for the plasma, blood, and bones, and is used as an aphrodisiac, and in the treatment of syphilis and gonorrhea.

There are many powerful Ayurvedic medicines that are combinations of metals and other compounds. These include Makaradwaj, Trivanga Bhasma, Laxshimi Vilas, and Arogya Vardini.

REFURBISHED PARTS
SURGERY, TRANSFUSIONS, TRANSPLANTS

Organs also have quality characteristics. The liver is associated with the FIRE quality as are the heart, eyes, and gallbladder. The colon is associated with the AIR quality, and the lungs, pancreas, and spleen with the EARTH quality.

Even with these general quality tendencies, organs from individuals with their own overall AIR, FIRE, or EARTH dominance will bring those qualities with them if they are transplanted into another individual. Thus, a heart from a donor who has been filled with FIERY anger will generate that quality when transplanted into the body of another person. Similar transplantation of qualities is said to occur with another's liver, kidneys, eyes and other organs. If transplanted organs (including blood and plasma) are filled with chemical or IPOD toxins, these abnormal substances can cause extra immune rejection.

Surgery across Energy Junction Points where the incision leaves a scar can interfere with the conduction of subtle energy. This interference can cause depletions in areas governed by the affected channels. For example, a horizontal hysterectomy scar may interfere with stomach, kidney, bladder and conception channels according to ayurvedic medicine.

Although it is rarely possible to pick and choose when receiving a donor organ, the unusual effects of some transplants can at least be understood on the basis of transplanted ayurvedic qualities.

CHAPTER 29: SPECIAL ADDITIVES
Special Remedies

GOOD NEWS!

I checked with my ayurvedic practitioner, and there are natural medicines that are available in India for Reggie's condition! They say they've been using these herbs and compounds for thousands of years with good success!

Luckily, ayurveda does quite well with this particular problem. Frequently, conditions that have reached this severity can't be helped by much of anything, even ayurveda.

It's so weird that you have to leave the country to get treatments that have been used elsewhere forever without known side-effects. Considering all the poisons that are used nowadays in pesticides, chemotherapy, and tuna fish cans, you'd think a whiff of humanized metal would be no big deal. Don't forget, they used mercury to treat syphilis in Europe about a hundred years ago, if I remember my history right. Maybe it actually does work for some things. It seems to work in India.

I guess people need to feel comfortable that their treatments are compatible with what they already know. But telling desperate people in pain that they shouldn't try something different when they're sick or dying and nothing else is working, is like telling someone hanging off a cliff that they can't use a rescue rope because it hasn't been thoroughly tested!

I just hope Regg is willing to give ayurveda a try. It does take a certain leap of faith.

…

Wait a sec. Here comes his nurse now! She looks pretty happy. We'll take that as a good sign.

POWERFUL ADDITIVES
SPECIAL REMEDIES

Each health system has its own special remedies for dealing with difficult problems. In ayurvedic medicine, there are many such treatments in all different areas of therapy, but a few stand out as being especially useful.

Caution must be used with any medication. Giving a heating substance to a person with a fever may be harmful. Refrigerating an AIR quality person will create complications, and feeding an EARTH quality person heavy substances is counter-productive. It should be remembered that everyone is different, and that each person's reaction to a substance is expected to be different as well.

SPECIAL FUELS
SPECIAL FOODS & SPICES

Ginger

Ginger is a very useful kitchen herb. Its circulatory stimulating quality is often helpful for all quality types. When used with salt, it relieves excess AIR quality. When used with rock sugar, fresh ginger helps cool the FIRE quality, and when mixed with honey, ginger helps balance excesses of EARTH quality.

It has been called a "universal medicine." It is excellent for stimulating the digestive ability of the stomach. It is also used as a treatment for belching, gas, and for spasmodic abdominal pain.

Fresh ginger is more balancing for all qualities, and dried ginger is more heating. Ginger tea is a good expectorant, and good for decreasing heavy EARTH type mucous. It is, therefore, a good dietary suggestion for nasal and sinus congestion. Its use with fever and sore throat is a bit more tricky.

It is also a vasodilator, and a stimulant for the circulation. Sweating is sometimes increased by ginger use, which is said to have a cleansing effect. In addition, those with inflammatory, ulcerative, or hemorrhagic conditions should not use ginger. Ginger's uses include:

Congestion	Heart disease
Colds	Gas
Flu	Headache
Indigestion	Pain
Vomiting	Blood clots
Belching	Coronary spasm
Abdominal pain	Osteoarthritis
Abdominal cramps	Hemorrhoids
Laryngitis	Cholesterol elevation
Obesity	Arthritis

Those with excess FIRE quality may not be able to use ginger in these situations.

Honey

Honey is sweet to the taste, but it has heating properties. It is therefore the savior of the sweet-hungry EARTH type. Sweet and heating! Honey should not be using in baking according to ayurveda, because it changes to a form that may be associated with coronary congestion.

Basmati Rice

Basmati rice is used frequently in Ayurvedic cooking. It is preferred over brown rice which is more difficult to digest, too heating for those with FIRE quality problems, and too heavy for those with an excess of the EARTH quality.

Basmati rice is lighter and sweet, so it is good for most, but when taken in excess, it can cause an excess of the EARTH quality.

Cardamom

This spice is used commonly in Ayurvedic cooking. It is therapeutic for sexual debility, bleeding disorders, burning urination, and nausea. It acts as a broncho-dilator, so it is useful in asthmatic conditions as well. When used with ginger and nutmeg, cardamom is said to neutralize the stress on the adrenal glands caused by drinking coffee.

Cardamom is somewhat heating, and can therefore be a problem if taken in excess by those with too much FIRE quality.

Clarified Butter
(Ghee, Drawn Butter)

Ghee is one of the greatest gifts that ayurveda brings. By cooking out much of the curd from butter and leaving the oil, ghee delivers the benefits of butter without many of the congestive disadvantages.

According to ayurveda, ghee is excellent for digestion as it helps to improve absorption and assimilation of nutrients. It is especially nourishing for nervous and connective tissue, and is good for improving the memory and for keeping the body flexible. It also strengthens immunity and digestion.

The penetrating properties of ghee make it a useful vehicle for delivering medications to the different tissues. Many herbs are cooked into ghee to allow them to penetrate deeply.

Ghee is sweet and cooling, and can therefore be used effectively to help balance conditions of excess AIR and FIRE. It should, however, be used cautiously by those with EARTH quality excess, and those with high cholesterol.

Pepper / Ginger / Long Pepper
(Trikatu)

This mixture combines black pepper, Indian Long Pepper, and dry ginger to form a mixture that is excellent for digestion. It is also used to help decrease body fat and as a coronary vasodilator. Trikatu has an affinity for the lungs and is useful in AIR and EARTH types of asthma.

Trikatu is heating, and it therefore increases the FIRE quality while decreasing the AIR and EARTH qualities

Licorice Root

Licorice is cooling, lubricating, and liquefies and stimulates secretions. It is good for many digestive, respiratory and nervous system symptoms. It also helps with some reproductive and excretory disorders. It has natural steroid-like effects, is also helpful with itching, spasms, and inflammation.

Licorice should not be used by those with high blood pressure, swelling, osteoporosis, diabetes, malabsorption, and steroid toxicity. It increases the EARTH quality, but decreases the AIR and FIRE qualities effectively.

Conditions that may be helped by licorice include:

Peptic ulcer	Muscle spasm
Hyperacidity	Abdominal pain
Glaucoma	Sty
Dizziness	Blepheritis
Motion sickness	Dry eyes
Hypoglycemia	Asthma
Cough	Hypothyroidism
Cold	Dry mouth
Urination, painful	Infertility
Bronchitis	Burns
Sore throat	Lacerations
Laryngitis	Diabetic ulcer
Teething	Constipation
Laryngitis	Gall bladder inflammation
Hyperacidity	Ulcerative colitis
Myopia	Hoarseness
Presbyopia	Goiter, cold
Hyperopia	Dysuria
Eye muscle tension	Vaginitis
Conjunctivitis	Debility

Cumin / Coriander / Fennel Tea

It's a good idea to have these three common kitchen herbs available. Not only are they the foundation of much of ayurvedic cooking, they are also very helpful for digestion, liver cleansing, and inflammations.

The seeds of these three herbs are mixed in equal proportions and steeped as a tea for almost any kind of dietary indiscretion. This tea is also a good treatment for internal hemorrhoids, bladder infection, itching, and heartburn.

Kitchari

This mixture of specially spiced basmati rice and yellow split mung beans is a basic part of the ayurvedic diet. It has good protein content, is easy to digest, and is balancing for the AIR, FIRE, and EARTH qualities. It is considered to be a complete food, and to provide strength and vitality while nourishing all the body's tissues.

Kitchari is an important part of the Five Cleansings procedure, and an important part of many modified fasting routines. It is said to help with cleansing and de-aging of the body tissues.

There are many different preparations of this nourishing food that enhance its balancing effects on the different qualities. The reader is referred to the works by Usha Lad and Amadea Morningstar in the bibliography.

Herbal Wine

Over a dozen ingredients are used to spice this special herbal wine known in ayurveda as "Draksha." These include ginger, cardamom, cinnamon, cloves, pepper, bay leaf, nutmeg and saffron. When taken before meals, the heating nature of the wine increases the digestive fire in the stomach. This promotes good appetite. When the wine is taken after meals, it promotes good digestion. Because proper digestion is the key to health in ayurvedic thinking, draksha wine can be very helpful.

In addition to its digestive benefits, draksha is a bronchodilator and can improve lung function. It also functions as a blood thinner, restores vitality and is especially balancing for excesses of the AIR quality.

Because it is heating, this (and other alcohol containing drinks) should be used with caution in conditions of excess of the FIRE quality. This same heating quality may be useful in improving circulation, relaxing nerves, and promoting regular menstruation.

✳

SPECIAL FUEL ADDITIVES
SPECIAL HERBS & COMPOUNDS

Aloe Vera

Aloe vera is available as a juice, gel, or (rarely) powder. It is bitter and cooling and therefore, especially good for FIRE quality excesses. Interestingly, it rarely aggravates the AIR or EARTH qualities. It is good for problems of the circulatory, digestive, excretory, and female reproductive systems. It is nutritive and rejuvenative.

Aloe is a good liver, gastrointestinal, and blood cleanser, and is helpful in most any inflammatory condition. Caution should be taken when using aloe during pregnancy or with any uterine bleeding.

Among the many conditions helped by are:

Menstrual cramps	Amenorrhea
Gallbladder disorders	Dysmenorrhea
Liver disorders	Menopause
Ulcers	Vaginitis
Gastritis	PMS
Colitis	Leukemia
Fever	Tumors (non-estrogen)
Constipation	Worms, intestinal
Obesity	Cough
Skin inflammation	Cold
Adenopathy	Congestion
Conjunctivitis	Burns
Bursitis	Cuts
Jaundice	Wounds
Hepatitis	Vaginal herpes
Hepatomegaly	Herpes
Splenomegaly	Venereal disease

Sitopaladi

This mixture of rock candy sugar, crystallized molasses, eye of bamboo, cardamom, cinnamon and Indian long pepper is used as an expectorant, bronchodilator, and decongestant.

It is a good treatment for EARTH-quality disturbances of the respiratory, cardio-vascular, and digestive systems. It is especially useful for dealing with congestion in the respiratory system. It is balancing for the AIR, FIRE, and EARTH qualities. It is used in many conditions including:

Bronchitis
Asthma
Post nasal drip
Pleurisy
Lack of taste capacity
Sinus congestion
Runny nose

Depression
Emphysema
Nicotine toxicity
Cough
Hoarseness
Weak voice
Lymphatic congestion

Ashwagandha

This herb is used to promote vitality and energy, to build tissue, as an age inhibitor, and as an aphrodisiac. It is a sedative, hypnotic, mind-clarifying root that promotes the development of muscle, marrow, and semen.

It is slightly provoking for the FIRE quality, but calming for the AIR quality. It affects many tissues in the body, and is especially effective on the nervous, reproductive, and respiratory systems.

It should be used with caution in the presence of EARTH-excess conditions, congestion, IPOD toxins, and avoided in excess FIRE quality and increased sex drive conditions.

It is used in many additional conditions including:

General debility
Sexual debility
Nerve exhaustion
Convalescence
Old age
Emaciation of children
Memory loss
Muscular energy loss
Muscle weakness
Paralysis
Spasms
Overwork
Tissue deficiency
Allergy
Eye weakness
Rheumatism
Skin problems
Cough

Insomnia
Anemia
Fatigue
Infertility
Pregnancy weakness
Fetal stabilization
Testosterone regeneration
Tissue healing
External wounds, sores
Spermatorrhea
Schizophrenia
Neurosis
Psychosis
Depression
Epilepsy
PMS
Asthma
Breathing difficulty

Triphala

This mixture of herbs is used daily by a large number of those taking Ayurvedic treatment. It is composed of the herbs amalaki, haritaki, and bibhitaki which are soothing for excess FIRE, AIR, and EARTH respectively. As a compound, it is therefore balancing for most all quality disorders.

In Ayurvedic folklore, it is said to carry away all diseases, possess all the properties of mother's milk, bring fearlessness, and promote de-aging. It achieves these and other changes primarily through its main function of removing IPOD toxins. It is a source of vitamins C, A, and B12, helps regulate cholesterol, and has laxative action.

Other indications for the use of triphala include cataract, constipation, and general toxin accumulation. Triphala is composed of fruits and therefore is not taken with any other foods or herbs.

Brahmi

This herb has wide-ranging effects, and influences all tissues except for reproductive. It is especially active on the blood, marrow, and nervous tissues. It has been described as rejuvenative and beneficial for the memory and intelligence. It strengthens the adrenals and supports immune function. It is an alterative and febrifuge as well as a diuretic.

It is close to being balancing for the AIR, FIRE, and EARTH qualities, but has a slightly cooling nature and is often used for conditions of excess FIRE quality.

Its other indications include:

Nervous disorders	Hair loss
Epilepsy	Skin disorders, persistent (paste)
Senility	Fever
Aging, premature	Bad dreams

Brahmi may keep one awake, so its use in the evening is restricted.

Jatamamsi

This is another herb that balances all three qualities. Like brahmi, jatamamsi is strengthening for the mind and promotes greater awareness. It clears and calms the mind, and improves intelligence. It is a mild sedative and relaxant as well as being another of the "de-aging" herbal medicines.

It is balancing and calming and is therefore often used in conditions of excess FIRE and AIR.

Other uses for jatamamsi include:

Nervous disorders	Spiritual growth
Hysterectomy	Erysipelas
Insomnia	Herpes zoster
Glaucoma	Herpes labialis
Alzheimer's disease	Herpes genitalis
Intracranial pressure increased	Insanity
Headache	

Chayavan Prash

This jam-like medicine is a combination of many Ayurvedic herbs. It is rich in vitamin C, and affects the digestive and circulatory systems. It is an anti-oxidant, a blood builder and lung rejuvenative. It also helps strengthen all the tissues especially the bones, brain, heart, lungs and kidneys.

It is the classic Ayurvedic tonic and rejuvenative strengthener. It increases the body's Composite Vital Strength and is also described as de-aging.

Guggulus

Guggulu is a resin that acts on bodily 'resins' such as the periosteum. Guggulus are similar to myrrh and affect all tissues. They are especially helpful for disorders of the nervous, circulatory, respiratory, and digestive systems. They are used most often in chronic conditions, and have many actions.

Guggulu is often compounded with other herbs to provide more specific effects. This has resulted in a proliferation of many types of guggulus that are most often used in specific types of arthritis and other conditions.

Guggulu is a stimulant, alterative, nervine, anti-spasmodic, anti-inflammatory, analgesic, astringent, and antiseptic. It is said to increase white blood cells and appetite. It clears the lungs, heals the skin and mucous membranes, and stimulates nerve regeneration. It reduces fat, toxins, and cholesterol. It removes toxins form the joints and it removes necrotic tissue from the body as well.

Other indications for its use include:

Osteoporosis	Bursitis
Rheumatism	Hemorrhoids
Gout	Pyorrhea
Lumbago	Skin diseases
Nervous disorders	Sores
Neurasthenia	Ulcers
Debility	Cystitis
Diabetes	Endometritis

Obesity
Bronchitis
Whooping cough
Dyspepsia

Leucorrhea
Tumors
Menstrual regulation

Caution should be taken when using guggulus in the presence of acute kidney infections or severe skin rashes.

Shilajit

Unlike most of the other herbal medications used in ayurveda, shilajit is a mineral pitch. It is ground into a powder and often combined with other herbs.

It is valuable for its tonic and rejuvenative functions and is cleansing and balancing for the urinary tract. It is a good source of calcium, magnesium, and zinc. It is also described as a "fat scraper" and is used in obesity. It is used for thyroid regulation, but not thyroiditis.

It is said to strengthen the immune system, improve sexual vitality and strengthen the reproductive system. It has also been described as an anti-hypertensive, anti-diabetic, anti-osteoporotic, and anti-aging medicine. It is an Ayurvedic aphrodisiac. Its use is often indicated in:

Fatigue, EARTH type
Obesity
Poor renal function
Poor bladder function
Diabetes
Urinary calculi
Sexual debility, EARTH-type

Cancer
Hypoglycemia
Hypertension
Cholesterol elevation
Prostatic enlargement
Kidney stones

Shilajit is AIR and EARTH-reducing, but can provoke the FIRE quality.

SPECIAL MOTOR OIL BLENDS
SPECIAL OILS

Oils are used extensively in ayurveda, not only for cooking and massage work, but for carrying herbal medications into tissues, organs and systems as well. In massage, oils help loosen, liquefy and remove toxins.

AIR types need lots of oil to balance their naturally dry nature, while FIRE and EARTH types may already have too much oil. Oils soothe and stabilize the tissues, and both internal and external oleation is considered important in ayurvedic treatment. Oils help decrease friction and avoid routine wear and tear.

Several types of oil are used including those from vegetables, animal fat, butter, and bone marrow. Applying oils to the mucous membranes can help increase membranous secretions.

Sesame oil

Sesame oil is used extensively in ayurveda because it is fairly penetrating to all tissue levels. It has a calming effect, is high in calcium and helps promote restful sleep. It strengthens the skin, the intelligence, the digestion, and the general health as well.

It is effective at rebalancing excess AIR and EARTH qualities, but it can be heating and is therefore not the best oil for those with excess FIRE.

Sunflower Oil

This is usually the oil of choice for those with excess or dominant FIRE quality, but it can be used for all body quality-types. Sunflower oil is light and cooling, high in vitamin E, and is used in the treatment of skin inflammations, cough, and excessive heat in the lungs.

Neem oil

Most herbs can be cooked into an oil using traditional ayurvedic techniques. When neem is cooked into oil, a medicine of great value is created. Neem increases the AIR quality, decreases the FIRE and EARTH qualities, and is used mostly for inflammatory conditions that result from a FIRE excess. It is bitter and cooling, and affects many systems including the digestive, respiratory, urinary and circulatory systems.

Neem has anti-inflammatory, antibiotic, anti-cancerous, and anti-fungal qualities. For these reasons, the oil is used for many skin rashes, hives, eczema, ringworm, scabies, tendonitis, poison oak, and inflammatory arthritis. It is also a good insect repellent, and mild sun blocker. It is used for scars, and congested lymph glands.

Mahanarayan (MN) oil

This heating oil is a mixture of many Ayurvedic herbs and is available from many Ayurvedic suppliers. It is soothing for aching joints, muscles, and tendons. It is used in AIR and EARTH imbalances in those areas, and for the nervous system. It is not used above the clavicles.

PIT STOP MAGIC
SPECIAL PROCEDURES

Five Cleansings Treatment

Although it has been mentioned previously in this text (Chapter 23), the *Five Cleansings* technique ("Panchakarma") is again noted for its central role in Ayurvedic healing. This process helps mobilize and remove toxins, and rebalance the AIR, FIRE, and EARTH qualities that have become excessive.

The process helps restore mental calm and clarity. Despite its sensual aspects, it is a detailed and serious procedure when done for medical reasons rather than spa pleasures.

Enemas

One of the techniques used in the *Five Cleansings* process is enema ("Basti"). In many countries, the therapeutic benefit of enema is more accepted than it is in the United States.

In addition to removing toxins that accumulate in the colon, medicated enemas can deliver therapeutic substances in the same way that modern medicated suppositories do. In addition, enemas are extremely useful for calming excess AIR quality conditions, because the colon is the primary site of AIR quality accumulation.

Because enema therapy is an "operation" in ayurvedic medical science, there are both pre-operative and post-operative measures to observe. It is only performed on an empty stomach and should be undertaken only with an experienced supervisor.

Nasal Medications

As most cocaine users know, the nose is a quick-access doorway to the brain. Ayurveda makes use of this fact to treat brain-associated conditions with medications. Usually the herbal medicines are combined with oil or ghee before being snorted, but on occasion, powdered herbs are taken directly into the nostrils.

Medications that are commonly given nasally ("Nasya") include brahmi, vacha, and various aromatic oils. Any of the quality imbalances can be helped by nasal medications depending on which herbs and carrier substances are used.

Nasal medications can be helpful in treating allergies, nasal obstruction, sinus conditions, asthma, migraine, nasal polyps, epilepsy, hyperactivity, and head bobbing among others.

Abdominal Lock

When certain muscle groups are held in contraction, changes in the movement of energy and on control of body functions are noted. There are several locks that have been described in the section above on this subject. The abdominal lock ("Udiana bandha") is especially good for strengthening the lungs and back muscles.

Mineral Waters

Mineral waters have long been used in traditional medicines for their various healing properties. Calcium, phosphorus and sulfur are among the minerals more commonly considered.

In ayurvedic medicine, pure gold and silver are boiled for one to three hours to produce therapeutic water, and copper water is produced by storing water in copper containers. Trace amounts of these metals in the water then exert therapeutic effects over time. These metals are also used therapeutically in ash form as described above in Chapter 28.

Gold has been used in modern medicine for the treatment of severe arthritis. In ayurvedic medicine it is used as a heart tonic and a vasodilator. It also helps in protein metabolism, bone mineralization, cholesterol regulation, immune function and skin conditions. Gold is good for those with AIR or EARTH quality issues. Yellow gold is generally heating, and white gold is more cooling.

Silver is used in ayurveda when cooling action is required. In ayurveda, it is used as an aphrodisiac and a brain tonic. It is also used to improve production of ova and sperm, and in many problems of the reproductive tract including infertility due to excessive FIRE quality, painful ovulation, and inflammation of the ovaries, tubes, testes, and epididymis. It is used to cool inflammations of the prostate, lungs, lymph nodes, brain, and meninges.

Copper is heating, and is therefore used to balance excesses of the AIR and EARTH qualities. It strengthens and cleans the liver and aids in iron absorption. It is said to support the immune system by keeping bacteria from attacking cell membranes.

Copper's central use is to "scrape fat" from the tissues. For this reason, it is used to treat obesity, increased cholesterol and triglycerides, lipomas, acne, and gallstones. It is also a treatment for hepatitis B and C, liver dysfunctions, enlarged spleen, and dull hair.

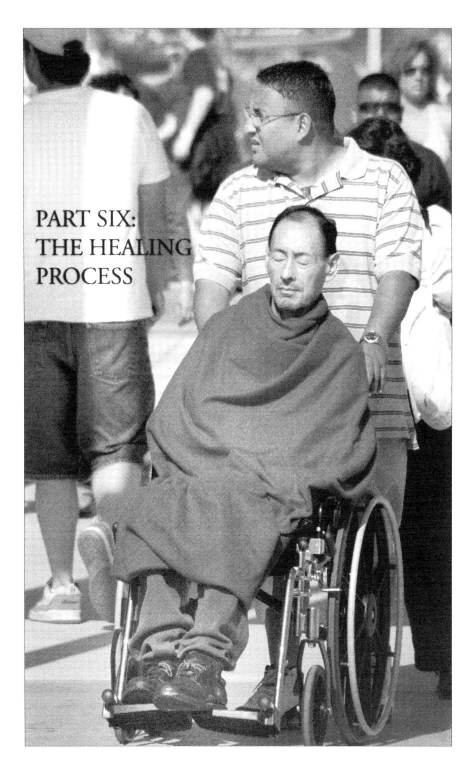

PART SIX:
THE HEALING
PROCESS

CHAPTER 30:
REPAIR GUIDE

REFORM SCHOOL

… I guess the reason I never did much to turn my health around was that I just didn't know how the hell to do it! That, plus the fact that I was always in so much frikin' pain that what I really wanted to do was just *die!* With that attitude, hurting myself bit by bit with bad habits made some sense.

I keep thinking of my health problems as a *physical* thing, even though I know that it's my *head* that's messed up. I know that the way I was raised is the reason that I do all that dumb shit. But even knowing that, I *still* can't seem to change!

Before all this happened, I never really believed that I had what people like Margo call a "spiritual" side. I was pretty sure that my body and my mind were all that there was, and that when I died and my body decayed like old refrigerator food, there would be nothing left. Nothing.

But when I fell in love, when I had kids, and when Dad died, I started to feel differently. I could see that there was something more than my body—something beyond the big sleep. I hated all the crap I had to put up with from people pushing their religion and morals on me. But who would have thought that the sons-a-bitches might be right?!

I guess when you face death like I am now, you can't avoid looking right at it. I don't think I'll be able to get clear about death before the surgery. I just hope that I get through it, and that I learn enough from this experience not to make the same damn mistakes. I guess I could always go back to hiding behind my pills and booze. Maybe I will. But maybe I'll do better this time.

Margo says it all depends on whether or not I find something worthwhile to do after this problem gets fixed. She says she does "community service," whatever that is.

Anyway, I'm glad there are people out there who know what they're doing with idiots like me … with my illness. They seem to have plenty of experience fighting this kind of problem. I used to think I was beyond needing help. Now, I can't bullshit myself anymore. Letting go of "Mr. Tough Guy" won't be all that easy. But, right now, I'm scared enough to give it a try.

Margo says that sometimes you have to hit bottom before you can change. She says that the smarter people are the ones who avoid the "crash-and-burn" approach to making changes. She says they already have that "spiritual" thing going.

But people like me, I guess we need to pay attention to what we're doing. I guess I need to have some faith in something beside myself. For me, that would be like driving on the left side of the road! Like they do in England and Ireland.
…

Hmm … I've always wanted to see Ireland … my family's from there. Maybe now's the time …   Hold on … someone' at the door...

"Reggie? … Knock knock! ... Hey Reggie! ... You've got quite a few visitors out here, dude! ... Go on in guys!"…

… What the…?

REPAIR GUIDE
THE HEALING PROCESS

Knowledge of the mind, body, and spirit's functions and malfunctions is needed to understand what our activities need to be, but actually *doing* them can be the hardest part. Setting up a program that helps overcome the barriers that obstruct healing is a process that requires significant awareness, effort, and maturity.

Healing programs usually involve making advances in several areas at once, just as we take several courses at once when we are in school. We don't work only on math until we've mastered advanced calculus. We do what we're ready for in each area, We do what life has chosen for us. If this type of multitasking becomes too difficult, we must drop a few courses and focus on the most important personal issues in the life curriculum.

In the same way that there are many methods of education, there are many ways to heal. A central ayurvedic principle is that no one method works for everyone. This section examines some techniques used in yoga and ayurveda, as well as some methods used in modern psychology.

Although folklore describes miraculous healings by saints and circumstances, most healing happens as a result of correct understanding, planning, and hard work. Healing involves *accepting some additional pain*. But there is already pain connected to the problem on which we are working.

All too often, the only reason for beginning a painful healing program is that the:

PAIN of the PROBLEM

Finally becomes greater than the

PAIN of the TREATMENT

Many times, present-day pain needs to be *much* greater than the treatment pain. Sadly, it may need to be disastrous in scope before we will accept any additional discomfort. Only the uncommonly wise and mature can overcome this behavior pattern and accept *ahead of time* that the:

PAIN of the PROBLEM

LATER

Will be MUCH greater than the

PAIN of the TREATMENT

NOW

But how does one get this future wisdom firmly implanted in the head and in the heart when the senses are constantly pulling us to give all of our attention to the immediate present?

The answer that ayurveda and yoga give is to gradually develop and maintain a consistent daily practice routine. But where does the energy and ability to do that come from when we are already weak in will power? It comes from the *belief that we are valuable*, and have something valuable to live for. Without this belief, overcoming the painful events of life can be very difficult. If we have something meaningful to work toward, we will not wander off to the sensory circus with Pinocchio and Paris. We must have a purpose!

Many of us decide to give our everyday lives purpose by being of service. It may be service to one's family or to the whole planet. It may be advancing scientific knowledge, or it may just be keeping out of trouble. Whatever the means, being of service helps give us the purpose and the sense of self-worth we need to undertake a healing program.

We are on this planet to do practical work on our personal and interpersonal problems. It's much harder to face these issues than it is to run off to the mall, but we must force ourselves to pass those tough classes in responsibility, communication skills, honesty, respect, and many other practical subjects if we are find the energy to heal ourselves.

ROAD TRIP EXPECTATIONS
WANTING GOOD HEALTH

Believe it or not, some people don't really want good health. They "enjoy" being sick, because it distracts them from even more difficult problems, and provides endless opportunities to complain. Very often, those problems turn out to be issues of prior injury, harbored resentment, or some other unfaceable variation of "I didn't do it right" or "I'm not good enough." They can't confront those issues, so they get sick.

For others, being sick is a way to get the attention that can't be obtained in healthier ways. Still others believe that they *can't* get well, or that their illness is terminal. For some, the difficulties involved in the healing process itself are just too great, so they accept their poor health.

We must believe that it is possible to succeed. Too often, the obstacles seem so complex that we give up, rather than attempt something with a high likelihood of "failure." We forget that failure is part of the learning process.

When someone has things to do that are more important than being sick, the motivation for healing arrives. If we don't have such goals, there is no reason to get out of a sick bed or off the couch. What drives the physical body is the mind, and what drives the mind is spiritual purpose. If there is no spiritual purpose, there is little need to keep the body-vehicle healthy.

The reasons that we decide to believe in the future are numerous. There are the many examples of those who have healed themselves by their faith in the future even against great odds. There are those who have risen out of all sorts of despair to become happy and content.

A REASON TO DRIVE SAFELY
SELF-ESTEEM & SELF-CONTROL

We must decide that we are worth the effort and the temporary discomfort of self-discipline. As little i-selves, if we think we don't really matter, then our minds will tell us that we might as well get as much pleasure as we can and forget self-discipline. We don't have the energy needed to practice healthy behavior, so we constantly cruise for more sensual experiences to cover the fear that our lives have no meaning. We forget that even when we lose the small i-self body, we will still be part of the omnipotent, eternal G-Self! If we are even *thinking* about such things as the Greater Self, we have done very well!

When we *do* remember that we are a part of the greater whole, we feel a larger sense of strength, value, and importance, and we gain the self-respect needed to take better care of ourselves.

SELF-RESPECT = GREATER-SELF–AWARENESS

We all have an internal memory of the stadium's G-Self roar! It's a matter of recalling that memory, and truly believing that we are a part of it.

MECHANICAL DIAGNOSTICS
UNDERSTANDING HEALTH PROBLEMS

In order to create an effective treatment plan for an illness, an understanding of the disease process is important. Many people know all about their symptoms, but don't know the cause of their problems or the names of their medicines. Blindly following a health care provider's directions without understanding one's disease pathology will ofen result in a repetition of the problem behaviors that caused and maintain the illness. Such blind therapy is also a statement that a patient is unworthy and unable to help himself.

For healing, one must also be clear that the diagnosis is correct, especially if the treatment is not going well. A full review of the history, and the clinical and laboratory data often reveal diagnostic errors that lead to faulty diagnosis and treatment. Taking the patient's whole situation into account ("Holistic" approach) allows the problem to be better understood and solved.

One must also be open to understanding the illness in whatever ways lead to improvements, with or without "proof" by a single prejudiced scientific method. One must be ready to let go of some of the labels that cubbyhole health problems in ways that are not accurate or constructive.

Modern Allopathic medicine maintains a biochemical and biomechanical point of view. Other health sciences rely on non-biochemical information such as psychology, spirituality, subtle energy flow, optimal nerve function, and proper bony alignment. Ayurveda looks at illness primarily as the result of imbalances in subjective qualities, problems with toxins, and inadequacy of physical and mental digestive transformations.

It helps to remember that health is cyclical; that it often comes and goes. It is important to be aware of the normal progression of a disease, but not to become so attached to predictions that a self-fulfilling disease state is created.

It is also important to understand that we are primarily responsible for our own health. No health care provider should be given total responsibility for curing someone else. In the final analysis, behavioral changes by the individual involved account for most of the sustained healing that happens. Ill health often comes from deeply entrenched bad health habits, so we need to develop the flexibility, willingness, and willpower to make the changes that are needed. Easy to say, difficult to do. That's the challenge.

By looking at the subjective qualities in our lives, ayurveda can help us create an internal balance that is different from the biochemical balance of the allopathic world. With an awareness of the importance of food qualities as well as food's biochemical nutritional content, ayurveda can treat illnesses using food as medicine without as many of the side effects inherent in modern medicinal approaches.

By understanding the ayurvedic principles of wrong digestion and the creation of Incomplete Products of wrong Digestion (toxic IPODs), we can avoid polluting our own bodies and causing autoimmune reactions. We can use ayurvedic cleansing techniques to repair and maintain our body-vehicles. We can also use the ayurvedic concepts of the progression of disease to more effectively interrupt the chain of pathological events.

ROAD HAZARD RECOGNITION
SUBCONSCIOUS TO CONSCIOUS

If we can't read the road signs, it will be difficult to avoid the hazards. If we are not aware of the early signs of an illness, or if we ignore them, then deeper problems will occur.

In the early stages of illness, ayurveda describes an "uneasiness" or a vague sense of aversion to those things that are becoming health problems for us. Since they tend to be minor, we tend to ignore them. It is important to learn to recognize these warning signs.

Even when illness worsens and progresses to overt disease, the powers of denial, anesthesia, and diversion can work to keep us from dealing with the problem. We can remain quite unaware of the behavior patterns or environmental circumstances that make our problems worse. It is even more unusual to recognize the absence of spiritual purpose as a cause of low self-esteem and self care.

Something must happen that allows a greater awareness of those concerns. Most often, it is a worsening of the problems that slaps us into reality. At other times, a true friend will risk a confrontation by pointing out the need for action.

Admitting that there is a problem, accepting the pain of the need to change, and giving effort and attention to health concerns is a crucial step for healing to happen. Often, it helps to express an acceptance of the problem to a trusted person. It is important to say out loud:

"I have a problem with . . . ."

TRAFFIC COURT CONFESSIONS
ADMITTING OUR PROBLEMS

Even if we recognize our problems in our conscious mind, it is still difficult to confess them in the court of public opinion. We are usually embarrassed to admit that we have not been "good enough," or that we "didn't do it right."

Embarrassment is a tough hurdle to jump, but it is important to remember that we are human, and all humans make mistakes. Our very purpose here is to make mistakes until we learn better behavior.

The mistakes we make are usually the ones that we make over and over again. They are our chronic problems. We should not feel too guilty that we have trouble with repeating the same mistakes. Children are not sent to school for a dozen years because they are bad people. They are sent because it takes time to understand and adapt.

Some philosophies hold that we bring our difficult issues with us from previous lifetimes. While this can become a convenient rationalization for problem behavior, it can also be useful in reducing the self-blaming that develops when we cannot understand our own difficult behavior or circumstances. Assigning an astrological or religious cause to our difficulties can have the same useful, guilt-assuaging effect.

Although we may blame ourselves for our problems, they are rarely entirely of our own making. We were raised by parents who had little training in the very difficult task of parenting. Often, they simply repeated the mistakes that their own parents made. Many of us were raised in difficult physical or emotional circumstances over which we had little control. We are products of difficult environments from both the recent and distant past.

Even after we have taken the important steps of overcoming the anesthetics and diversions that keep us from facing our problems, we must still stand before some traffic court judge and admit our mistakes. Since there is little need or use for extended guilt, this overt statement should not be viewed as a "confession" of sin. We are human! We make mistakes.

The declaration of a problem to the outside world should be semi-public. Standing in front of a private group or a trusted individual and admitting, "I am an alcoholic" (or whatever), removes the weight of secrecy from one's existence. It also opens the door to being tutored in the subject on which we need the most help by the people who have experience dealing with our issues.

The fear of external judgment often keeps us from taking this courageous action even though we are already judging ourselves. But admitting a weakness is a necessary step to take. When we take it, we are almost always surprised to discover that we have survived without the cataclysmic pain our ego-mind told us we'd experience. The mind is good at creating such fear. It takes a courageous leap of faith to get the mind to stand in front of the congregation and ask for help.

WHO'S RIDING SHOTGUN?
GETTING SUPPORT

Easy changes are rarely a problem for us to make by ourselves. But when the needed changes are difficult, we have to be able to look for and accept help from others.

The choice of a support person for our efforts at self-improvement is an important one. We must first recognize that any support person we choose does not bear the primary responsibility for making the changes that are needed. That is our personal responsibility. We must somehow develop the strength within ourselves to overcome our own problems.

That being said, the helpers we choose must have certain qualities. If the prospective support person is unknown to us, he or she should come to us by way of a reference from someone that we know who has already had a positive connection with that support person. We should have a sense of trust that the chosen helper has a genuine interest in our well-being. Working with someone who is really giving something of him/herself rather than just running a psychology business is much more helpful. That trust should extend to a feeling that complete confidentiality will be maintained at all times.

Although it is important for a support person to provide information, opinions and advice, it is just as important that they be non-judgmental about our situation. This is usually the case if we choose someone who has already success-fully dealt with significant problems of their own. If we can find someone who has dealt with the same problem we are confronting, then their having "been there" will often yield better advice and greater tolerance.

Our support person should also be available, reliable, and someone who embodies the qualities that we desire for ourselves. If heavy mind issues will be approached, our support person should have training in clinical psychology. We should also be clear about the therapeutic orientation of people whose support we are considering since there are many ways of approaching problems. Is the counselor oriented toward rapid results, deeply analytic inquiry, and biofeedback?

If a minister is helping out, it is important that his/her religious orientation be consistent with our own spiritual point of view. Spiritual connection and personal compatibility are important for assisted behavior changes.

Of course, it may be difficult to find all of these qualities in one person. A close friend or relative will not be able to remain objective. Keeping some personal distance from a support counselor is also important.

We should also reserve the right to change helpers if, over time, the process remains problematic. It should be expected that making such changes will be uncomfortable, but one must feel that positivity is pervasive in the therapeutic relationship.

Support groups can be very helpful in getting us where we need to go. They help us to realize that we're not the only ones in the world who have trouble with a problem. They can add friendship to the process, advise us of additional approaches, references, and resources. They can help us say "No."

EXPLORING REPAIR OPTIONS
EXPLORING HEALTH CARE OPTIONS

Once we have made a commitment to ourselves and to others to improve our health, it is important to explore all of our options.

If we are already involved in some type of treatment program that is not working, then we must search for something else in the same way that Patty searched for a cure for her diabetic foot ulcer in the beginning of Volume One of this book.

The internet may provide us with an overview of what is available as well as some of the specifics of each approach. Introductory seminars are widely available on many of the health treatment areas. Attending some of these gives us an opportunity to ask questions, and to meet people with health care needs that are similar to our own. They can share their experiences, and point us toward healing resources.

The shelves at local book stores are full of self-help books on specific disorders. They also give references for further assistance. Health care centers such as hospitals and clinics also offer programs on approaches to specific illnesses. It is important to remember that most all of these centers are promoting themselves in order to expand their business and sell their products. Many of them do not admit when their approach is not right for specific individuals.

It is important to look for a few basic things when searching for an alternative solution. There should be some understandable, logical reason why a proposed treatment works. Most often, isolated success stories constitute the basis for trying a new method, and scientific evidence that the program consistently works is often lacking. This does not mean that a new program won't work for specific individuals, but the more evidence that it is effective for large groups, the better. Programs that have been around a while are also more likely to have been helpful. Ayurveda has been in use for over 5000 years.

Once a program has been chosen, it is important to give it the time, energy and attention that is necessary for any program to work. It is important to avoid looking for an instant cure. Most conditions that develop over long periods of time take long periods of time to resolve. Give it some time, but expect to see some results within a few weeks or months of starting the program.

MAPS
CREATING A HEALTH PLAN

Once an area of treatment is selected, it is important to set up a well-defined plan to carry it out. Expect that making significant life changes will be difficult. Every detour has twists, turns, and potholes.

A time-line for change is usually a good idea. Decide when to expect results. Be aware of the steps that are involved in getting those results. Often, small steps are taken in improving long-term problems.

It is important to set goals that are reasonable. Trying to do too much or be too perfect too fast will often lead to failure. It can actually make the process more difficult.

If it feels like improvement is happening, but not fast enough, it is important to be a patient patient. On the other hand, a different practitioner in the same area may add a fresh perspective to help move things along if progress seems too slow.

Monitor your progress by marking your daily calendar (see below). Each day, mark your calendar when you have done what you have set out to do. This part of the process cannot be over emphasized. Put a small mark on each day on the calendar when you have indulged in a negative behavior, or succeed in doing the desired practice. It's OK to feel discouraged when your calendar reveals a "failure" to make progress. Examine those pointless feelings of inadequacy, decide what the obstacles were, make changes, and try again.

DRIVING SCHOOL
USING ILLNESS, PAIN, AND ANXIETY

Another important part of the healing process is the *attitude* that we adopt toward our illness. It is important that we examine the emotions that may have generated our problems in the first place, as well as the emotions that the illness itself generates. If we don't face this painful process, it is likely to recur.

Ayurvedic psychology encourages a view of these painful healing times as messages from the body and mind for change. If we see our illness in that light, we can begin to educate ourselves more thoroughly about our behavior. Hopefully, we can envision potential growth in the way we take care of ourselves.

We can even view health difficulties as a means to resolve conflicts within us by changing our difficult behavior patterns. Instead of viewing illness as total misfortune, we can appreciate how the body gives us feedback on our behavior. We can learn to accept our limitations and imperfections, and to accept ourselves for what we are rather than for what we think we should be.

One definition of stress is a state in which the energy spent worrying is greater than the energy spent on other activities. When that is the case, it is important that we use that anxious energy for changes and improvement! Don't be afraid of it! Anxiety is there to help us get moving! We must work hard to avoid seeing anxious energy as negative, and we must avoid covering it over with anesthetics, or dissipating it with unproductive diversions.

Ayurveda and yoga occasionally use semi-"painful" techniques such as fasting, and isolation to help us learn the benefits of pain messages. Many of the other yogic/ayurvedic techniques could be described as "uncomfortable" for those of us who are lazy or out of shape, but they only require a little discomfort to yield significant results.

USING THE CONTROLS
SELF-CONTROL, DISCIPLINE & ROUTINE

All of these yogic/Ayurvedic techniques require self-control, discipline, and routine. For that matter, so does the achievement of *anything* important.

Accepting that self-control, discipline, and routine are the basis of most healing changes is an important and difficult step for many of us to take. We are conditioned to believe that a "magic bullet" medication is the way to approach our health problems. We are trained this way by the people who are selling these magic pills for profit. It's the lazy way. It asks us to avoid *any* pain or discomfort. Pain is a messenger. Don't miss the message!

One message is: "Get your bleepin' act together!" This is simply the process of developing healthy routines. Routines lead to discipline and self-control. Every day, like it or not, "painful" as it may be, we must do our postures, breathing, meditation, etc. It may only take twenty minutes, but it *must* be done. Getting up early is an important way to make these changes.

Routines need to be practiced, and "practice" means that we don't always succeed. Some days we may blow off our daily practice. That's our humanity. The challenge is to stay with it and to rise above human laziness to become a person who is in conscious control of him/herself.

Even taking "healthy" herbal medicines is lazier than taking a closer painful look at our problem habits and changing them. If we use medicines in this way, we are chasing our own behavior tails.

Yogic/ayurvedic discipline begins with the classic "Restraints" discussed in Chapter 15:

> Non-violence
> Non-deception
> Non-stealing
> Sexual control
> Non-hoarding

The discipline practice continues with the "Observances" of:

> Cleanliness
> Contentment
> Minimizing desires
> Study
> Surrender

These "Ten Commandments" of yoga are lifestyle practices that develop discipline as well as positive character. They may take years to develop in the same way that it may take years to get through high school or college.

The more advanced yoga techniques of sensory reduction, concentration, and meditation are much more easily achieved if the Ten Commandments curriculum has been passed. Practicing discipline increases further discipline.

Another basic and essential area in which we all face disciplinary challenges is diet. If we can control our eating habits, we have the capacity for true self-control. If we cannot manage our food issues properly, the odds are we will have all sorts of self-control problems in other areas.

A mental understanding of healthy behavior and practices is a good start, but an awareness *with action* is one manifestation of "enlightenment." It comes with repeated effort.

Practice

Makes a ladder
to attain peace

Every day's Practice
makes one step of the ladder

If we miss one day
we lose one step.

*

The mind will always
make excuses

"Not today –
tomorrow for sure."

And tomorrow doesn't come.

So we need someone
To remind

"Look, tomorrow is today,
so do your practice."

- Baba Hari Das

PERFORMANCE TRACKING
CALENDARING BEHAVIOR

Routine is essential in the military, in educational institutions, and in health care programs where behavior control is a major goal. Without the discipline of a daily routine, significant or lasting changes in behavior are rarely achieved.

We must also develop a way to monitor our progress ourselves. Since a daily effort is required, the Calendar Action Method (CAM) is an essential part of this process. Most of us already use a calendar to keep track of our obligations, plans, appointments and significant events. A few underachievers try to get by without that much planning. If you don't use a calendar, start.

844

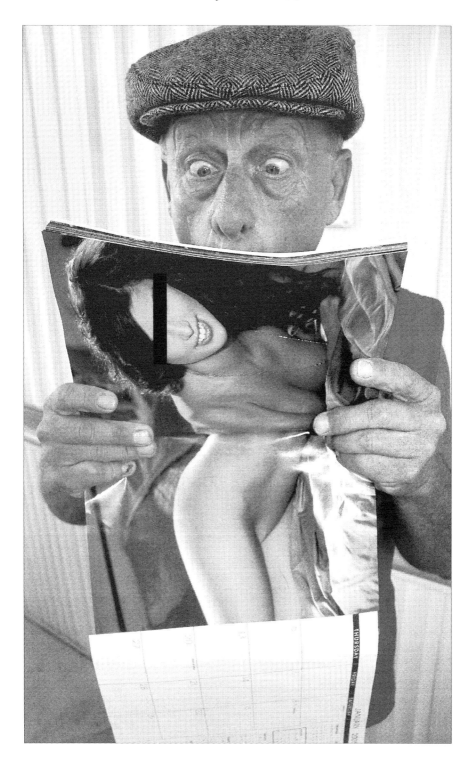

Your regular calendar may have one page or one square for each day. The month at a glance graphic format works better for behavior modifications since it gives an overview of the goal and the progress. Use the four corners of each page or day-square to keep track of up to four behaviors. Limit your behavior control efforts to no more than four problem activities. Changing one behavior pattern is hard enough. Changing a dozen would be like taking a dozen classes at a time in school. Trying to do too much in too many areas often leads to failure in all subjects.

Choose the one behavior that needs changing the most and mark it in the upper left corner of the day-square or page. Put the second difficult behavior in the upper right corner. In the lower corners, it is a good idea to designate *positive* behaviors that you can do to replace the negative ones. Alternatively, you can add more negative behaviors to the lower corners. Use as many or as few of the corners as you can handle comfortably. You may want to start with just one.

Designate the corners for each behavior on one blank page or blank square. For example, if smoking and drinking are the problems, put an "S" for smoking in one corner, and a "D" in the other. If walking around the block, and writing in a journal are the positive behaviors, then put a "W" in a lower corner, and a "J" in the other.

FIGURE 30-1: **CALENDAR MARKING**

Define your terms. "No Drinking" may mean not taking anything alcoholic. "No Smoking" might mean not smoking tobacco cigarettes, but continuing to indulge in marijuana. Whatever you decide.

Keep track of the number of times you remain human and do things the lazy way, by putting a number in the corner of that day's page or square for each time that you do that problem behavior. At the end of each day, guesstimate the number of slipups as best you can.

FIGURE 30-2: **CALENDAR NUMBERING**

S 15 (15 CIGARETTES)   D 3 (3 DRINKS)

JANUARY 1

9-5   Work - Project due

5-7   Dinner with Alice

7-7:10   Work on taxes

8:00   NA Meeting

W   (NO WALKING)   J ⊘ (NO JOURNALING)

Each day, write in the numbers. Do this at the same time of day that you routinely consult your calendar. Make a minor ritual out of it.

When you notice a particularly good or bad day for behavior control, try to remain non-judgmental about it. Instead, notice what events triggered the good and bad results. Be on the lookout for these triggers when they occur. When they do happen, catch yourself as you begin to do your negative anesthetic or diversion response. Even if you proceed with that negative behavior, become aware of the relationship between the trigger and the response. Eventually, you will be able to identify the trigger in time to fashion a more positive response to it.

It will take time for the numbers to change. Be patient. Love yourself. From now on, whether you mark them or not, each corner of the page or the square will remind you of your behavior issues. You might as well keep track of them.

DRIVING TIPS
BEHAVIOR CONTROL METHODS

No matter how long it takes to change a behavior, the task must be faced every day in individual moments when behavioral decisions are made. In each of those moments, a DoG (Delay of Gratification) decision is often necessary. Finishing each successive moment in a positive way eventually adds up to many days of success.

Repeating a mantra-like catch phrase in that decision-making moment can be helpful in maintaining a long-term perspective:

"I am strong enough to say 'No' (to my immediate sensual desires)."
"I am worth saying 'No' (to my own sensual desires)."
"I want a future!"
"The divine in me is strong!"
"I will practice my beliefs!"

Such an easy to remember reminder can help us get through those difficult present moment decisions. Positive phrases are preferred over the negative, and over self-blaming.

It is also important not to excuse our own behavior by blaming those who cause us pain and push us to escape into anesthesia or diversion. Blaming diverts us from taking responsibility for our part of the problem. Those who bring us challenges may be seen as bringing a message on how *not* to behave, or on the importance of looking closely at our own behavior.

Don't sit around trying *not* to do something. Become active in doing something positive. Walking, working on hobbies, or going out in public to museums, concerts, or performances moves us away from our struggles. Taking a course on a subject of personal interest, going to a gym, and doing physical chores can also be helpful. If we are in a situation of immobility, depression, and lassitude, then we usually need activity rather than rest.

Volunteering for a charity-oriented organization almost always improves self-esteem and lifts the spirits. Doing something to improve personal appearance can have the same effect. Going to support groups on a regular basis is also very helpful. Even doing something frivolous just to get out of the behavior pressure cooker can be worthwhile.

It helps to have a long-term project that is readily available. When the anxiety of avoiding a difficult behavior arises, go to that project and add to it. An alternative project can be helpful in case the primary positive diversion cannot be done. These options are especially good if anxious insomnia is a complication of getting straight. If you just can't sleep, get up and use that anxious energy on something that will make you feel better or tired.

Getting things done makes us feel better about ourselves and thereby decreases the need for soothing negative behavior. Getting up early is difficult, but it gives us more time to get those things finished. There is no easy way to get up early, but going to sleep earlier can help. "The early bird catches the worm" and "early to bed, early to rise …" describe the sacrifices required for success.

Getting sufficient rest is important especially if we are overworked and stressed out. Escaping on a vacation is OK if health and a little self-discipline are a part of it. There are many health getaways available that have both short and long-term fitness benefits. The wild and crazy disco-driven fun centers only leave us more exhausted and disappointed with our ability to respect our health issues.

Try a yoga resort!

Telephone help is also key. Just having someone available to listen is beneficial, even if they give no advice. Being able to quickly connect with a person who has experience with our problem area is helpful when difficult decisions need to be made.

It is important for each of us to *become the observer* of our own emotions and behavior. If we feel anger and resentment, we need to learn to observe the presence of those emotions; "Yes, I feel angry." There is no need for judgment about the fact. It is simply there. Be on the lookout for those events that *trigger* our negative behavior. Cut the negative response short, or block it entirely before the response gets started.

Recognize loneliness when it appears, as it often does during the process of recovering from negative behavior. When we give up a long-standing, negative behavior, we give up an old "friend." We should also recognize loneliness itself as a cause of negative behavior.

While we are in the process of kicking one bad habit, it is important not to replace it with another *bad* one. Quitting drinking and starting smoking may be acceptable in the short term, but healthier replacement choices can certainly be made.

Letting go of guilt and self-pity over our negative behavior is important. Guilt is only useful to remind us of the need for change. After that, it's a waste of time. We must accept our human fallibility and the fact that we are here to fail—and then learn from it. Don't feel guilty. Feel the message! Remember the consequences of the unhealthy behavior that we are trying to avoid.

It is also useful to practice *gratitude* whenever possible. Even when things are tough, there are good things that we take for granted. We must remind ourselves of those things on a regular basis, and writing down our blessings can be transformative. Recognizing the misfortunes of others is helpful, but it doesn't erase our own personal pain.

Getting professional help as described above is usually a very good idea. Eventually, we must all learn to lean on ourselves and put into practice those insights that have been obtained with qualified help.

Take things slowly, a step at a time. Remember that it took time to build up the negative behavior, and it will take time to replace it. Outcomes depend on our attitudes and persistence. Change the things you can change, and accept the things that you can't. This famous "Serenity Prayer" defines one of our major challenges.

There are essentially two approaches to removing unhealthy behaviors:

Decreasing Amounts Method (DAM)

or the

Total Abstinence Method (TAM)

The choice of which method to try first centers around the type of problem being approached, and the person doing the self-correction.

If a problem such as overeating is present, then total abstinence for more than a short period of time may be impractical and unhealthy, so the Decreasing Amounts Method (DAM) must be used.

When trying to DAM up this type of behavior, it is crucial that an accurate, compulsive, and quantitative calendar be kept. External checks and controls must be in place. The DAM rewards must be clear, frequent, and progressively greater.

For someone to be successful with the DAM method, he or she has to have a clear sense of the triggers for their problem behavior, and an equally clear motivation for change. There should also be an ability for such a person to consistently observe his/her own behavior, and to understand the clearly defined limiting that must happen.

For other issues, the Total Abstinence Method (TAM) may be best. This means physically staying *completely* away from the problem behavior or substance. Those who are less aware of their triggers, and improvement motivations must use this method to simplify and "Just Say No!"

Those who use the TAM must have even greater external controls and reinforcements. In the case of problems such as alcohol addiction, the challenge must be simplified by there being nothing available for abuse. "No exceptions!"

The problem is that there will *always* be "exceptions." We almost always slip up and fall off the wagon. To think that we can stay totally free of our problem behavior at all times forever, is to deny our human fallibility. It takes tremendous strength to consistently deny the lure of an ingrained habit! Finding that strength is what Discipline 101 is all about.

Many times, a combination of DAM and TAM are used. A gradual decreased is used to get to a point where total abstinence is attempted. In either case, many of the above-described techniques must be used, and failures are expected and accepted. We are here to make mistakes, and learn from them. As many times as it takes.

REST STOPS
REWARDING SUCCESS

Being good to ourselves in a constructive way is also key in the healing process. Learning to reward our successes is an important step that gives us some added incentive to endure the rigors of sensory denial, and self-discipline.

As with most behavior modification techniques, "rewards" for good behavior must meet certain requirements. All rewards should be directly connected to the chosen behavior. We only get the reward if we exercise the desired control.

"Success" should be clearly defined in advance. For example, an initial success might be defined as simply skipping one cigarette a day—say, the after lunch smoke. When lunch has been finished, and the desire for the cigarette has just been overcome, a phone call can be made *immediately* to the support person who can offer congratulations and encouragement. Alternatively, money can be added to a jar, a favorite magazine can be purchased, or a dessert can follow the meal instead of the cigarette. A mark should be made on the calendar to record the success.

When the goal is achieved, the reward should happen *without major delay*. It is difficult enough to avoid the desire for immediate anesthesia or diversion at the moment of decision. As time goes by and more self control is developed, the delay in receiving the reward can be lengthened.

The reward should be something positive, fun, stimulating, and/or special. It should be specific and meaningful for the individual. If possible, it should also have some of the characteristics of the avoided behavior. For example, if the after-lunch cigarette functions as a stimulant, a stimulating specialty coffee may work well as a substitute. If the smoke worked as a sedative, then a sweet, calming dessert can be taken as the reward.

Initially, rewards should be fairly concrete. Physical evidence of achievement is reassuring, whereas theoretical rewards provide little in the beginning.

When using a "replacement" reward, it is important to choose one that is better than the behavior being replaced. Replacing smoking with drinking or vice versa has a limited effect on improving self-esteem, although for a short time, it might provide some breathing space. Choose something that is an improvement. For example, replace the bad breath of smoking with sucking on a stimulating lozenge, or chewing gum.

Cumulative rewards can also be useful. Getting tokens or chips to commemorate different durations of positive behavior can create a continuing series of goals. The chips used by the "Anonymous" groups for different lengths of abstinence have proven useful for this purpose. As time goes by, it usually becomes easier to get to the next step. Success breeds success, but it is useful to always have another goal in the future. Group recognition of achievements can also be helpful.

If we are using the Decreasing Amounts Method of behavior control, then the reward can even be an indulgence in the avoided behavior. The coveted end-of-the-day cigarette to reward the skipping of the daytime smokes is an example. The end-of-the-week piece of chocolate cake can signify previous dietary success. But it is usually better to find a different type of reward so that movement to the Total Abstinence Method can be accomplished.

The yogic/ayurvedic tradition often puts an emphasis on attaining distant and lofty rewards; discipline is developed to attain "peace" and "awareness." External rewards are seen as internal business transactions, and are much less important than these spiritual gratifications. Taking care of ourselves is important because it allows us to "serve others" and to progress toward "enlightenment." Seeking any benefit for ourselves is an uncommon yogic goal. Doing the right thing is, itself, the reward.

Seeking the abstract as a reward is an exercise for the advanced practitioner of self-discipline. For most of us, we need to start simply and concretely before we can consistently deny our sensory desires in return for a thought or an image. When we get up in the morning, it is important for us to feel good about the person we see in the bathroom mirror. Eventually, the divinity in that image will be reward enough.

It is a good idea to create a formal health plan on paper. The forms in Figures 30-3 & 30-4 are examples of such a plan. The plan is divided into beginning, intermediate, and long-term goals with rewards assigned for each stage. This is often a difficult and time-consuming form to complete as many of us are not used to being specific about our problems, goals, and methods of achieving them. Make a copy and take the time to fill in the blanks. Give yourself enough time to reasonably achieve these goals. Mark your goals and achievements on your calendar.

FIGURE 30-3: **HEALTH PLAN**

General Health Goal: _____

Reason for Goal:_____

Specific Issue: _____ _____ _____ _____

Starting Point: _____ _____ _____ _____

Beginning Goal: _____ _____ _____ _____

Reach Goal by: _____ _____ _____ _____

Support Resources: _____ _____ _____ _____

Replacement Behaviors: _____ _____ _____ _____

Methods, Meds, Mind: _____ _____ _____ _____

Reward for Beginning Goal: _____ _____ _____ _____

Intermediate Goal: _____ _____ _____ _____

Reach Intermed. Goal by: _____ _____ _____ _____

Support Resources: _____ _____ _____ _____

Replacement Behaviors: _____ _____ _____ _____

Methods, Meds, Mind: _____ _____ _____ _____

Reward for
Intermediate Goal: _____ _____ _____ _____

Long-term Goal: _____ _____ _____ _____

Reach Long-term Goal by: _____ _____ _____ _____

Support Resources: _____ _____ _____ _____

Replacement Behaviors: _____ _____ _____ _____

Methods, Meds, Mind: _____ _____ _____ _____

Reward for Long-term Goal: _____ _____ _____ _____

FIGURE 30-4: **HEALTH PLAN EXAMPLE**

General Goal:	Improved health	Reason for Goal:	I am important for my kids	
Specific Issues:	Stop smoking	Lose weight	Stop drinking	Do Yoga Posture
Starting Point:	3 cigs per day	209 lbs	3 drinks/ night	
Beginning Goal:	2 cigs per day	199 lbs	2 drink/ night	Every 3rd day
Date to Beginning Goal:	2 weeks	4 weeks	4 weeks	2 weeks
Support Resources:	Mom/Bob	Mom	Ed	Susan
Replacement Behaviors:	Pipe	Gum/Walking	Gum	-
Methods, Meds, Mind	Pineapple/honey	Licorice candy	Bitter ghee	Set alarm early
Reward: Beginning Goal:	Camera lens	New Jacket	Football tickets	Yoga weekend
Intermediate Goal:	1 cig every 2 days	190 lbs	1 drink/night	Every other day
Date to Intermed. Goal:	1 month	2 months	2 months	1 month
Support Resources:	Mom/Bob	Mom	Ed	Susan
Replacement Behaviors:	Pipe	Gum/Walking	Gum	-
Methods, Meds, Mind:	Lung tincture	Sweet Ease form.	Bitter ghee	Set alarm early
Reward: Intermed. Goal:	Printer	Camera body	Massage x 2	New suit
Long-term Goal:	No cigs x 2 weeks	180 lbs	2 drinks/week	Every day
Date to Long-term Goal:	1 month	4 months	3 months	2 months
Support Resources:	Mom/Bob	Mom	Ed	Susan
Replacement Behaviors:	Rose/neem cigs	Gum/Walking	Gum	-
Methods, Meds, Mind:	Lung tincture	Sweet Ease mix.	Herbal Antabuse	Set alarm early
Reward: Long-term Goal:	Cruise	Long weekend	Fancy dinner	$250 shopping

NORMAL WEAR & TEAR
NATURAL HEALING & DISEASE

Once a healing program has been created, it is important to remember that healing is a naturally occurring event. Sometimes, all it takes is removing the barriers to natural good health for healing to happen.

Healing is an inherent capacity of life up to a point. In most cases, damaged skin will repair itself, and broken bones will mend. Even the DNA molecules that direct the repair process can repair themselves. The healing system is always operating. It is constantly at work recognizing damage and imbalances as they occur. The immune system is almost always ready to fight off any illegal aliens that get past the body's borders.

The molecules that make up our body parts are constantly being replaced over time with new molecules. This continuous turnover of molecules in the body provides one of the key opportunities for healing. In many cases, the main objective of becoming healthy is to simply provide top-quality molecules to replace the damaged ones. If we want the finest health, we need to use the finest ingredients to make it happen. If we want our vehicles to run well, we need to buy the best parts and use the best fuel.

We also need to be aware of the natural processes of digestion. We need to practice correct digestion so that the proper molecules can replace the IPODs that have been downloaded into our hard drives.

By understanding our own natural quality-type and our current state of quality imbalance, we can re-balance our bodies so they can return to their natural states.

In the same way, we must remember to feed our *minds* natural, healthy food. If the mind is nurtured by natural things, it thrives. Nurture and nature go together. Many of us take our vacations in places of great natural beauty because such places are healing for the mind and spirit. Those places stand in stark contrast to the media-soaked cities where the cattle are fed bad news around the (never-resting) clock.

But all things natural are not necessarily beneficial. The enthusiasm for natural cures should be tempered by the reality of natural degradation and imbalance. Avoiding unnatural disease-preventing vaccines may result in a very natural case of meningitis. Natural childbirth may result in natural child death or injury.

We do not live in a perfect world, and everything that lives decays. Even thousand-year-old redwood trees, and hundred-year-old tortoises move on to other adventures. The forces of nature are always pulling us out of balance with excess AIR, FIRE, or EARTH qualities. On this planet, no one lives forever, and, despite our desires to believe otherwise, there is no such thing as absolutely perfect health.

Part of the healing challenge is to *accept* some of the imperfections of life, and the reality of natural decay and transformation. The rest of the challenge involves learning to effectively delay this decay as long as possible. Of course, there needs to be a spiritual reason to hang around. We are here to learn.

PAINFUL REPAIRS
PAIN THERAPIES

One of the main subjects we are here to learn about is pain. This has been discussed in detail in Chapter 18 and elsewhere, but dealing with pain is so important that it must be carefully included in any healing process.

Healing usually involves some additional pain, and it is rarely pleasurable initially. In addition to the physical changes that happen, the mental effort involved in a healing program is often uncomfortable.

The life changes that healing brings can be equally uncomfortable. When we move out of a sickness comfort zone and into health we have to say "goodbye" to some negative familiar emotional companions. Letting go of negative habits can be frightening. There are fewer excuses, and we have empty time slots to fill. But moving up to something better effectively replaces these crutches once they have been discarded.

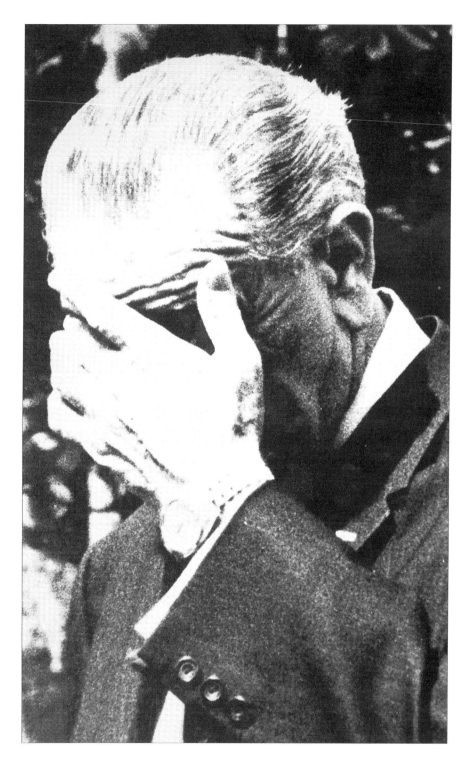

Getting better is also *pleasurable*. Some of the ayurvedic rejuvenation procedures are so pleasurable they are used as spa treatments! Quitting smoking, drinking, and overeating, improve the senses and bring new energy. The relief from the removal of the illness problems eventually makes the initial pain worthwhile. Removing the fear of disability and death that go with illness is also pleasurable.

When embarking on a difficult healing program, remember that pain is here to teach something. Because we can be lazy, we don't want to learn those lessons, we just want to ditch those difficult classes and move on. If we ditch, we flunk the class, and we wind up repeating the behavior again and again.

PASSENGER CARE
SPIRITUAL THERAPIES

According to ayurveda, consciousness is primary, and everything, including healing, is derived from one's state of our consciousness. We need an inspirational reason to be mentally and physically healthy. Without that sense of spiritual purpose, we are fighting an uphill battle for health.

Just as physical and mental training are needed to develop a healthy mind and body, *spiritual* exercises and processes are necessary to improve our guiding principles and practices. A course of formal spiritual study is often a helpful addition. This can take the form of religious or philosophical training that can be helpful or narrowing in its effect on our spirit.

There are many paths to a spiritual goal. As long as they are essentially positive in nature, we should remain open to whatever they can teach us about spiritual matters.

Some of the spiritual tools that can be used to become healthier, are summarized in Table 30-5 below. Of the many pieces of the spiritual puzzle, ayurveda and yoga concern themselves primarily with a special subset of spiritual practices.

"Devotion" is a committed and loving dedication to the divine aspect of our existence. Whatever constitutes "God" for each of us should command our continued respect and attention. As seekers, we enthusiastically aspire to live the qualities that bring us spiritual contentment and bliss. We continuously try to tune ourselves to the vibrations of whatever we consider to be divine.

As a part of that effort, we *surrender* ourselves to that which is greater than ourselves. There is a limit to our ability to control our lives. Try as we might, things happen that are difficult or disastrous. We can choose to rail against the injustices of life, or to accept the fact that some of it is either random, or beyond our comprehension. We may even choose to believe that it all happens by intent or for a purpose. In any case, if we try to take responsibility for controlling everything, we will wear ourselves out in short order.

It is also important to develop and fortify the spirit through the use of ritual. It need not be religious in nature, but a regular recognition of the spiritual aspect reinforces spirit as a part of our lives. Rituals put us in the proper frame of mind to receive the energy that comes from our deeper consciousness. Rituals can include prayers, repeated phrases, chants, offerings, or anything else that helps us give time to thoughts of the divine.

We must also learn to become loving souls. In point of fact, that is what we are. We don't just *experience* love, we *are* love. All of those things that reinforce our loving nature are worth practicing. Compassion for the problems of others, and selflessly serving their needs are among the greatest ways we can strengthen our spiritual nature.

The Eight-fold Yogic Path (see Chapter 23) is not only a way to develop a strong mind and body, it is a means to develop inner tranquility. It's culmination in deep meditation can connect us to our true spiritual selves, and to the common consciousness.

True forgiveness is another one of the more difficult spiritual mountains we need to climb. If we can truly let go of our resentments and anger towards life's indignities, then this release of negative feelings can free up health-giving energy that is wasted on preoccupation with the past.

We can learn to go beyond logic and the mind, and live at least part of our lives with the faith that there is a purpose to it all. Without that faith, our reasons for living remain superficial and the process becomes tedious. We run to anesthetics and diversions, and our health fails.

TABLE 30-1: **SPIRITUAL THERAPIES**

1. Love
2. Compassion
3. Service
4. Renunciation
5. Faith
6. Surrender
7. Dispassion
8. Forgiveness

9. Non-Duality
10. Non-Judgment
11. Equitability
12. Purity
13. Mental Digestion
14. G-Self-Awareness
15. Identity as Spirit
16. Cosmic (Astrological) Awareness

17. Yoga Practices
18. Religious Practices
19. Meditation
20. Witnessing Awareness
21. Distinguishing the Mundane from Magnificent
22. Dumping the DEA (Desire, Ego, Attachment)
23. Perceptual & Attention Choices (positive)
24. Developing a Positive Ruling Love

25. Isolation
26. Silence
27. Lifestyle
28. Right Intention, Action, etc.
29. Ritual
30. Prayer
31. Phrase Repetition
32. Devotion

33. Learning from an Exemplary Teacher
34. Living from the Heart
35. Living in the Present Moment
36. Death Contemplation/Acceptance
37. Seeing Life as a Mind Reflection
38. Accepting Life as the Appropriate Lesson
39. Seeing Divinity in Everything

TABLE 30-2: **BEHAVIOR CHANGE TOOLS**

1. Facing Pain
2. Getting Information
3. Getting Help, Counseling
4. Renouncing Effortless Change Desire

5. Quality-type Evaluations, Mind & Body
6. Mental Digestion
7. Kicking Anesthesia
8. Diversion Awareness
9. Philosophy & Religion
10. Ayurvedic Mental Health Techniques
11. Eight-part Yoga Practices
12. Mind Food

13. Mental Quality Rebalancing
14. Five Cleansings Techniques
15. Mind Improvement Herbs
16. Nature Therapy
17. Sounds, Colors, Gems, Patterns

18. Exercise
19. Mind-Healing Foods
20. Work
21. Workplace Adjustments
22. Relationships & Associations Adjustments

23. Meditation
24. Austerity
25. Isolation & Reflection
26. Discipline & Daily Routine
27. Fasting
28. Gem Therapy
29. Sound Therapy
30. Phrase Repetition Therapy
31. Visual Pattern Therapies
32. Music Therapy

33. Stopping Negative Stories
34. Ending Attachment, Ego, & Desire
35. Acceptance
36. Impermanence Recognition
37. Journey as Destination
38. Enjoying Life
39. "Self"-love

DRIVER TRAINING SCHOOLS
MIND THERAPIES

According to yoga and ayurveda, the mind is a condensation of spiritual energy. If the spirit is in a good place, then the mind will follow suit. In a similar way, the mind is influenced by the body. A body that is plagued by illness will often pollute the mind into a mental illness.

Healing the mind, therefore, involves healing the spirit (as described above) and the body (as described in Section Two).

First, the body is purified of environmental and dietary toxins. This can be done with the various Ayurvedic cleansing techniques, and by maintaining a diet that promotes proper digestion, and by balancing the individual's qualities. The body should be strengthened with yoga postures, breathing, and cleanliness.

The feeding of the mind must be equally well-managed. Over-stimulating or anesthetic TV should be reduced as much as possible. Mental digestion must be maintained by facing one's mind issues, and not avoiding them with extra diversions, or covering them over with anesthetics. Constructive activities should be chosen.

The mind should be quieted with sensory reduction and one-pointed meditation on a daily basis. Stimulating food should be limited to daytime use, and mind-altering drugs kept to a minimum.

The qualities of our minds should be identified and balanced with the appropriate mental and physical food. Excess EARTH heaviness in the mind should be balanced with stimulating mind activities. Too much AIR-like mind chatter should be soothed with calming mental activities. Intense FIRE minds should be cooled with soothing and cooling mental and physical activities.

Associations with people and situations that are positive and uplifting are also essential for mind healing. Behavior choices that promote positivity rather than unconscious activity or negativity are also important. Using psychology counselors with a sense of spirituality to provide feedback and suggestions for mind therapy issues is often helpful.

We can learn to observe our minds as if they were symbiotic creatures living and operating inside our heads. We are not primarily our mind, even though the mind takes up most of the air time between our ears. When we can recognize our responses to painful problems and identify them as anesthetic or diversionary, then we can begin to move beyond those responses toward constructive ways of dealing with pain (Table 22-2). We can change our behaviors using many of the techniques that yoga and ayurveda have to offer (Table 30-1).

We must learn to view our own behaviors as a reflection of our state of mind. If we have taken in the healthy mental food, then we can expect to feel the positive qualities mentioned in Table 30-3.

TABLE 30-3: **FINDINGS OF GOOD MENTAL INTAKE**

1. Mental Lightness
2. Peace
3. Luminosity
4. Perceptual Clarity
5. Creativity
6. Satisfaction
7. Sleep Deep, Dreamless
8. Imagination Controlled
9. Sensory Function Sharp

If, on the other hand, our mental intake has been less than ideal, we can expect to see some of the findings in Table 30-8.

TABLE 30-4: **FINDINGS OF POOR MENTAL INTAKE**

1. Mental Heaviness, Dullness
2. Disturbed or Dark Thinking
3. Perceptual Cloudiness
4. Creativity Absence
5. Violent Entertainment Cravings
6. Sleep Disturbed
7. Imagination Uncontrolled, Disturbed
8. Sensory Function Poor

We can learn to deal with the emotional issues described in Chapter 19, and somehow develop a faith and optimism that will carry us forward through difficult times. We must continually work to overcome fear and guilt.

An important part of the healing process is to avoid letting the mind get comfortable with our illnesses. Our lives must have a focus beyond healing ourselves physically. Our support groups should not become our only family.

An approach toward mental management of pain is also central to healing. Pain is an omnipresent force in our lives, and we need to use it in a positive manner rather than run from it with frivolous diversions, or hide it under deadly anesthetics. We must recognize these responses when we use them, and gradually opt for something better.

We must become aware of the causes and consequences of our attitudes, and accept at least part of the responsibility for our problems. At the same time that we face difficult issues such as abuse and violence, we must be careful not to superficially label and pigeonhole these issues to avoid looking at them closely. In the face of issues such as these, we must somehow learn to understand, trust, and accept intimacy. We should also learn to relinquish some control over our lives and accept things as they are.

We must learn to give ourselves time to solve our difficult issues. We need to learn to subdivide our issues rather than think of life as one overwhelming problem. It is important to recognize that physical energy often comes from mental energy. We can re-energize our bodies by clearing up our mental issues.

When our egos are diminished, our minds are quieted. When our Life Force Energy becomes more balanced, our intelligence becomes clarified, and our perceptions are sharpened. We can derive additional energy from our interactions with others who cultivate positive energy.

We need to learn to focus on the positive strengths that we possess, and to view the changes that we need to make as an adventure rather than a burden or obstacle.

BODY SHOPS
BODY THERAPIES

When it comes to control of our bodies, the senses are usually dominant. Initially the senses served to protect and nourish the body, but because survival is no longer so dependent on the senses, they have become pleasure-seeking devices that demand feeding rather than providing assistance.

The inability to control sensory needs is the cause of most illness and disease. That inability comes from a mind that is without discipline, and a spirit that is without purpose.

At the same time that we are developing purpose and discipline, we must learn the principles of basic and advanced body maintenance discussed in Section Two of this book. There are many ayurvedic choices for us to utilize on the way to improving our health.

The importance of matching body type and food fuel cannot be overestimated. Proper digestion principles can help us avoid building up the IPOD TOXINS that are equally to blame for our health problems. Daily routine is the key to our health maintenance. There is no substitute for the beneficial effect on the body of yoga postures, breathing exercises, and meditation techniques.

When the basic concepts of ayurveda are understood and put into practice, then a balanced lifestyle will result. It takes significant effort to put these changes into practice, and it takes patience to see changes in the chronic illnesses that we create over many years. Immediate improvements are also seen once these principles become a lifestyle.

TABLE 30-5: **BODY THERAPIES**

1. AIR-Excess Treatment Principles
2. FIRE-Excess Treatment Principles
3. EARTH Excess Treatment Principles

4. Body Type / Food Matching
5. Proper Digestion
6. Daily Routine

7. Oils
8. Aromas
9. Massage

10. Five Cleansings Technique
11. Rejuvenation
12. Body Regeneration

13. Acupressure
14. Herbal Medications
15. High-potency Ash Medications
16. Polarity

17. Yoga Postures
18. Breathing Practices
19. Medicinal Carriers
20. Medicinal Ash Preparations
21. Metal Therapy
22. Color Therapy

23. Homeopathy
24. Primary Energy Centers
25. Energy Junction Points
26. Polarity Energy System
27. Energy Poses
28. Body Locks

DRIVE THRU'S
FOOD AS MEDICINE OR POISON

Medicines can be anything from complex, artificially created chemicals to faith healing prayers. It is important to stay open-minded, and to use whatever works best for any individual problem, be it natural or artificial.

The unique nature of the ayurvedic healing science is its emphasis on identifying the different *qualities* that each individual has, and custom tailoring a dietary approach to rebalancing those qualities. When the right food-fuel is put into the correctly identified engine, then we're off to the races! When the wrong fuel is used, our engines stall, clog up, and fall apart. According to ayurveda, most illness and disease come from wrong diet or wrong digestion!

It's just a matter of knowing which fuel to use, and then overcoming our habits and our sensory urges by putting that knowledge into practice. It seems so simple. We can do it easily with our cars, but with our body-vehicles, we must build considerable self-control, self-esteem and discipline. This is because we identify ourselves primarily with the sensual body and/or mind. Food is sensual.

When a noble life purpose remains in the forefront of our consciousness, we have a *reason* to pull up to the right fuel pump instead of heading for the junk-food drive thru. When we truly and continuously are nourished by the love that we are, then our engines will vibrate smoothly, and our life-journey becomes a joy ride.

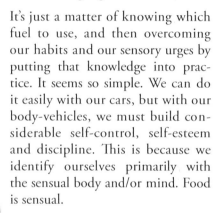

✳

CHAPTER 31:

DUDE, HERE'S MY CURE!

Health Journey Summary

LOVE WHAT YOU DO

… Well, Reggie's feeling better now, and he sure looks a lot better. A celebrity visit can work wonders. The doctors did a great job of pulling his bacon out of the fire –*this* time! No one knows how he's going to do now, but he says he's ready to give up some of his nasty habits and try some new things.

And now that he has no choice, he's finally going to take some time off. Who knows? He may not come back to work at all! He says he's always wanted to travel, and now would be a good time, once he gets his strength back.

He does seem happier and more comfortable with himself and the decisions he's making, now that he's had a near death experience. He's finally getting a chance to do what he really wants – not work all the time! That company disability policy sure helped a lot, and his divorce lawyer says that he'll only have himself to support now. Free at last.

Hmm…

After he recovers, he says he's going to do "whatever it takes" to stay alive and healthy. We've all heard *that* before. I can tell you from my own experience that words are cheap! Finding the strength and self-respect to stick to a healthy life-style is the junior high school course that most of us have blown a time or two. I hope Reggie understands that this could be his last chance to learn those lessons, or he flunks out to continuation school!

Figuring out what to do with yourself. Not easy. Going out there and finding that job-that-gets-your-enthusiasm-going-enough-to-get-you-out-of-bed-before-the-snooze-alarm-is-worn-out. That's the trick.

It reminds me of a TV show I saw a long time ago. Old George Burns is nearing his hundredth birthday, and is asked, during an interview, for the secret of his longevity. He smiles, pulls the cigar out of his mouth, looks directly into the camera and says:

"Love what you do for a living."

And puts the cigar back in.

Amen, George. Amen.

…

Well, speaking of doing what you love for a living, I'd better get back on the radio.

"Hey, Alan! You out there, dude? … Alan?"

PRIMARY AUTOMOTIVE INTELLIGENCE
AYURVEDIC HEALTH PRINCIPLES

5000 years ago, there was no trimethoprimsulfamethoxazole, a commonly used antibiotic in modern medicine. But 5,000 years ago, penicillin mold *was* growing on old food. There was no Viagra back then, but ashwagandha, bala, vidhari, Laghu Malini Vasant, and the system of yogic body locks were in common use.

Back then, they had no Walgreen's pharmacies, but they had a whole forest full of natural medicines like chamomile, valerian, nutmeg, and ephedra. Finding healing medicines was an issue of survival, so the people of that era gradually learned what worked best in specific situations, and for which kinds of people.

Although the people of ancient times did not have our modern knowledge and remedies, we still have theirs. The ayurvedic medical system they developed still applies to modern health because it is based on health principles that are timeless (Table 31-1).

TABLE 31-1: **TIMELESS HEALTH PRINICPLES**

1. Eat whole, natural, fresh food.

2. Digest food properly.

3. Eat what balances YOUR qualities.

4. It's easier to stay healthy than it is to cure an illness.

5. Create a routine and a lifestyle to maintain health.

6. Develop mental and physical discipline.

7. It can take a long time to fix long-standing problems.

8. Don't eat poison. (chemicals, pesticides)

9. If you do become polluted, do a cleansing procedure.

10. Given a chance, the body will usually heal itself.

11. Use whatever works.

These enduring health principles form the core of the first organized health science, ayurveda. It has been used for thousands of years because it works effectively and naturally to maintain health, and to cure illness. Today, many of our health issues are the same. Diet is still a common, modern controversy so the time-tested science of ayurveda , a discipline based on customizing diet, makes it very relevant today.

COMMENCEMENT
HEALTH GOALS

We want to be in a place where pleasure is dominant, and where we are not distracted by nagging illness. It is vital that we have such goals, even if they are just the small-self-satisfying goals of pleasurable, healthy living.

We need to train our minds in ways that allow us to keep track of our health, and to maintain and improve it. Like athletes in training for the Olympics, we must develop a routine that allows us to protect our health.

Hopefully, we've enrolled in life-school because we want to learn, and not just because we happen to be here. Since we're already on the planet, we might as well learn something! It can be anything that works for us, but some of our classes will no doubt be about health.

Getting rid of our health problems allows us to focus on greater things. Some of

us may be able to do generous service, or to work to make the world a better place. For many of us, just getting by without suffering is enough of a goal.

Ayurveda can effectively augment the strong points of other health disciplines, and fill in the areas where they are weak. It offers us an opportunity for us to find alternative treatments where no other solutions exist.

Just as it has done for thousands of years, Ayurvedic medicine shows us the way to the elusive cures and the healthy lifestyle that we seek. Both yoga and ayurveda offer us the opportunity to find health, happiness, contentment, peace, and the tingling, goose-bump-bliss of the Greater-Self cheering within us in every present moment.

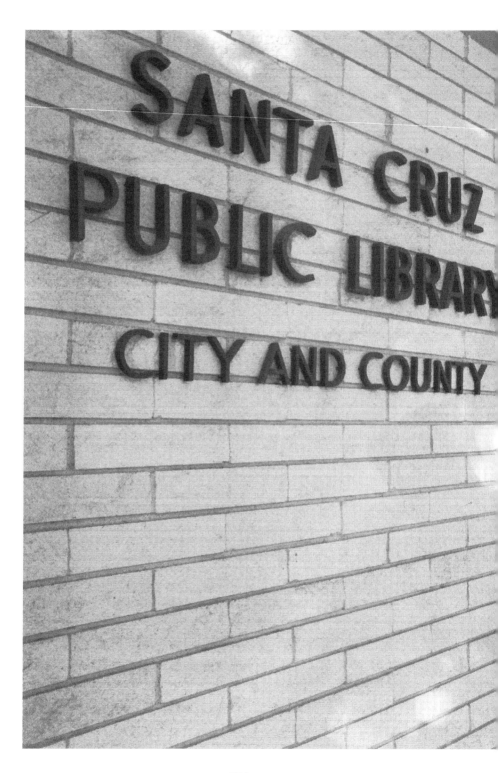

874

INFORMATION APPENDIX TWO

TABLE A-1: **SUMMARY OF QUALITY GROUP CHARACTERISTICS**

	AIR-Type	FIRE-Type	EARTH-Type
PHYSICAL QUALITIES	Mobile Fast Light Cold Rough Dry Clear Aromatice, dispersing Subtle Sparse Bitter Irregulat Unpredictable Flaxible Astringent Weaker Fatugues easily Hair thin, black/brown Skin thin, dry Teeth irregular/ large Voice weak Sleep light Appetite irregular Memory short	Spreading Steady medium Hot Sharp Liquid Penetrating Oily Definite Moderate Hot-spicy Regular Predict Soft Salty Moderate strength Moderate stamina Hair medium, red/blonde Skin medium, fail, oily Teeth regular / yellowish Voice forceful Sleep moderate Appetite strong / regular Memory excellent	Stationary Slow Heavy Cold Smooth / slimy Liquid Cloudy / sticky Oily Gross Dense / hard Sweet Steady Consistent Sturdy Stable Strong Strong stamina Hair thick Skin thick, oily Teeth white Voice deep, strong Sleep heavy Appetitie constant Memory long-term
MENTAL QUALITIES	Moods variable Alert Intuitive Spiritual Fearful Creative Restless Sensitive Fickle Happy Gregarious Active Talkative Unsure Blunt Spends money easily	Moods focused Argumentative Perceptive Artistic Aggressive Articulate Driven Reactive Irritable Determined Social Leads Directive Certain Superior, comparing Spends on luxury	Mood prolonged Foggy Appreciative Constructive Loving Forbearance Passive Less sensitive Accepting Sad Reclusive follows Listener Patient Modest Conservative
ILLNESS QUALITIES	Spasm Cracking Cramping Pain Moving Pain Nervousness Constipation Dry Arthritis Nervous Disorders	Inflammation Burning Burning Pain Sharp Pain Acid Stomach Diarrhea Hot Arthritis Hormonal Disorders	Congestion Congealing Constant Pain Dull Pain Mucous Bulky stools Thick Arthritis Congestive Disorders

TABLE 3-2:
PHYSICAL CHARACTERISTICS
OF THE QUALITY TYPES

CATEGORY	AIR	FIRE	EARTH
Frame Shape	Thin	Medium	Round
Weight	Light	Medium	Heavy
Size	Small	Medium	Large
Movement	Active	Directed, moderate	Steady, less
Skin	Thin	Medium	Thick
Body Temperature	Cold	Hot	Cool
Environment Preferred	Warm	Cool	Warm
Appetite	Irregular, weak	Regular, Strong	Constant
Thirst	Irregular	Strong	Moderate
Bowel Movements	Small, hard	Medium, soft	Large, soft
Urine	Little, pale	Moderate, yellow	Moderate
Facial Lines	Many	Nasal Bridge Creases	Few
Fingernails	Brittle	Soft	Soft, thick
Hips	Narrow	Medium	Wide
Shoulders	Narrow	Medium	Wide
Lower Legs	Narrow	Medium	Wide
Teeth	Crooked	Straight, yellowish	Straight/strong/white
Eyes	Small	Medium	Large
T O T A L	_____	_____	_____

TABLE 3-3:
MENTAL CHARACTERISTICS
OF THE QUALITY TYPES

CATEGORY	AIR	FIRE	EARTH
Mood	Variable	Focused	Prolonged
Attention	Alert	Quick	Foggy
Speed	Fast	Quick	Slow
Precision	Random	Accurate	Certain
Compulsion	Common	Common	Rare
Memory, short-term	Good	Good	Fair
Memory, long-term	Poor	Good	Excellent
Sleep quantity	Less	Moderate	More
Sleep quality	Active	Good	Heavy
Temper	Unpredictable	Fiery	Cool
Attitude	Blunt, Creative	Superior, Purposeful	Modest, Forgiving
Speech	Talkative	Direct	Listener, Patient
Social	Gregarious	Social climber	Reclusive
Spirituality	High	Low	Moderate
Attachment	Little	Moderate	High
Ego	Moderate	High	Low
Competitiveness	Low	High	Low
Status concern	Low	High	Moderate
Clothing	Creative	Neat	Relaxed
Generosity	High	Purposeful	Low
Spending	Easily	Luxuries	Sparingly
Demeanor	Fearful	Aggressive	Loving
Manner	Fickle	Irritable	Accepting
Sensitivity	Sensitive	Reactive	Compassionate
T O T A L	_____	_____	_____

TABLE 6-1:
GENERAL FOODS FOR BALANCING BODY QUALITY TYPES

	AIR-Balancing		FIRE-Balancing		EARTH-Balancing	
	AVOID	TAKE	AVOID	TAKE	AVOID	TAKE
FRUIT	Dried Fresh Bitter	Soaked Cooked Sweet	Sour	Sweet Bitter	Sweet Sour Cooked	Bitter Dried Fresh
VEGETABLES	Raw Bitter	Cooked Juicy Sweet	Spicy-hot	Sweet Bitter	Sweet Juicy	Spicy-hot Bitter
GRAINS	Drying	Sweet	Heating	Sweet	Sweet	Drying Heating
ANIMAL FOODS	White Meat Lighter	Dark Meat Heavier Seafood Eggs	Red Meat Egg Yolk Seafood	White Meat Egg White Freshwater fish	Red Meat Egg Yolk Seafood	White Meat Egg White Freshwater fish
LEGUMES	Most All	Black & Red Lentils	Lentils	Most	Kidney Beans Black Lentils	Most
NUTS	None	All	Most	Coconut	All	None
SEEDS	None	All	Most	Sunflower Pumpkin	Most	Sunflower Pumpkin
SWEETENERS	None	Most	Honey Molasses	Most	Most	Honey
CONDIMENTS	Cooling	Heating	Heating	Cooling	Cooling	Heating
DAIRY	None	All	Sour Salty Fermented	Sweet	Most	Ghee Goat's Milk
OILS	None	All	Heating	Cooling	Most	Almond Corn

TABLE 6-2:
FRUITS FOR BALANCING QUALITIES

AIR Balancing (heating, sweet, spicy)	FIRE Balancing (cooling, sweet, tart, bitter)	EARTH Balancing (heating, sweet, spicy)
Apples (sweet)	Apples (sweet)	-
-	Apples (tart)	Apples (tart)
Apricot	-	Apricots
Bananas	-	-
Blackberries	-	-
Blueberries	Blueberries	-
Cherries	**Cherries**	**Cherries**
Cranberries	-	Cranberries
Currents	Currents	-
Dates	Dates	-
Figs (raw)	Figs (raw)	-
Gooseberries	Gooseberries	-
Grapes (sour)	-	-
Grapes (sweet)	Grapes (sweet)	-
Grapefruit	-	-
Kiwi	-	Kiwi
Guava	Guava	-
Lemon	-	Lemon
Lime	**Lime**	**Lime**
Loquat	Loquat	-
Mango	Mango	-
Melons	Melons	-
Mulberries	Mulberries	Mulberries
Nectarines	Nectarines	Nectarines
Oranges (sweet)	Oranges (sweet)	-
Oranges (sour)	-	-
Papaya	-	-
Peaches	-	Peaches
-	Pears	Pears
-	-	Persimmons
Pineapple (sour)	-	-
Plums (sweet)	Plums (sweet)	-
Plums (sour)	-	-
-	Pomegranate	Pomegranate
-	Prunes	Prunes
Quince	**Quince**	**Quince**
-	Raisins	Raisins
-	Raspberries	-
Rhubarb	-	-
Strawberries (sour)	-	-
Strawberries (sweet)	Strawberries (sweet)	-
Tangerine	Tangerine	-
Watermelon	Watermelon	-

TABLE 6-3:
VEGETABLES FOR BALANCING QUALITIES

AIR Balancing (heating, sweet, spicy)	FIRE Balancing (cooling, sweet, tart, bitter)	EARTH Balancing (heating, sweet, spicy)
Acorn Squash	Acorn Squash	Acorn Squash
-	Alfalfa Sprouts	Alfalfa Sprouts
Algae	**Algae**	**Algae**
-	Artichoke (cooked)	Artichoke (cooked)
-	Artichoke, Jerusalem	Artichoke, Jerusalem
Asparagus	**Asparagus**	**Asparagus**
Avocado	Avocado	-
Beets	-	Beets
-	-	Beet Greens
-	Bitter Gourd	Bitter Gourd
-	Borage	Borage
-	Broccoli	Broccoli
-	Brussels Sprouts (cooked)	Brussels Sprouts (cooked)
-	Cabbage	Cabbage
Carambola	**Carambola**	**Carambola**
Carrots	-	Carrots
-	Cauliflower	Cauliflower
-	Celery	Celery
Charole	**Charole**	**Charole**
Cilantro Leaf	**Cilantro Leaf**	**Cilantro Leaf**
-	Corn	Corn
Cucumber	Cucumber	-
-	-	Dandelion Greens
Dulce	**Dulce**	**Dulce**
-	Eggplant	Eggplant
-	Endive	Endive
Fennel	Fennel	-
Ginger (raw)	-	Ginger (raw)
Green beans	**Green beans**	**Green beans**
-	Kale (raw)	Kale (raw)
Kelp (cooked)	**Kelp (cooked)**	**Kelp (cooked)**
-	-	Kohlrabi
Kombu (cooked)	-	Kombu (raw)
-	Leafy Greens	Leafy Greens
Leeks (raw)	-	Leeks (raw)
-	Lettuce	Lettuce
-	Mushrooms	Mushrooms
Mustard Greens (raw)	-	Mustard Greens (raw)
Okra	**Okra**	**Okra**
Olives (in oil or brine)	-	-
Onions	-	Onions
Parsley (raw)	Parsley (raw)	Parsley (raw)
Parsnips (raw)	Parsnips (raw)	-
Peas	Peas	Peas

AIR Balancing (heating, sweet, spicy)	FIRE Balancing (cooling, sweet, tart, bitter)	EARTH Balancing (heating, sweet, spicy)
Peppers (hot)	-	Peppers (hot)
-	Peppers (sweet)	Peppers (sweet)
Plantain (raw)	Plantain (raw)	-
Potatoes (sweet)	Potatoes (sweet)	-
-	Potatoes (white)	Potatoes (white)
Pumpkin	Pumpkin	-
Radishes	Radishes	Radishes
Rutabaga (cooked)	**Rutabaga (cooked)**	**Rutabaga (cooked)**
Scallions (raw)	-	Scallions (raw)
Seaweed (raw)	**Seaweed (raw)**	**Seaweed (raw)**
-	Spinach	Spinach
Spirulina	-	Spirulina
-	Sprouts	Sprouts
Squash, acorn (cooked)	**Squash, acorn (cooked)**	**Squash, acorn (cooked)**
Squash, summer	**Squash, summer**	**Squash, summer**
-	-	Tomato
-	-	Turnips (cooked)
-	-	Turnip Greens (raw)
Watercress (raw)	-	Watercress (raw)
-	Wheatgrass (raw)	Wheatgrass (raw)
Zucchini (raw)	Zucchini (raw)	-

TABLE 6-4:
GRAINS FOR BALANCING QUALITIES

Amaranth (cooked)	**Amaranth (cooked)**	**Amaranth (cooked)**
-	Barley	Barley
-	-	Buckwheat
-	-	Corn
-	Gram, black	-
-	-	Millet
-	Muesli	Muesli
Oats	Oats	-
-	Oat Bran	Oat Bran
-	-	Polenta
-	Popcorn	Popcorn
Quinoa	-	-
Rice, Basmati	**Rice, Basmati**	**Rice, Basmati**
Rice, brown	Rice, brown	-
Rice, white	Rice, white	-
-	-	Rye
-	Sago	Sago
Seitan	Seitan	Seitan
Wheat	Wheat	-
-	Wheat bran	Wheat bran
Wheat, durham	**Wheat, durham**	**Wheat, durham**

TABLE 6-5:
BEANS/LEGUMES FOR BALANCING QUALITIES

AIR Balancing (heating, sweet, spicy)	FIRE Balancing (cooling, sweet, tart, bitter)	EARTH Balancing (heating, sweet, spicy)
-	Adzuki	Adzuki
-	Black	Black
-	Black-eyed peas	Black-eyed peas
-	Fava	Fava
-	Garbanzo	Garbanzo
-	Green	Green
-	Kidney	Kidney
Lentils, red	**Lentils, red**	**Lentils, red**
-	Lentils, brown	Lentils, brown
-	Lima	Lima
-	-	Miso
Mung	**Mung**	**Mung**
-	Navy	Navy
-	Pinto	Pinto
-	Soy	Soy
-	Tempeh	Tempeh
-	Tofu	Tofu
Tur dahl	-	Tur dahl
Urad dahl	-	-
-	White	White

TABLE 6-6:
ANIMAL PRODUCTS FOR BALANCING QUALITIES

Beef	-	-
Buffalo meat	Buffalo meat	-
Chicken (dark meat)	-	-
-	Chicken (white meat)	Chicken (white meat)
Duck meat	-	-
Eggs	-	-
Egg white	**Egg white**	**Egg white**
Fish (freshwater)	**Fish (freshwater)**	**Fish (freshwater)**
Frog meat	-	-
Goat meat	**Goat meat**	**Goat meat**
Horse meat	-	-
Kidney	-	-
Liver	-	Liver
Pork	-	-
-	Rabbit	Rabbit
Sardines	-	-
Salmon	-	-
Seafood (other)	-	-
Scallops	-	-
Shellfish	-	-

AIR Balancing (heating, sweet, spicy)	FIRE Balancing (cooling, sweet, tart, bitter)	EARTH Balancing (heating, sweet, spicy)
Shrimp	**Shrimp**	**Shrimp**
Snails	-	-
Sweetbreads (pancreas)	-	-
Tongue	-	-
Tuna	-	-
Turkey (dark meat)	-	-
-	Turkey (white meat)	Turkey (white meat)
-	Venison	Venison

TABLE 6-7:
DAIRY FOR BALANCING QUALITIES

Breast milk	Breast milk	Breast milk
Butter (salted)	-	-
Butter (unsalted)	Butter (unsalted)	-
Buttermilk	-	-
Cheese (hard)	-	-
Cheese (soft)	Cheese (soft, unsalted)	-
Cream	Cream	-
Cottage Cheese	**Cottage Cheese**	**Cottage Cheese**
Ghee	**Ghee**	**Ghee**
Goat's cheese (unsalted)	**Goat's cheese (unsalted)**	**Goat's cheese (unsalted)**
Goat's milk	**Goat's milk**	**Goat's milk**
-	Ice Cream	-
Milk	Milk	-
Sour Cream	-	-
Yogurt	-	-

TABLE 6-8:
OILS/FATS FOR BALANCING QUALITIES

Almond	-	Almond
Apricot	-	-
Avocado	Avocado	-
Canola	**Canola**	**Canola**
Coconut	Coconut	-
-	-	Corn
-	Flax Seed	-
Ghee	**Ghee**	-
Olive	Olive	**Ghee**
Primrose	Primrose	-
Primrose	Primrose	-
Safflower	-	-
Sesame	Sesame	-
?	Sunflower	Sunflower
?	Soy	Soy
Walnut	Walnut	-

TABLE 6-9:
NUTS & SEEDS FOR BALANCING QUALITIES

AIR Balancing (heating, sweet, spicy)	FIRE Balancing (cooling, sweet, tart, bitter)	EARTH Balancing (heating, sweet, spicy)
Almonds	-	-
Brazil nuts	-	-
Cashews	-	-
Charole	**Charole**	**Charole**
Chia	-	-
Coconut	Coconut	-
Filberts	-	-
-	Flax	Flax
Hazelnuts	-	-
Macadamia	-	-
Mustard	-	Mustard
Peanuts	-	-
Pecans	-	-
Pine nuts	-	-
Pistachio	-	-
Poppy	-	Poppy
Pumpkin	**Pumpkin**	**Pumpkin**
-	Psyllium	-
Sesame	-	-
Sunflower	**Sunflower**	**Sunflower**
Tahini	-	-
Walnuts	-	-
Walnuts, black	-	-

TABLE 6-10:
SWEETENERS FOR BALANCING QUALITIES

Barley malt	Barley malt	-
Fructose	Fructose	-
Corn Syrup	Corn Syrup	Corn Syrup
Fruit Juice Concentrate	**Fruit Juice Concentrate**	**Fruit Juice Concentrate**
Honey	-	Honey
Jaggary	-	-
Maple syrup	Maple syrup	-
Molasses	-	-
Rice syrup	Rice syrup	-
Stevia	Stevia	Stevia
Sucanat	Sucanat	-
Sugar, white	Sugar, white	-
Sugar, brown	-	-
Sugar, turbinado	Sugar, turbinado	-

TABLE 6-11:
DRINKS FOR BALANCING QUALITIES

AIR Balancing (heating, sweet, spicy)	FIRE Balancing (cooling, sweet, tart, bitter)	EARTH Balancing (heating, sweet, spicy)
Almond "milk"	Almond "milk"	-
-	Apple Juice	Apple Juice
Apple Cider	-	Apple Cider
Apricot juice	**Apricot juice**	**Apricot juice**
-	-	Beer
-	Carob	Carob
-	-	Carrot juice
Chai milk	Chai milk	-
Cherry Juice	**Cherry Juice**	**Cherry Juice**
-	-	Coffee
-	-	Cranberry Juice
Grape juice (purple)	Grape juice (purple)	Grape juice (purple)
Grapefruit juice	-	-
Lemon juice	-	-
-	Lime juice	-
Mango juice	**Mango juice**	**Mango juice**
Milk (cow's)	Milk (cow's)	-
Orange juice	-	-
Papaya juice	-	-
Peach juice	Peach juice	Peach juice
Pero (grain coffee)	**Pero (grain coffee)**	**Pero (grain coffee)**
Pineapple juice	-	-
-	Pomegranate juice	Pomegranate juice
-	Prune juice	Prune juice
Rice milk	Rice milk	-
-	Soy milk	-
-	-	Tea (black)
-	Water (cool)	
Water (hot)	**Water (hot)**	**Water (hot)**

TABLE 6-12:
SPICES & TEAS FOR BALANCING QUALITIES

Ajwan	-	Ajwan
Allspice	-	Allspice
Almond Extract	-	Almond Extract
Anise	-	Anise
Asafoetida	-	Asafoetida
Basil	-	Basil
Bay Leaf	-	Bay Leaf
Black leaf	-	Black leaf
Black pepper	-	Black pepper
Cardamom	**Cardamom**	**Cardamom**
Cayenne pepper	-	Cayenne pepper

TABLE 6-12: **SPICES & TEAS** (cont):

AIR Balancing (heating, sweet, spicy)	FIRE Balancing (cooling, sweet, tart, bitter)	EARTH Balancing (heating, sweet, spicy)
Cinnamon	-	Cinnamon
-	Alfalfa	Alfalfa
Bancha	**Bancha**	**Bancha**
-	Barley	Barley
Basil	Basil	Basil
-	Borage	Borage
-	Burdock	Burdock
-	Catnip	Catnip
Chamomile	**Chamomile**	**Chamomile**
-	Chicory	Chicory
-	Chrysanthemum	Chrysanthemum
Cinnamon	-	Cinnamon
Clove	-	Clove
Comfrey	Comfrey	-
Coriander	**Coriander**	**Coriander**
Cumin	**Cumin**	**Cumin**
-	Dandelion	Dandelion
Dill	**Dill**	**Dill**
Elder Flower	**Elder Flower**	**Elder Flower**
Eucalyptus	-	Eucalyptus
Fennel	**Fennel**	**Fennel**
Fenugreek	-	Fenugreek
Garlic	-	Garlic
Ginger (dry)	-	Ginger (dry)
Ginger (fresh)	**Ginger (fresh)**	**Ginger (fresh)**
-	-	Ginseng
Hawthorne	-	Hawthorne
-	Hibiscus	Hibiscus
-	Hops	Hops
-	-	Hyssop
-	Jasmine	Jasmine
Juniper berry	-	Juniper berry
Kukitcha	**Kukitcha**	**Kukitcha**
Lavender	**Lavender**	**Lavender**
-	Lemon balm	Lemon balm
Licorice	**Licorice**	**Licorice**
Mace	-	Mace
Marjoram	-	Marjoram
Marshmallow	Marshmallow	-
Mint	**Mint**	**Mint**
Mormon	-	Mormon
Mustard seed	-	Mustard seed
-	Nettle	Nettle
Nutmeg	-	Nutmeg
Oat straw	**Oat straw**	**Oat straw**

AIR Balancing (heating, sweet, spicy)	FIRE Balancing (cooling, sweet, tart, bitter)	EARTH Balancing (heating, sweet, spicy)
Orange peel	-	Orange peel
Oregano	-	Oregano
Paprika	-	Paprika
Parsley	**Parsley**	**Parsley**
Pennyroyal	Pennyroyal	Pennyroyal
Peppermint	**Peppermint**	**Peppermint**
Pippali	-	Pippali
Poppy seeds	-	Poppy seeds
Raspberry	-	Raspberry
-	Red clover	Red clover
Rose hips	-	-
Rosemary	-	Rosemary
Saffron	**Saffron**	**Saffron**
Sage	-	Sage
Salt	-	-
Sarsaparilla	**Sarsaparilla**	**Sarsaparilla**
Sassafras	-	Sassafras
Savory	-	Savory
Spearmint	-	Spearmint
Star anise	-	Star anise
Tarragon	-	Tarragon
Thyme	-	Thyme
Tumeric	**Tumeric**	**Tumeric**
Vanilla	**Vanilla**	**Vanilla**
Wintergreen	**Wintergreen**	**Wintergreen**

TABLE 6-13: **SUPPLEMENTS FOR BALANCING QUALITIES**

-	Algae, blue-green	Algae, blue-green
-	Aloe vera juice	Aloe vera juice
Amino acids	-	Amino acids
-	Barley green	Barley green
Bee pollen	-	Bee pollen
-	-	Brewer's yeast
Calcium	**Calcium**	**Calcium**
Copper	-	Copper
Iron	-	Iron
Royal jelly	-	Royal jelly
Spirulina	Spirulina	Spirulina
Vitamin A	-	Vitamin A
Vitamin B	-	Vitamin B
Vitamin C	-	Vitamin C
Vitamin D	**Vitamin D**	**Vitamin D**
Vitamin E	**Vitamin E**	**Vitamin E**
Zinc	**Zinc**	**Zinc**

TABLE A-14: **EIGHT BRANCHES OF YOGA**

EIGHT CYLINDER ENGINE

1. RESTRAINTS

   Non-violence
   Non-stealing
   Non-hoarding
   Truthfulness
   Sexual Control

2. OBSERVANCES

   Purity
   Contentment
   Austerity
   Study
   Surrender

3. POSTURES

4. BREATHING

5. SENSORY WITHDRAWAL /
   INWARD FOCUS

6. CONCENTRATION

7. MEDITATION

8. UNION

TABLE A-19: **AYURVEDIC SANSKRIT TERMS**

Abrak	Mica
Abhyanga	Oil massage
Agni	Digestive, transformative fire
Ahara	Unprocessed
Akasha	Space, ether
Alochak Pitta	Eye fire, vision
Ama	Toxin
Amala	Sour
Amashaya	Stomach
Ambu Vaha Srotas	Water carrying channels
Anahat	Heart chakra
Anna Vaha Srotas	Digestive system
Apana	Downward-moving energy
Apa	Water
Arishta	Fermented herbal medicine
Artava	Female reproductive tissue
Asana	Yoga posture
Asava	Juice
Asthi	Bone
Avalambak Kapha	Lung/cardiac EARTH quality
Avila	Cloudy
Ayuh	Life
Ayurveda	Life knowledge
Bhasma	Medicinal ash preparation
Bheda	Deformity stage of illness
Bodhak Kapha	Mouth EARTH quality
Brajak Pitta	Skin FIRE quality
Buddhi	Discriminating intellect
Chakra	Major energy vortex
Chit	Conscious mind aspect
Chikitsa	Treatment
Churna	Powdered mixture
Dosha	Quality grouping
Dushti	Disorder
Dhatu	Tissue
Dina Charya	Daily routine

TABLE A-20: **AYURVEDIC TERMS IN ENGLISH**

ENGLISH	ABREVIATION	SANSKRIT
Incomplete Product of Digestion	IPOD	Ama
Air-like Qualities	AIR	Vata
Fire-like Qualities	FIRE	Pitta
Earth-like Qualities	EARTH	Kapha
Composite Vital Strength	CVS	Ojas
Life Force Energy	LiFE	Prana
Transformational Intelligent Energy	TIE	Tejas
Digestive Transformational Energy	DTE	Agni
Devine Mind View	DMV	—
Taste	—	Rasa
Thermal effect	—	Virya
Destination effect	—	Vipak
Mind-Tongue alliance	MTA	—
Energy Center	—	Chakra
Energy Junction Point	EJP	Marma
Purity	—	Satva
Activity	—	Rajas
Negativity	—	Tamas
Genetic Mind Quality	—	Manas Vikruti
Neurotransmitter	NT	—
Delay of Gratification	DoG	—
Individual Consciousness	self (individual self)	Paramatman
Sum of all Consciousness	Self (Greater Self)	Atman
Five Actions Cleansing Techn.	FACT	Pancha Karma

INDEX to CHARTS/TABLES & FIGURES/ILLUSTRATIONS

Volume One

VOLUME TWO

Volume Two (cont)

BIBLIOGRAPHY

1. Abramson, Edward. Emotional Eating: What You Need to Know Before Starting Another Diet, Jossy-Bass, San Francisco.

2. Balch, James F., and Mark Stengler. Prescription for Natural Cures, Wiley, Hoboken, 2004.

3. Ben-Ze'ev, Aaron, The Subtlety of Emotions, MIT Press, Cambridge, 2000.

4. Bhishagrantna, Kaviraj K. The Shusruta Samhita, Cowkhamba, Varanasi, 1981.

5. Bodian, Stephan. Meditation for Dummies, Wiley Publishing, New York, 1999.

6. Chopra, Deepak. Ageless Body, Timeless Mind, Harmony Books, New York, 1993.

7. Chopra, Deepak. The Seven Spiritual Laws of Success, Amber-Allen.

8. Chopra, Deepak. Perfect Digestion, Harmony Books, New York, 1995

9. Chopra, Deepak et al. The Chopra Center Cookbook, John Wiley & Sons, Hoboken, 2002.

10. Chopra, Deepak. The Path to Love, Harmony Books, New York, 1997.

11. Chusid, Joseph G. Correlative Neuroanatomy & Functional Neurology, Lange, 1985.

12. Copony, Heita. Mystery of Mandalas, Theosophical Publishing House, Wheaton, 1988.

13. Cox, Kathleen. Vastu Living, Marlow, New York, 2000.

14. Dali Lama. How to Practice, Atria, New York, 2002.

15. Dash, Bhagwan. Massage Therapy in Ayurveda, Conept Publishing Company, New Delhi, 1992.

16. Dash, Bhagwan. Concept of Agni in Ayurveda with Special Reference to Agnibala Pariksa, Chaukhamba Amarabharati Prakashan, Moujpour Delhi 1993.

17. Dash, Bhagwan. Ayurveda for Mother & Child, Delhi Diary Publishers, New Delhi, 1975.

18. Dash, Bhagwan. Ayurvedic Cures for Common Diseases: A Complete Book of Ayurvedic Remedies, Hindu Pocket Books, Delhi, 1997.

19. Dash, Bhagwan. Fundamentals of Ayurvedic Medicine, Konark, Delhi, 1978.

20. Devraj, T.L. The Panchakarma Treatment of Ayurveda, Sri Satguru Publications, Delhi, 1998.

21. Douillard, John. Perfect Health for Kids, North Atlantic Books, Berkeley, 2004.

22. Epstein, Donald M. The 12 Stages of Healing, Amber-Allen, San Rafael, 1994.

23. Fairburn, Christopher. <u>Overcoming Binge Eating</u>, Guilford Press, New York, 1995.

24. Frawley, David. <u>Ayurveda and the Mind: the Healing of Consciousness</u>, Lotus Press, Twin Lakes Wisconsin, 1997.

25. Frawley, David. <u>Ayurvedic Healing</u>, Moroson Publishing, Salt Lake City, 1989.

26. Frawley, David. <u>From the River of Heaven</u>, Passage Press, Salt Lake City, 1990.

27. Frawley, David and Vasant Lad. <u>The Yoga of Herbs</u>, Lotus Press, Santa Fe, 1986.

28. Frawley, David et al. <u>Ayurveda and Marma Therapy</u>, Lotus Press, Twin Lakes, WI, 2003.

29. Frawley, David and Sandra Summerfield Kozak. <u>Yoga for Your Type: An Ayurvedic Approach to Your Asana Practice</u>, Lotus Press, Twin Lakes, WI, 2001.

30. Gerrish, Michael. <u>The Mind-Body Makeover Project</u>, Contemporary Books, Chicago, 2003.

30.1 Gogte, V.M. Ayurvedic Pharmacology and Therapeutic Use of Medicinal Plants, Chaukhambha Publications, New Delhi.

31. Gravitz, Herbert L. and Julie D Bowden. <u>Recovery: A Guide for Adult Children of Alcoholics</u>, Simon & Schuster, New York, 1985.

32. Guyton, Arthur C. and John E. Hall. <u>Textbook of Medical Physiology</u>, W.B. Saunders, Philadelphia, 2000.

33. Hari Dass, Baba. <u>Ashtanga Yoga Primer</u>, Sri Rama Publishing, Santa Cruz, 1981

34. Hari Dass, Baba. <u>Fire Without Fuel</u>, Sri Rama Publishing, Santa Cruz, 1986

35. Hari Dass, Baba. <u>The Path to Enlightenment is Not a Highway</u>, Sri Rama Publishing, Santa Cruz, 1996.

36. Hirschi, Gertrud. <u>Mudras: Yoga in Your Hands</u>, Weiser Books, Boston, 2000.

37. Joshi, Sunil V. <u>Ayurveda and Panchakarma: The Science of Healing and Rejuvenation</u>, Lotus Press, Twin Lakes WI, 1997.

38. Johari, Harish. <u>Tools for Tantra</u>, Destiny Books, Rochester, 1986.

39. Kabat-Zinn, Jon. <u>Coming to Our Senses</u>, Hyperion, New York, 2005.

40. Kaplan, Harold I. and Benjamin J. Sadock. <u>Comprehensive Textbook of Psychiatry</u>, Williams & Wilkins, Baltimore, 1985.

41. Kumar, Abhimanyu. <u>Child Health Care in Ayurveda</u>, Sri Satguru Publications, Delhi, 1994.

42. Lad, Usha and Vasant Lad. <u>Ayurvedic Cooking for Self-Healing</u>, The Ayurvedic Press, Albuquerque, NM, 1994

43. Lad, Vasant. <u>Ayurvedic Perspectives on Selected Pathologies</u>, The Ayurvedic Press, Albuquerque, 2005.

44. Lad, Vasant D. <u>Ayurveda: The Science of Self-Healing, A Practical Guide</u>, Lotus Press, Wilmot Wisconsin, 1984.

45. Lad, Vasant. <u>The Complete Book of Ayurvedic Home Remedies</u>, Harmony Books, New York, 1998.

46. Lad, Vasant. <u>Lectures on Ayurveda</u>, Mount Madonna Center, 1992-2007.

47. Lad, Vasant and Anisha Durve. <u>Marma Points of Ayurveda: The Energy Pathways for Healing Body, Mind and Consciousness with a Comparison to Traditional Chinese Medicine</u>, Ayurvedic Press, Albuquerque, NM, 2008

48. Lad, Vasant.<u>Textbook of Ayurveda, Vols. 1 & 2</u>, The Ayurvedic Press, Albuquerque, 2002.

49.Lad, Vasant. <u>Secrets of the Pulse: The Ancient Art of Ayurvedic Pulse Diagnosis</u>, The Ayurvedic Press, Albuquerque, 1996.

50. Ladinsky, Daniel. <u>The Gift</u>, Penguin Putnam, New York, 1999.

51. Lele, Avinash, <u>The Lost Ayurveda Secrets of Marma</u>, International Academy of Ayurveda, Pune, 1999.

52. Levine, Stephen. <u>Guided Meditations, Explorations, and Healings</u>, Doubleday, New York, 1991.

53. Lidell, Lucinda. <u>The Book of Massage</u>, Ebury Press, London, 1984.

54. Mahan, L. Kathleen and Marian T. Arlin. <u>Krause's Food, Nutrition & Diet Therapy</u>, W.B. Saunders, Philadelphia 1992.

55. Miller, Light and Bryan Miller. <u>Ayurveda and Aromatherapy: The Earth Essential Guide to Ancient Wisdom and Modern Healing</u>, Lotus Press, Twin Lakes, WI, 1995.

56. Mohan, A.G. <u>Yoga for Body, Breath, and Mind</u>, Rudra Press, Portland, 1993.

57. Monte, Tom. <u>The Complete Guide to Natural Healing</u>, Boston Common Press, New York, 1997.

58. Morningstar, Amadea. <u>Ayurvedic Cooking for Westerners: Familiar Western Food Prepared with Ayurvedic Principles</u>, Lotus Press, Twin Lakes, WI, 1995.

59. Morningstar, Amadea and Urmila Desai. <u>The Ayurvedic Cookbook: A Personalized Guide to Good Nutrition and Health</u>, Lotus Press, Wilmot, WI, 1990.

60. Morningstar, Amadea. <u>The Ayurvedic Guide to Polarity Therapy: Hands-on Healing</u>, Lotus Press, Twin Lakes, 2001.

61. Murthy, K.R. Srikantha. <u>Vagbhata's Astanga Hrdayam</u>, Krishnadas Academy, Near Golghar.

62. Myss, Caroline. <u>Why People Don't Heal and How They Can</u>, Three Rivers Press, New York, 1997.

63. Myss, Caroline. <u>Anatomy of the Spirit</u>, Three Rivers Press, New York, 1996.

64. Nadkarni, K.M. and A.K Nadkarni. <u>Indian Materia Medica</u>, Popular Prakashan, Bombay, 1982.

65. Rakel, Robert E., Ed. <u>Conn's Current Therapy</u>, W.B. Saunders Company, Philadelphia 1993.

66. Ram Dass. <u>Miracle of Love</u>, E.P. Dutton, New York, 1979.

67. Ranade, Subhash and Sunanda Ranade. <u>Ayurveda and Yoga Therapy,</u> Nandurkar, Pune, India 1995.

68. Ros, Frank. <u>The Lost Secrets of Ayurvedic Acupuncture</u>, Lotus Press, Twin Lakes Wisconsin, 1994.

69. Sachidananda, Sri Swami. <u>The Yoga Sutras of Patanjali</u>, Integral Yoga Publications, Buckingham, 1999.

70. Sachs, Melanie. <u>Ayurvedic Beauty Care: Ageless Techniques to Invoke Natural Beauty</u>, Lotus Press, Twin Lakes, WI, 1994.

71. Saraswati, Swami Satyananda. <u>Asana Pranayama Mudra Bandha</u>, Bihar Yoga Bharati, Munger, 1997.

72. Shah, J. T. <u>Therapeutic Yoga</u>, Vakils, Feffer & Simons,, Mumbai, 1999.

73. Shanbhag, Vivek. <u>A Beginner's Introduction to Ayurvedic Medicine,</u> Keats Publishing, New Canaa, 1994.

74. Sharma, Ram K., Vaidya Bhagwan Dash (tr. & ed.) <u>Caraka Samhita</u>, Chowkhamba, Varanasi, 1988.

75. Siegel, Michele. <u>Surviving an Eating Disorder</u>, Harper and Row, New York 1988.

76. Sills, Franklyn. <u>The Polarity Process</u>, Element, Shaftesbury, 1989.

77. Stein, Diane, <u>Essential Reiki</u>, The Crossing Press, Freedom, 1996.

78. Surya Das, Lama. <u>Awakening the Buddha Within</u>, Broadway Books, New York, 1997.

79. Svoboda, Robert E. <u>Aghora II: Kundalini</u>, Brotherhood of Life, Albuquerque, 1993.

80. Svoboda, Robert E. <u>Ayurveda, Life, Health and Longevity</u>, Arkana, London, 1992.

81. Svoboda, Robert E. <u>Prakruti: Your Ayurvedic Constitution</u>, Geocom, Albuquerque, NM, 1989.

82. Swedenborg, Emanuel. <u>The Worlds in Space</u>, University Press, Cambridge, 1997.

83. Tierra, Michael. <u>Planetary Herbology</u>, Lotus Press, Santa Fe, 1988.

84. Tirtha, Swami Sada Shiva. <u>The Ayurveda Encyclopedia: Natural Secrets to Healing, Prevention, & Longevity,</u> Ayurveda Holistic Center Press, Bayville New York, 1998.

85. Tolle, Eckhart. <u>The Power of Now</u>, New World Library, Novato, CA, 1999.

86. Treadway, Scott and Linda Treadway. <u>Ayurveda and Immortality</u>, Celestial Arts, Berkeley, CA, 1986.

87. Vaishali. <u>You Are What You Love</u>, Purple Haze Press, Naples, FL, 2006.

88. Verma, Vinod. <u>Ayurveda A Way of Life</u>, Weiser, York Beach, 1995.

89. Watt, Bernice K. and Annabel L. Merrill. <u>Composition of Foods</u>, United States Department of Agriculture, Washington, D.C., 1963.

90. Weil, Andrew. <u>Eight Weeks to Optimum Health</u>, Knopf, New York, 1998.

91. Weil, Andrew. <u>Spontaneous Healing</u>, Knopf, New York, 1995.

92. Yogananda, Paramahansa. <u>Man's Eternal Quest</u>, Self-Realization Fellowship, 1975.

93. Image licensed from Wireimage.

94. Image licensed from Getty Images.

95. Image licensed Alamy Images.

96. Hanuman Foundation

MASTER MECHANICS

DEDICATIONS

DR. VASANT LAD

This book is dedicated to Dr. Vasant Lad of Pune, India. He has given his life to the advancement of ayurvedic medicine. He left his homeland and endured many hardships so that he could bring the benefits of ayurveda to the west. He has established the premier center in the U.S. for ayurvedic education and treatment in Albuquerque, N.M.

Few people in any area of study are so completely intimate with the workings of their art. If you know a spiritual leader who lives every minute of every day according to the doctrines of his or her faith, then you have a sense of the essence of Dr. Lad. If you know a spiritual leader who has also memorized the sacred texts of his faith, and can sing its verses in their original ancient language, then you have a sense of the depth of Dr. Lad's knowledge of the origins of ayurveda. It is an honor to be his student.

DR. JULIUS HOFFMAN

This work is also dedicated to Dr. Julius Hoffman of Bethesda, Maryland. Dr. Hoffman was a physician and ultra-specialist. He was American Board Certified in five medical specialties.

He came from an era in which medicine was still an art as well as a science. In that age, clinical findings were used instead of scanners and sophisticated lab tests to make a diagnosis. This skill yielded a deep understanding of the intricacies of the human body. Yet he also embraced the astounding achievements of modern technical medicine, and the practical benefits they could offer.

As a teacher of medicine at several universities, he shared his knowledge with anyone who showed a genuine interest. His passion for knowledge carried him and his many students to areas of greater understanding and appreciation for the workings of the human form and mind.

His integrity lifted him to a level above those who traded the gifts and responsibilities of medical science for wealth and status. He exemplified propriety and responsibility as a physician, and he cared deeply for the many patients who benefited from his experience and wisdom.

Dr. Vasant Lad

RAY NAOMI HOFFMAN

This work is also dedicated to Ray Naomi Hoffman, also of Bethesda, Maryland. As an experienced nurse, social worker, writer, artist and parent, she continues to exemplify sensitivity, compassion, wisdom, and creativity in all things.

We are all the beneficiaries of the experience of those who have come before us and who have shared their knowledge and wisdom with us. Without them, we would all need to re-learn the basics. With them in our hearts and minds, there is no limit to the places to which we can travel.

Acknowledgements

Significant medical treatises are rarely created by one individual, but with the cooperation, encouragement, and contributions of many.

This effort was only possible due to the support and contributions of:

Vaishali	Karen E. Egan
Jaisri M. Lambert	Jerri-Jo Idarius
Sarita Sreshta	Ray N. Hoffman
Vasant D. Lad	Julianna Fomenko
Ram H. Singh	Peter R. Hoffman
Vivek Shanbhag	Deborah A. Hoffman
Robert Hoffman	Mark Hazelbaker
Akwia Diane Knipe	Sarah A. Hoffman
Donald Treolo	Jaye Apte
Baba Hari Das	Della L. Tracy Davis
Lee F. Hoffman	

Ray Naomi Hoffman

About the Author

Dr. Paul L. Hoffman has been educated in both Western allopathic medicine and in ayurvedic medicine.

He graduated from Oberlin College, the University of Cincinnati College of Medicine, and from the Good Samaritan Hospital of Cincinnati Residency Program in Pediatrics. He did his subspecialty training in Newborn Intensive Care at the University of Colorado at Denver Children's Hospital.

He was founding Director of the Newborn Intensive Care Unit at the Good Samaritan Hospital of Santa Clara Valley, San Jose, California, where he worked for 19 years providing high-tech care to critically ill newborn babies.

He studied ayurveda under Dr. Vasant Lad, and opened Alternative Health Services in Los Gatos, California, in 1994.

He has lectured on ayurveda at Stanford University College of Medicine, the University of California San Francisco Medical Center, San Francisco State University, the American Pediatric Society, the National Ayurvedic Medical Association, Five Branches Institute of Traditional Chinese Medicine, Twin Lakes College, Mount Madonna Institute, Kerala Ayurveda Academy, and other educational institutions.

Currently, he treats patients with chronic, poorly responsive health problems at Alternative Health Services in Boulder Creek and Santa Cruz, California. He also practices allopathic pediatrics in the San Francisco Bay area, and lectures at other institutions on the value of Ayurvedic medicine.

Dr. Hoffman has been honored by the California State Legislature for his work with underpriviledged children in East San Jose.

Currently, he serves as the Medical Director of the Mount Madonna Institute College of Ayurveda in Watsonville, California.

Dr. Paul L. Hoffman

BUYER'S GUIDE

NOTICE OF NO WARRANTY - "AS IS" CONDITION
(Disclaimer)

Although ayurvedic medicine can be an effective form of treatment for many problems and illnesses, it is not the answer for everything or everyone. The information in this book is not intended to replace standard medical treatments, especially in serious illness. Ayurveda is especially useful as an additional form of treatment in combination with other types of medicine, as well as being useful on its own.

All Hail Lawyers!

As always, it is the responsibility of each individual to make a personal judgment concerning what course of therapy to pursue, and to assume full responsibility for those decisions.

It is also the responsibility of each individual to follow through with the suggested course of treatment if positive results are to be expected.

CUSTOMER SERVICE
(Dedication)

This work is for all seekers of health who strive to understand the workings of the body, the mind and beyond. The book is only for those who are willing to step outside the apparent safety of their known medical world and discover the knowledge and healing that different thinking may bring.

AUTOMOTIVE TECHNICAL LANGUAGE

(Sanskrit Language)

Many fields of endeavor have their own technical language. Ayurveda is no exception. Because it was developed thousands of years ago in ancient India, many ayurvedic terms are in the ancient Sanskrit language. Like the Latin of the Catholic Church, Sanskrit is now a specialized language of scholarly works, and not one of common usage.

It is difficult enough to learn an entirely new health system without having to learn an entirely new language as well. For this reason, Sanskrit terms are mentioned only briefly in this work. The English terms that have been created to replace the Sanskrit are less compact, and often less accurate than the original terminology.

The serious student of ayurveda who wishes to become more familiar with the deeper workings of the science will do well to learn the important Sanskrit vocabulary. Many of these terms are given in the Glossary. Sanskrit words are said to have their own special vibrations and unique descriptive applications for Ayurvedic health science concepts.

MISSING THE FOREST for the TREES

The BODY is shaped by MIND & CONSCIOUSNESS

Our immediate concerns usually center around the comfort of our physical bodies. Sensory discomfort elicits a primitive avoidance response and gets our attention quickly. We are hard-wired to get rid of pain as quickly and easily as possible.

Relief from physical discomfort puts a temporary end to the immediate pain problem, so we often close the book on that particular health issue and ignore the behavior(s) that created it. We forget that the physical body is shaped by the habits the mind creates.

The mind, in turn, is shaped by the consciousness, but we don't go into the mind/consciousness aspects which caused the physical problems because these areas are much less concrete. When issues are less mechanical, less rarely predictable, and hard to define, they are seen as too difficult to approach. So, we just move on.

But if the mind retains the habits that hurt the body, the same problems will recur. Therefore:

Long-term healing often has a mental basis.

The care and feeding of the mind is very important, but difficult. This is because it is difficult to perceive, measure, and explain subtle mental activity. The mind exists to help us perceive, measure and explain the physical body, but what do we have that observes the mind?

Consciousness is the observer of the mind.

The mind can only be trained and healed if we are "aware" of it. Somehow, we must be able to step back from our situation and observe our own actions and the mental patterns that create them. Only then can we train the mind differently.

This stepping-back process is the movement to a wider (higher) consciousness. It involves quieting the chattering mind and opening ourselves to planes of existence even more subtle than the mental. Once this is accomplished, a purpose for existence is perceived, and a unity with "non-self" is recognized.

When the consciousness imparts a sense of purpose and unity to the mind, we perceive ourselves as both belonging and important. We then have good reason for healthy behavior! Without purpose or a sense of belonging, the mind will follow Pinocchio back to the sensory circus.

A healthy and connected consciousness imparts a sense of cosmic order that brings a feeling of belonging and a sense of peace. If these are absent, the mind will feel alone, become agitated, and misbehave.

Consciousness must bring a sense of self-esteem to the mind. If we don't love ourselves, there is little reason for self care. A connection with the "Greater Self" brings us this needed sense of importance.

Most readers will ignore all of this, and be content with the considerable benefits of following the physical Ayurvedic path described in Volume One. But when the problems recur or shift to another place in the body, the enlightened health-seeker will turn to Volume Two and begin the greater journey within.

INDEX

A

Abdomen 160, 164, 259, 271, 788
  distension 270, 364, 390, 401, 465
  lock 322
  pain 160, 164, 270, 274, **291,** 364,
    386, 401, 467, 784, 816, 818
Abhivati 306
Abortion, threatened 274, **292**
Abscess 196, 268, 271, **292**
Abrak 199, 212, 276-77, 281, 283,
    286, 304, 307, 313, 320-21, 326,
    335, 339, 351, 359, 368, 389-91,
    397, 399, 461
Absorption 384, 810
Abundance 673, 742
Acacia 280, 352, 412
Acceptance 552, 631-3, **674,** 697, 739,
    767, 833, 863
Acclaim 690
Accumulation 725
  stage of disease 160
Accupuncture 40, 349, 790
Aching 195, 825
Acid 127, 155, 259, 316, 366, 378,
    439
  indigestion 155, 164, 274, **292,**
    416, 435811, 818
  reflux 129, 291, 343
Acidophilus 276, 317
Acne 195, 207, 268, 271, 274, **293,**
    389, 427, 429, 812
Acorn squash 110, 451
Action 55, 697, 725, 748, 801, 806,
    843, 848
Achievement 57, 787
Activity 64, 503, 515, 523, 698-700
    772, 876
Acupuncture 212, **251, 277,** 783-5,
    790, 868
Addiction 150, **295,** 380, 398, 603-5,
    630, 789, 850

Adhesions 164
Adrenal glands 146, 207, 213, 314,
    333, 414, 540, 585, 786, 788,
    795, 817, 822
  insufficiency 274, 296
Adzuki beans 112, 422
Affirmation 146, 664
Agenesis 270
Agate 811
Aggression 521, 807, 876
Aging 71, 147, **166,** 243, 777, 821-24,
    274, 337, 390, 429, 455
Agitation 570, 587
Agni **127-28** (see also "DTE")
Agni tundi 129, 279, 283, 341, 368
Ahamkar 544
AIDS (see also " HIV") 274, **296-7,**
    778
Air 35, **55,** 38-39, 51, **154-55,** 221,
    503
Ajna (see "Third eye energy center")
Ajwain 115, 279, 299, 301, 312, 317,
    323, 343, 389, 401, 412, 422,
    455, 462, 465, 476, 479
Akasha 365 (see also "Space")
Albumin 777
Alcohol 33, 57, 98, 106, 129, 234, 274,
    293, **297-98,** 300, 317, 331, 337,
    346, 353, 363, 391, 399, 405,
    410, 423, 431, 435, 453, 469,
    592, 593-4
Algae 117, 422
Alfalfa 110, 116, 316, 394, 422
Algae 110, 281, 302, 389
Allergies 147, 174, **298-300,** 347, 400,
    425, 428,788, 821, 826
Alligator pose 472
Allopathy 56, 96, 103, 136, 172, 182,
    240, 291, 304, 318, 836
Allspice 115, 465, 476
Almond 108, 113-15, 196, 198, 200,
    209, 274, 278-79, 285, 290, 294,
    305, 325, 328, 339, 359, 363,

913

Brahmi (cont.) 297-98, 300-1, 304, 308, 312, 319, 329, 333-34, 336-37, 347-49, 353, 356-57, 358, 360, 362, 365, 369-71, 373, 375, 378, 383, 385-86, 389, 391-95, 397, 399, 400, 402-4, 413, 459-60, 462, 478, 585, 660, 739, **822**

Brain 125, 207, 212, 241, 258, 269, 300, 335-37, 378, 395, 397-98, 400, 428-29, 440, 462, 466, 468, 776, 789, 797, 827

tumor 789

Brazil nut 114, 424, 454

Bread 96, 131, 219, 320-21, 332

Breakfast 99-100, 129, 144-45, 342, 382, 444-46

Breast 196, 268-70, 390, 462, 467, 788

abscess 275, 311

cancer 276, **312**

fibrocystic disease 195, 197, 268, 279, **341**

feeding 276

milk 113, 193, **312**, 466

Breath bad 275, 309, 468

Breathing (see also individual breathing types) 40, 131, 144, **149, 172,** 212, 233, 235, 256, **259-60, 276,** 287-88, 294, 297-99, 304, 308, **312-13,** 317, 335, 357, 365, 382, 398, 402, 471, 596, 678, 736, 780, 794, 821, 868

bellows 259

control 531, 586, 660, 664

therapy 333, 532, 737, 791, 865

difficulty 160, 164, 324

Brewer's yeast 117

Bridge pose 292, 294, 322, 366, 472

Bringaraj 277, 279-80, 284, 287, 290, 300, 302, 310, 322, 336-37, 346, 349, 353, 355-56, 363, 365, 373, 389, 393, 395, 402, 404, 411, 462-63, 585

Broccoli 39, 99, 110, 195, 219, 234-35, 293, 324, 331, 334, 384, 414, 424, 454, 456

Bronchiectasis 275, 313

Bronchi 211, 227

Bronchitis 174, 212, 276, 299, **313,** 425-26, 428, 465-66, 795, 818, 820, 823

Bronchodilator 154, 156, 307, 817, 819, 820

Bruising 268, 271, 276, 313

Brussels sprouts 98, 110, 195, 219, 234, 293, 324, 334, 424, 454

Buckwheat 111, 382, 424

Buddhism 552, 633, 646, 676, 703, 706, 717, 746, 748, 769

Buffalo

meat 112, 294, 424

milk 424

Bulimia 345, 788

Bundle branch block 199, 269

Bunion 269

Burdock 116, 307, 313, 316, 334, 406

Burning 227, 412, 416, 631

Burning foot syndrome 276, 313

Burns 276, 414, 468, 818, 820

Burping 125, 386, 816

Bursitis 196, 268, 276, **314,** 820, 823

Business 135, 145, 228, 574, 579, 635, 637, 743, 839, 841, 853

Butter 113, 233, 293, 320, 324, 353, 424

Buttermilk 113, 145, 278, 289, 316, 332, 352, 469-70

Buttocks 196

By-products 124, 126, 128, 192-97, 199, 200, 208, 339

C

Cabbage 110, 195, 219, 234, 289, 293, 324, 334, 343, 346, 408, 414, 424, 454, 456

Caffeine 134, 146, 276, **314,** 389, 424, 453, 456

Calamus (see also "Vacha") 249, 306, 329, 331, 390, 476, 479

Calcium 117, 177, 190, 268, 275-76, 294, 305, 309, 314-15, 346, 356,

D

E

H

J

Jade 805

Jaggary 114, 301-2, 314, 430, 457

Jasmine 116, 233, 235, 241, 274, 277, 279, 281, 283, 289, 301, 319, 344, 355-56, 369, 389, 408, 411, 478-79

Jatamamsi 199, 200, 275, 278, 282, 284, 287-89, 298, 300, 303, 308, 310, 329, 333-34, 346, 357-58, 360, 362-63, 367, 369-71, 373, 375, 383, 385-87, 389, 391, 395, 399, 402-3, 407, 459, 462-63, 478, 585, 660, 739, 822

Jaundice 282, **365,** 426, 436, 470, 820

Jaw clenching 282, 365

Jesus (see "Christ")

Jet lag 282, 466

Jock Itch 282, 365

Joints 147, 150, 196, 197, 207, 268, 270-71, 282, 304-5, 339, 457, 469, 776, 791

weakness 268, 282, 365, 403

Journey 675, 726, 863

Joy 157, 571, 587, 642, 697, 801, 863

Judgment 57, 329, 515, 521, 551, 669, 672, 735, 751, 789, 839, 862

Judaism 676, 703, 706, 769

Juice 134, 316, 420, 469, 671

vegetable (see individual fruits & vegetables) 134, 146, 297, 329, 660

Juniper 116, 241, 394, 430, 476, 479

Jyotishmati 199, 285, 287, 362, 371, 388, 395, 459-60, 739

K

Kaknasha 280, 345

Kale 110, 234, 384, 430, 454

Kama dudha 199, 200, 277-78, 281-84, 287-88, 290, 292, 314, 323-24, 326, 333, 336-37, 350, 354-55, 358-60, 363, 374, 378, 383-85, 391, 396, 408, 411-12, 459-60, 462

Kanchanar 312, 335, 345, 369, 385, 408-10

Kantakari 312, 345, 361, 408

Kapha (see "Earth quality) 59

Kapikachu 282, 285, 288, 297, 317, 360-62, 368, 371, 383, 387, 407

Karma 276, 602, 639, 699

Katuka 297, 336, 345, 354, 357, 368, 396

Kefir 430

Kelp 110, 430, 451, 454

Ketchari mudra 285, 388

Khadiradi 355, 362

Khus 199, 200, 355, 458-61

Kidney 69, 112, 146, 163, 176, 210, 238, 242, 268, 301, 314, 335, 339, 344, 410, 417, 423, 426-27, 434, 462, 596, 786, 788, 823, 824

bean 107, 108, 112, 456, 470

Kidney (cont.) energy 282, 339, 366

failure 282, 366

infection 282, 291, 366

stone 59, 156, 282, 291, 356, 366, 423-24, 436, 440, 467

Kitcheri 131, 300, 326, 339, 353, 451, 454, **455,** 819

Kiwi 109, 317, 430

Knees 269, 339, 382

Knee-chest pose 257 , 309, 325, 394, 473

Knowledge 16, 32, 43, 89, 96, 171, 190, 206, 217, 222, 231, 237-38, 260, 272, 295, 330, 481, 697, 724, 750-1, 789

Kohlrabi 110, 430

Kokam 457

Kombu 110, 430, 456

Koshas 781-2

Krishna 703

Kriyas 664

Krumi kuthar 317, 386

Kumari asava 276, 312

Kum Kum 360, 361

Kundalini 145, 786, 813

Kushtha 275, 311, 354

Kutaka 316, 336, 365

Kutki 197, 278, 279, 281, 286-87, 290,

M

O

P

T

U

Ulcer 31, 129, 164, 234, 268, 289, 291, 363, 408, 430, 423, 434, 436, 441, 469, 795, 818, 820, 823
  apthous 289, 408
  diabetic 9, 331, 414, 811
  duodenal 31, 289, 291, 408, 788
  gastric 31, 155, 285, 289, 291, 788, 811
  mouth 789
Ulcerative colitis 163, 289, **408,** 469, 811, 818
Ultrasound 342
Umbilical energy center 787
Unbalanced state 1-895, **82,** 298-99, 305, 311, 411
Union 44, **261-62,** 471, 672, 697, 772
Unity 683, 690, 757, 892
Upper respiratory infection 322, **324-25,** 818, 820-21
Urad dahl 112, 290, 413, 457-59
Ureter 210, 462
Urethra 155, 200, 208, 210, 270, 271, 289, 427, 462, 466
Urine 52, 67, 69, 87, 88, 159, 205, 211, 213, 221, 271, 314, 351, 408, 429-30, 441-42, 460, 462, 466, 469-70, 788, 795, 824-26
  burning 270, 289, 426-27, 466, 469
  frequency 271, 289, 372
  incontinence 289
  infection 270, 289, 410, 426-27, 469
  retention 289
  stones 271, 289, 824
Urticaria 289, 210
Uterus 200, 289, 410, 462, 469
Uveitis 289, 410
Uvula 268

V

Vacation 245, 646-47, 670, 726, 848, 858

Vacha 199, 275-81, 283, 285-88, 298, 300, 304, 306, 308, 311, 317, 319, 322-23, 325, 327, 333, 337, 342-44, 348, 362, 367-68, 370-71, 373, 375, 377-79, 386, 388, 393, 397-98, 400, 403, 458-59, 462-63, 660
Vagina 200, 208, 270, 361, 382, 462
  dryness 200, 289, 410
  warts 289, 410
  vaginitis 200, 289, 317, 411, 818, 820
Vajrasana 309, 396
Valerian 196, 199, 277, 280, 282, 285, 289, 304, 329, 333, 342, 357-58, 363, 365, 373, 376, 385-86, 389, 394, 411, 476-77, 479, 660
Validation 600, 639, 641, 672
Vamsha rochna 249, 323, 328
Vamsha lochana 304, 312
Vanilla 117, 468, 476
Varicose veins 195, 289, 411, 788
Variability 16, 53, 55, 66-68, 173, 232, 416, 874
Vasculitis 290, 331, 411
Vas deferens 208, 462
Vasodilitation 8303, 16, 818, 827
Vata (see "Air") 55, 503
Vegetables 96, 107, 131, 145, 146, 316, 322, 329, 351, 353, 414, 455, 470
  juice 297
Veins 195, 206, 213, 268, 287, 289, 310, 352, 388, 401, 411, 461, 788
Venereal disease 820
Vengence 735, 743
Venison 113, 293
Ventricular septal defect 270
Vertebrae 249, 394, 788
Vertigo 270, 290, 795, 812
Vetraga 316
Vibration 502, 690, 799, 802-3, 808, 859, 893
Vidanga 277-78, 285, 301, 317, 320, 328, 334, 336, 369, 386, 396, 460

Z

X

Y

GET RID OF YOUR FAT PANTS

Frostred
Angry
Overwhelmed

I'm just so thankful
I know this sounds cheesy but I feel like
a million bucks — I really do

Dr. IanSmith —   Shred —
Tweet some of Program   The Revolutionary
                          Diet.

—>   Secret weapon <—

Diety is 80% mental
Not loosing — You're Shredding — Ha —
Why is it so effecu — This Diet Does
follaor require prefullon easy to
           require prefullon
* Don't eat Same Fords every day
Posy metabolism
                    WAT TOO Long to eat
        when you eat you Spike Insulin
Week — 1+2 Protein Drinks
With 3 —
     4
     5) Cleanse —

Detox –
Flaxseed oil
lemons
water
or ground flax seeds

Hibsus Tea
1 cup pure cranberry juice

3 S's – (3 secrets to shred)

apples
Blue Berry   smoothie
Bananas

8 prawns
choc Banana
Pizza made on Gluten free muffin
Soups

SciFringi.   18.00 hour.
                        B.B.7.

User/Review (5/9)   T,150.00 OK

Bannu/poster (6/5)   135.00
Graphics (6hours)

Kids show — (6/9)

B BT.   ___   400. (2)

Embody 5/16